Forensic Musicology and the Blurred Lines of Federal Copyright History

Forensic Musicology and the Blurred Lines of Federal Copyright History

Katherine M. Leo

LEXINGTON BOOKS
Lanham • Boulder • New York • London

Chapter 2: Portions of this chapter were previously published in, or are adapted from, Katherine Leo, "Musical Expertise and the 'Ordinary' Listener in Federal Copyright Law," *Music and Politics* 13, no. 1 (Winter 2019): 1–19. https://doi.org/10.3998/mp .9460447.0013.108.

Chapter 3: Portions of analysis for Arnstein v. Porter were previously published in, or are adapted from, Katherine Leo, "Musical Expertise and the 'Ordinary' Listener in Federal Copyright Law," *Music and Politics* 13, no. 1 (Winter 2019): 1–19. https://doi .org/10.3998/mp.9460447.0013.108.

Chapter 6: Portions of this section and the one following have been previously published in, or are adapted from, Katherine Leo, "Musical Expertise and the 'Ordinary' Listener in Federal Copyright Law," *Music and Politics* 13, no. 1 (Winter 2019): 1–19. https://doi .org/10.3998/mp.9460447.0013.108.

Published by Lexington Books
An imprint of The Rowman & Littlefield Publishing Group, Inc.
4501 Forbes Boulevard, Suite 200, Lanham, Maryland 20706
www.rowman.com

6 Tinworth Street, London SE11 5AL, United Kingdom

British Library Cataloguing in Publication Information Available

Library of Congress Cataloging-in-Publication Data Available

Library of Congress Control Number: 2020948537

ISBN 978-1-7936-1940-2 (cloth : alk. paper)
ISBN 978-1-7936-1941-9 (electronic)

♾™ The paper used in this publication meets the minimum requirements of American National Standard for Information Sciences—Permanence of Paper for Printed Library Materials, ANSI/NISO Z39.48-1992.

Contents

List of Figures

Acknowledgments

Research and publication are impossible without the expertise and support of many people and institutions, to all of whom I am profoundly grateful. This book is the culmination of studies first conducted for my PhD dissertation in musicology, which I completed in 2016 at The Ohio State University with generous funding from its Graduate School, College of Arts and Sciences, and School of Music. I have presented various sections at annual meetings of the American Musicological Society, the Society for American Music, and the Society for Music Theory; others have been previously published in *Music and Politics*, which are recognized with citation. Through each of these phases, I received valuable and constructive feedback from colleagues that have shaped this final result.

Much of the archival source material discussed herein is contained in available case files, which are housed at various courts and National Archives and Records Administration facilities. Judicial opinions as to the outcome of each case and more recent records are also available on legal research databases, including Westlaw and Public Access to Court Electronic Records (PACER), as well as other online repositories active at the time of this book's publication. In particular, the invaluable open-access Music Copyright Infringement Resource (MCIR) website (https://blogs.law.gwu.edu/mcir/) features judicial opinions with partial recordings and scores for much of the music involved in each case. Because of this book's intended interdisciplinary audience, I have used a blended vocabulary and citation style that incorporates elements of the Bluebook, used by legal scholars and practitioners, and the Chicago Manual of Style, used in many humanities disciplines, including musicology.

I appreciate the ongoing support of the many librarians, archivists, professors, scholars, colleagues, friends, and family that have encouraged this research since I was a graduate student. This book would not have been possible without the support of my fellow faculty members at Millikin University and colleagues with diverse specialties, who have answered questions, offered critiques, shared materials, helped format figures, and reviewed copious drafts, especially Charles Atkinson, Joe Bennett, Graeme Boone, Charles Cronin, Andrew Farina, Dan Monroe, Guy Rub, Mark Rubel, Mark Rudoff, Alex Stewart, and Jessa Wilcoxen. And finally, my infinite love and thanks to John, Stuart, KJ, Cathy, and Mom.

Introduction

From its commencement in 2013 to its final ruling in December 2018, the federal music copyright lawsuit between collaborators Pharrell Williams and Robin Thicke against Marvin Gaye's estate, centered on the hit song, "Blurred Lines," has garnered ongoing public attention. Scholars, industry specialists, and pop culture buffs alike have worried about the ramifications of this case, now legally referred to as *Williams v. Gaye*, for the protection of musical style and the future of artistic creativity in U.S. commercial music. Some of these concerns stemmed from comparative analyses produced by musical expert witnesses that revealed noticeable stylistic similarity in the rhythmic grooves and instrumentation of both songs, but few congruences in their melodies or harmonies. The 2015 trial, however, resulted in a surprising jury finding of infringement that three years later would be affirmed by the Ninth Circuit. While the prevailing Gaye estate called this decision "a victory for the rights of all musicians,"[1] the Ninth Circuit dissenting judge characterized it as "a devastating blow to future musicians and composers everywhere"[2] because it "allow[ed] the Gayes to accomplish what no one has before: copyright a musical style."[3]

The question at the heart of this case, as in so many federal music copyright lawsuits, involved negotiating the putative similarities and differences between songs as intellectual property. Yet this issue is far from a recent legal dilemma. Nearly two-hundred years of music copyright infringement claims expose shared musical boundaries as contested space in which lines between lawful stylistic commonality and unlawful appropriation are blurred. Although the U.S. federal court system has developed methods designed to assist factfinders—either judges or jurors—in their legal evaluations of similarity, the outcomes of such cases are not only insistently variable but also

1

reflect unsettled debates over how, and by whom, musical similarity should be assessed.

Since the first music copyright cases heard in the nineteenth century, courts have consistently welcomed the detailed, systematic analyses presented by performing artists, publishers, teachers, and scholars as musical expert witnesses. Their comparisons are now considered an essential task of forensic musicology, or the study of music in conjunction with matters of law. Despite ostensibly objective evidence produced by these experts intended to elucidate matters of musical structure, stylistic idiom, and creative process, due to cumulating legal limitations, the totalizing and subjective perceptions of non-expert factfinders now determine the outcome of each case. Given this situation, what is the role of forensic musicology in federal copyright infringement cases, how have musical expert witnesses understood it, and what issues have they encountered?

This book aims to address these questions by mapping the historical terrain of forensic musicology in federal music copyright litigation. Drawing on interdisciplinary research methods from musicological and legal scholarship, it situates musical expert witnesses in the U.S. judicial system as a dynamic, adversarial environment that poses unique analytical issues. Rather than provide a comprehensive review of hundreds of music copyright infringement claims for which there survives some degree of documentation, this book instead maps a vast terrain of people, music, and events, memorialized in illustrative and precedential cases arranged chronologically from the mid-nineteenth century through the early twenty-first century. It unfolds across six chapters divided according to landmark lawsuits and issues that impact conceptions of expertise and musical identity. It concludes by returning to an analysis of *Williams v. Gaye* according to this map, which reveals both the essential role of musical expert witnesses and the contemporary issues they face.

Historical study of musical expert testimony demonstrates that, despite revisions to federal statutory and common laws pertaining to copyright, forensic musicology continues to fulfill a longstanding role surveying contested musical boundaries for courts. Cast into the adversarial judicial system, musical experts must negotiate precarious ethics surrounding the ostensibly impartial evidence they produce, which will be exposed to the subjectivities of partial attorneys and factfinder interpretations. Through their essential task, which might be referred to collectively as forensic similarity analysis, experts do not make final determinations about infringement; rather, in a prior legal step, they set out to clarify the intellectual property lines between songs by locating markers of similarity and difference. Judicial concerns since the early twentieth century about expert witness partiality, confusingly intricate analyses, and public policies favoring the evaluations of nonexpert factfinders, have all led to limitations on the scope and application of such analyses, however. Experts have understood and adapted to these restrictions by applying analytical techniques that are increasingly complex and at times abstract. While these techniques have distinguished the boundaries between music with greater precision, many cases have demonstrated that such analytical sophistication might do as much to inform as to mystify courts.

In its historical narrative of forensic musicology, this book navigates the ways in which legal practitioners and expert witnesses have approached music as intellectual property. It sheds light on the courtroom as a public forum for musical analysis, and elucidates the understudied, yet often significant, relationship of musical expertise to the U.S. judicial system. For nearly two centuries, musical experts have promoted a system acutely aware of musical styles and theories, creative processes, and the implications of copyright protection for musicians. In so doing, their role is not simply to survey musical boundaries to assess similarity or meet expectations of legal objectivity, but also to refine public conceptions of musical identity as intellectual property. It is through deeper consideration of this role that contemporary forensic musicologists and courts may be better equipped to clarify the, indeed, blurred lines of federal music copyright.

THE INTERDISCIPLINARY STAKES IN FORENSIC MUSICOLOGY

Although musical experts have played an integral role in federal copyright litigation for the entirety of its nearly two-hundred-year history, the discipline of forensic musicology has only been recognized consistently since the late twentieth century. Its apparently recent emergence has contributed to a relative dearth of academic study on its history, methods, and important figures. Yet the issues musical experts face not only permeate contemporary litigation; they have persisted through much of the discipline's history and have impacted not simply the expert witnesses themselves, but also the judges, attorneys, jurors, and musicians in each case and across time.

This limited scholarship is also due in part to the fundamentally interdisciplinary nature of forensic musicology, which draws on rich bodies of knowledge in both music and law to answer its core questions. While there is enduring scholarly interest in intellectual property, most scholarship focuses on the respective disciplinary occupations of its researchers to the detriment of such cross-disciplinary exploration. Historians typically offer broad, policy-centric accounts of copyright statutes that accord to music only modest amounts of attention.[4] Research that does address music copyright in more focused ways is more likely to emphasize only a few cases or statutory provisions, or to paint music industry history and popular culture with broad strokes, while devoting relatively little attention to the details of litigation and theoretical analysis in landmark cases.[5] Other scholarship tends to focus on the philosophical or sociocultural underpinnings of copyright, authorship, and ownership, including policy-driven issues of power relations, piracy, and audience consumption rather than on the practical implications of those concerns for the construction of laws or forensic analysis of music.[6] In the subdiscipline of legal history, few authors have focused on intimate portraits of attorneys and plaintiffs, rather than on tracing the evolution of issues fundamental to musical expertise.[7]

Legal scholars, by contrast, often focus on contemporaneously relevant issues and their proposed solutions, while rarely sifting through matters of U.S. music history, cultural context, or analytical techniques.[8] To that end, they have written extensively on the contours of the legal similarity inquiry, but comparatively less on the musical expert testimony central to it.[9] Legal scholarship specific to the past and present role of musical experts is sparse and generally focuses on legal, rather than musicological questions.[10] Although some scholars have commented on problems specific to the legal structure of music copyright litigation, they prefer to foreground matters of musical borrowing and creativity over distinctions, left unclarified, between composition and performance.[11]

Among the exceptions in this research climate are a small number of scholars and sources that recognize forensic musicology, or engage in research adjacent to it, which typically involves drawing on their own legal and musical training. Likely in an effort to remain relevant to a legal audience, articles by these scholars tend to minimize the discipline's history and are limited in their scope of application.[12] Some musical expert witnesses have commented on the practicalities of their work for a predominantly contemporary legal audience.[13] A similarly small number of music scholars have seriously considered what expert witnesses and courts actually do, and those that have tend to focus on a few cases as a means to extrapolate broad recommendations regarding best practices for forensic similarity analysis.[14] In an effort to promote further study of music copyright and forensic issues, however, some public-facing specialists have curated case opinions alongside audio and visual resources in an open access online format.[15]

As a result, scholars across disciplines and legal practitioners may be asking many of the same research questions central to forensic musicology, but their underlying epistemologies, methods, and source materials promote distinctly different orientations. This book offers an interdisciplinary solution that provides a coherent historical narrative and shared vocabulary with the aim of bringing together these disciplinary paths. On the one hand, it offers legal audiences an explanation of forensic similarity analysis and musical-theoretical concepts in recognizable contexts and identifies patterns in litigation; on the other, it lays out legal procedures and precedents, and it explains critical matters of law for nonspecialist audiences.

OVERVIEW

For most of music copyright history, musical expertise has been synonymous with legal service as an expert witness. Noted early twentieth-century Judge Learned Hand characterized the "rise of expert testimony [as] no more than the gradual recognition of such testimony, amid the gradual definition of rules of evidence."[16] Since the introduction of expert witnesses to litigation practice, regulation of expert witness qualifications and contributions has been subject to each court's discretion. Federal evidence law, established both through statutory laws drafted by Congress and common laws presented by judges, applies to all federal legal proceedings and structures when and what kinds of evidence an expert may present in the litigation process. In general, a witness may be admitted as an expert where his or her specialized skill, qualification, or experience is recognized by the court as offering a technical perspective to evaluating the evidence at issue. Since the nineteenth century, however, courts, scholars, and legal commentators have critiqued the inclusion of expert witnesses, characterizing their testimony as confusingly detailed and often partial to the party in the lawsuit that hired them.

These evidentiary rules regulate the qualifications and contributions of expert witnesses in music copyright cases, which became possible in 1831 when Congress designated music as copyrightable intellectual property. Litigation regarding the publication of sheet music, addressed in chapter 1, soon followed. Courts in this era sought first to define the fundamental principles of copyright, to establish a formalized means to decide whether alleged musical copying met the legal definition of infringement, and to determine whether that decision-making process should be the same for other expressive works or specific to musical compositions. In these nineteenth-century cases, courts turned to musical experts, often performers, teachers, or publishers, for assistance in analyzing similarity, or offering what one attorney described as "forensic discussion"[17] of music.

From the first cases involving music, expert witnesses were hired by one or the other party, either a plaintiff, who commenced a lawsuit, or a defendant, who responded to claims against them. Their participation typically began early in the litigation process by helping the parties and their attorney(s) assess the strength of their legal positions. To that end, early expert witnesses clarified boundaries between music primarily by locating note-for-note melodic congruences identified on sheet music, presented to the court through spoken testimony and diagrams with strategically colored ink to show points of overlap. Expert witnesses offered limited review of stylistic resemblances between the music at issue and prior compositions. Decisions as to the outcome of these cases reveal strong judicial reliance on expert contributions as neutral or scientific, despite analyses that appeared to be rendered strategically in favor of the hiring party.

Chapter 2 follows this narrative into the first half of the twentieth century, approximately between the enactment of the 1909 Copyright Act until 1945. While courts continued to implement legal procedures for evaluating similarity established in the prior century, they became increasingly interested in matters of access to competing musical works and in disparities in listening skill when assessing similarity. Case opinions during this time reveal the influence of the music appreciation movement sweeping across the United States that implied a division between elite, trained listeners as experts and the majority of the American public as "average" or "ordinary" listeners, or nonexperts presumed to be the audience for music implicated in copyright infringement cases. Shifts in analytical techniques applied by expert witnesses in these cases reveal increasingly sophisticated music-theoretical comparisons that emphasized the interrelatedness of melody, formal structure, and style, and their theoretical status as more indicative of similarity than seemingly secondary musical features, such as key, meter, or tempo. These analyses, represented on sheet music, sometimes with coloration, were met with growing judicial skepticism regarding expert partiality, due to the potential for manipulating representations of similarity to aid the hiring party and the extent of analytical sophistication necessary for legal determinations regarding infringement.

The middle of the twentieth century brought about two pivotal cases that codified a legal process, or "test," for evaluating similarity applicable to music as well as all other copyrightable media: *Arnstein v. Porter*, decided by the Second Circuit in 1946, and *Sid & Marty Krofft Television Productions, Inc. v. McDonald's Corp.*, decided in 1977 by the Ninth Circuit. Chapter 3 analyzes these two cases and their immediate impact nationwide. *Arnstein* introduced a judicial test that required analyses from expert witnesses cast as legally objective, yet paradoxically prevented experts from commenting on the ultimate issue of infringement; instead, such determinations were relegated to the subjective evaluations of nonexpert jurors. In a later attempt to refine *Arnstein*, the *Krofft* court introduced a new layer of complexity by narrowing expert analyses to the nonprotectable musical idea distinguished from nonexpert comparisons of its protectable expression. Although to the *Krofft* court this division appeared to be a mere refinement of the *Arnstein* test, the judgment had the effect of creating a new test that further limited the influence of musical expert witnesses according to legal presumptions of objectivity and impartiality. Together, these cases shifted the decision regarding similarity from judges to jurors, exacerbating issues with unpredictable outcomes across cases as well as the detailed, abstract nature of expert analyses. While these decisions galvanized the participation of expert witnesses in such cases with the goal of producing legally objective evidence, in practice, they reduced the clarity that experts could offer.

From the sweeping revisions enacted in the 1976 Copyright Act through the turn of the twenty-first century, courts struggled to apply, and refine, the *Arnstein* and *Krofft* tests. Cases analyzed in chapter 4 demonstrated that although both parties hiring their own experts had become normative practice, the peculiar balances of access and similarity on the one hand, and the evaluations of expert witnesses and nonexpert factfinders on the other, prevented expert witnesses from having any consistent, measurable impact on case outcomes. This was particularly true for the Ninth Circuit, where expert witnesses appear to have struggled to adapt their analytical techniques in ways that met legal notions of the ineffable musical idea. Despite, and because of, sophisticated analytical innovations among expert witnesses, cases during this time could be said to serve more to intensify than to clarify legal problems with evaluating similarity according to *Arnstein* and *Krofft*.

During the late twentieth century, music copyright infringement jurisprudence, or judicial philosophy, became fragmented as courts concurrently addressed ongoing issues with evaluations of similarity as well as new compositional processes and evolving conceptions of musical expertise. The rise of cases involving digital sampling in the 1990s, and continuing into the twenty-first century, presented a significant challenge to courts and musical experts alike. As the focus of chapter 5, sampling cases reveal courts, still functioning with problematic legal tests, reliant on expert witnesses to locate newly contested boundaries of music based on close and minute, yet sometimes still perceptible, similarities between compositions heard on record. The claims in these cases provided courts an opportunity to reconsider notions of similarity and refine the limits of copyright protection, including the *de minimis* exception for small portions of congruent musical content and fair use as an affirmative defense. They likewise motivated changes to the credentials and analytical techniques shared among musical expert witnesses, now including audio specialists. As a result, expert witnesses presented audio-based analytical techniques, which incorporated digital waveform analysis that seemed to promise greater analytic precision, alongside, and in opposition to, more traditional notation-based comparisons. Regardless of analytical technique for comparison, however, the stylistic context provided by expert witnesses has proven to be most informative for courts in their assessments of sampling as potential infringements.

At the same time that sampling cases drove new legal approaches to simi-larity, other courts have introduced heightened legal standards surrounding musical expertise. Lawsuits heard in the past three decades represent more recent efforts to reconceive of aging, yet still binding, *Arnstein* and *Krofft* tests, which had previously established musical expertise as a binary opposi-tion. Some contemporary courts have instead favored heightened listener-observer standards, such as an "intended audience" or "more discerning observer," which seem to expand legal notions of listener acuity and, in practice, the roles of knowledgeable listeners previously treated as unknowl-edgeable nonexperts. These landmark cases, addressed in chapter 6, highlight enduring problems with legal decision-making processes and the role of musical expert witnesses, now typically academic- or career-forensic musi-cologists, while contemporaneous cases reveal efforts toward the codification of forensic musicology as a discipline unique to music copyright. Courts and attorneys alike have begun referring to notation-based analytical techniques as "standard musicological procedure," which has been as instrumental in establishing expertise as undermining it through partial challenges to alterna-tive analytical methods. These legal confrontations, propelled by attorneys in legal documents and witness examinations, seem to confound the ostensible impartiality of expert analyses. Both of these standards for nonexperts and experts emphasize ongoing legal reliance on musical acuity and awareness of stylistic commonality by expanding the role of expertise in copyright and reaffirming the essential role of forensic musicology in such litigation.

The intersecting legal, analytical, and ethical paths of this historical nar-rative lead to an analysis of *Williams v. Gaye* in the Conclusion. In light of this context, the outcome of the case is recast as far from shocking; rather, it may be understood as a result of issues fundamental to copyright and foren-sic musicology alike regarding how, and by whom, musical similarity is to be assessed. Complex procedures, subjective legal standards, and abstract, conflicting expert analyses created the conditions for the now-famous jury verdict that stylistic commonality between "Blurred Lines" and "Got To Give It Up" amounted to infringement.

NEGOTIATING THE BLURRED LINES OF MUSICAL IDENTITY

Historical study of forensic musicology demonstrates that expert witnesses have an essential role in the legal decision-making process regarding copy-right infringement, but one that is riddled with challenges. With specialized knowledge regarding music theory, style, history, and culture, forensic musicologists as expert witnesses negotiate the boundary lines of music to assist factfinders in understanding the particularized nature of musical similarity in each case. In so doing, they offer critical, albeit at times mystifying, insight into musical similarities, seeking to clarify divisions between commonality and appropriation. Because their ostensibly objective contributions are cast into an adversarial litigation process, musical expert witnesses have the ability to influence factfinders and the outcome of each case that promise to impact the future of federal copyright litigation. It is through this deeper understanding of their role, cultivated at least in part through historical study, that forensic musicologists will be able to more effectively assist courts in clarifying the intellectual property lines of musical identity.

NOTES

1. Nick Romano, "'Blurred Lines' Copyright Lawsuit Ends: Robin Thicke, Pharrell Williams to Pay $5 Million," *Entertainment Weekly*, December 13, 2018, https://ew.com/music/2018/12/13/blurred-lines-copyright-lawsuit-robin-thicke-pharrell-williams-pay/; see also Ingrid Monson, "Personal Take: On Serving as an Expert Witness in the 'Blurred Lines' Case," in *The Cambridge Companion to Music in Digital Culture* (Cambridge: Cambridge University Press, 2019), 58.

2. *Williams v. Gaye*, 885 F.3d 1150, 1183 (9th Cir. 2018) (Nguyen, J., dissenting).

3. *Williams*, 885 F.3d at 1208 (Nguyen, J., dissenting).

4. See, for example, Benedict Atkinson, *A Short History of Copyright: The Genie of Information* (New York, NY: Springer, 2014); Mark Rose, *Authors and Owners: The Invention of Copyright* (Cambridge, MA: Harvard University, 1993).

5. See, for example, J. Michael Keyes, "Musical Musings: The Case for Rethinking Music Copyright Protection," *Michigan Telecommunications and Technology Law Review* 10 (Spring 2004): 407–47.

6. See, for example, Alex Sayf Cummings, *Democracy of Sound* (Oxford: Oxford University Press, 2013); Joanna Demers, *Steal This Music: How Intellectual Property Law Affects Musical Creativity* (Athens, GA: University of Georgia, 2006); Simon Frith and Lee Marshall, eds., *Music and Copyright*, 2d ed. (Edinburgh: Edinburgh University Press, 2004); Barry Kernfeld, *Pop Music Piracy: Disobedient Music Distribution since 1929* (Chicago, IL: University of Chicago Press, 2011); Lawrence Lessig, *Free Culture* (New York, NY: Penguin, 2004); Kembrew McLeod, "Musical Production, Copyright, and the Private Ownership of Culture," in *Critical Cultural Policy Studies: A Reader* (Malden: Backwell, 2003), 240–52; Kembrew McLeod, *Owning Culture: Authorship, Ownership, & Intellectual Property Law* (New York, NY: Peter Lang, 2001); Siva Vaidhyanathan, *Copyrights and Copywrongs: The Rise of Intellectual Property and How It Threatens Creativity* (New York, NY: New York University, 2001), 17–34, 117–84.

7. See, for example, Gary Rosen, *Adventures of a Jazz Age Lawyer: Nathan Burkan and the Making of American Popular Culture* (University of California Press,

2020); Gary Rosen, *Unfair to Genius: The Strange and Litigious Career of Ira B. Arnstein* (New York, NY: Oxford University, 2012).

8. See, for example, Mark A. Lemley, "Our Bizarre System for Proving Copyright Infringement," *Journal of the Copyright Society of the USA* 57 (Summer 2010): 719–35; Irina D. Manta, "Reasonable Copyright," *Boston College Law Review* 53 (September 2012): 1303–60. Legal scholar Olufunmilayo Arewa's work on orally transmitted traditions presents a notable exception. See Olufunmilayo Arewa, "A Musical Work is a Set of Instructions," *Houston Law Review* 52, no. 2 (2014): 467–535; Olufunmilayo Arewa, "Blues Lives: Promise and Perils of Musical Copyright," *Cardozo Arts and Entertainment Law Journal* 27 (2010): 573–624.

9. See Matthew W. Daus, "The Abrogation of Expert Dissection in Popular Music Copyright Infringement," *Touro Law Review* 8 (Winter 1992): 615–46; William Patry, *How to Fix Copyright* (Oxford: Oxford University, 2011).

10. See, for example, Mark Avsec, "'Nonconventional' Musical Analysis and 'Disguised' Infringement: Clever Musical Tricks to Divide the Wealth of Tin Pan Alley," *Cleveland State Law Review* 52 (2004–2005): 339–71; Maureen Baker, "La[w] – A Note To Follow So: Have We Forgotten the Federal Rules of Evidence in Music Plagiarism Cases?," *Southern California Law Review* 65 (March 1992): 1583–640; Michael Der Manuelian, "The Role of the Expert Witness in Music Copyright Infringement Cases," *Fordham Law Review* 57 (October 1988): 127–47.

11. See Robert Brauneis, "Musical Work Copyright for the Era of Digital Sound Technology: Looking Beyond Composition and Performance," *Tulane Journal of Technology and Intellectual Property* 17 (Fall 2014): 1–51; E. Scott Fruehwald, "Copyright Infringement of Musical Compositions: A Systematic Approach," *Akron Law Review* 26 (Summer 1992): 15–48; Margit Livingston and Joseph Urbinato, "Copyright Infringement of Music: Determining What Sounds Alike Is Alike," *Vanderbilt Journal of Entertainment and Technology Law* 15 (Winter 2013): 227–302.

12. Charles Cronin, "I Hear America Suing: Music Copyright Infringement in the Era of Electronic Sound," *Hastings Law Journal* 66 (June 2015): 1187–255; Charles Cronin, "Concepts of Melodic Similarity in Music-Copyright Infringement Suits," *Computing in Musicology* 11 (1997–1998): 187–209; Chris May, "Jurisprudence v. Musicology: Riffs from the Land Down Under," *Music and Letters* 97 no. 4 (2017): 622–46; Eleanor Selfridge-Field, "Substantial Musical Similarity in Sound and Notation: Perspectives from Digital Musicology," *Colorado Technology Law Journal* 16 (2018): 249–83.

13. Alexander Stewart, "'Been Caught Stealing': A Musicologist's Perspective on Unlicensed Sampling Disputes," *University of Missouri Kansas City Law Review* 83 (Winter 2014): 339–61; Judith Finell, "Using an Expert Witness in a Music Copyright Case," *New York Law Journal* 11 (May 1990): 5–6.

14. See, for example, Guillaume Laroche, "Striking Similarities: Toward a Quantitative Measure of Melodic Copyright Infringement," *Integral* 25 (2011): 39–88; M. Fletcher Reynolds, *Music Analysis for Expert Testimony in Copyright Infringement Litigation* (Ph.D. Diss., University of Kansas, 1991).

15. Charles Cronin, ed., *Music Copyright Infringement Resource*, https://blogs.law
.gwu.edu/mcir/.

16. Learned Hand, "Historical and Practical Considerations Regarding Expert
Testimony," *Harvard Law Review* 15 (May 1901): 51.

17. Francis M. McCormick, Jr., *George P. Reed v. Samuel Carusi: A Nineteenth
Century Jury Trial Pursuant to the 1831 Copyright Act*, Last modified January 2005,
http://digitalcommons.law.umaryland.edu/mlh_pubs/4/, 12–13 (quoting William
Frederick Frick).

Chapter 1

The Foundations of Music Copyright Law and Musical Expertise

The U.S. Copyright Act was first passed in 1790, rooted in European conceptions of intellectual property and market economies. The Act derived its power from the "Science Clause" of the Constitution, which established rights for creators to control information presented as their own original, expressive works. After its passage, creators could enforce limited rights to control the distribution of the intangible works they produced, or their intellectual property. Among those rights was a fourteen-year period where the copyright holder could control the "printing, reprinting, publishing, and vending"[1] of a protected book, map, or chart, with an additional fourteen-year period for renewal. Copyright holders could also sue alleged infringers of these rights.

Music did not receive legal protection, however, until the first major revision of the Copyright Act, which was enacted in 1831.[2] Among its changes, the 1831 Act afforded musical authors the same protections as were accorded to other reproducible expressive works covered by copyright. These "musical compositions," taking the form of notated sheet music thought to embody less tangible musical sound, did not receive individualized provision for controlling live performance, let alone nascent recording technology that would appear later in the century. Instead, courts tasked with enforcing these new rights for musical compositions would treat them identically to other expressive works.

MUSIC COPYRIGHT LITIGATION BEGINS

Shortly after enactment, legal issues began to be raised about the extent of rights protection for copyrightable music. These actions marked the start of federal music copyright litigation. The cases that ensued during this century show courts struggling to define a legal process by which the contours of copyright infringement could be determined, especially for music. By the middle of the century, courts had settled on similarity as the central inquiry for infringement cases as applied to all protectable works. Thus, a piece of music, or any other copyrightable work, was believed to have infringed on another work if the two pieces were sufficiently similar as to indicate copying.

Attorneys and courts during this time turned to the technical skill and experiential knowledge of musical experts, typically avocational or professional performers, composers, and music publishing company clerks, to offer more systematic, seemingly well-informed comparisons to clarify the subtle distinctions between musical works. Experts were almost always called as witnesses in these early cases, but there seems to be little standardization as to their contributions. Such expert witnesses typically performed the two pieces of music at issue to provide an aural means of comparison for factfinders, either judges or jurors, or provided explanations of fundamental music theory. More significantly, however, expert witnesses also conducted analytical comparisons based on the printed text of the music and offered their own conclusions as to whether the similarity amounted to copying. The relative lack of common law precedent for conducting infringement analysis, however, posed a problem for reaching equitable decisions across cases and for managing the kind and purpose of evidence presented by experts.

Even without a functional means to ensure legal uniformity across cases, trends began to develop in the role that musical experts played in each lawsuit. During the nineteenth century, cases involved then-popular styles, from songs typically heard in parlors or theaters to band music. Most expert witnesses approached the similarity inquiry as locating the extent of musical congruence, predominantly through note-by-note melodic comparison usually conducted separately from the harmonic and formal dimensions of the song. The analytical techniques they used often correlated to their party affiliation: the plaintiff's experts demonstrated putative congruences, while the defendant's experts often recast those putative points of similarity as a matter of stylistic commonality by showing resemblance between the music at issue and prior compositions. In so doing, expert witnesses marked features of the shared musical boundaries between pieces at issue and mapped unclear territory between commonality and infringement. Although the contributions of musical experts were not necessarily determinative in any case, their influence on case outcomes is explicit in some judicial opinions.

AN EARLY HISTORY OF EXPERT WITNESSES

Although the first documented use of an expert witness dates to early seventeenth-century England, judicial reliance on individuals with specialized knowledge began much earlier.[3] Fourteenth-century courts initially deter-mined the nature of expertise, as well as the admissibility of expert testi-mony, on the grounds of general relevance of evidence.[4] The concept of an expert witness derived from the idea of a "special jury," where jurors were required to have particular qualifications before making legal decisions, as separate from a "mixed jury" of guild members and merchants, or a "jury of matrons."[5] Instead of witnesses providing the jury with special information, as a modern expert witness might do, these jurors were the ones to bring expertise to courtroom.

This self-informing jury practice faded over time in favor of more passive, nonexpert jurors, and along with it came the rise of nonpartisan expert "advi-sors" to the court.[6] In these cases, there was no special process for distin-guishing an expert from a nonexpert, and no differentiation between the kinds of technical, specialized evidence presented by an expert as separate from any other kind of admissible evidence, including that which a nonexpert, or lay, witness might present. The court simply needed to determine whether the evidence was relevant to the legal inquiry.

Through the nineteenth century, as attorneys took greater and more strate-gic control over the production of evidence, expert witnesses grew increas-ingly common. They also became a common point of critique for courts and legal commentators, often because of a perceived failure on the experts' part to provide objective, clarifying evidence. In 1857, a U.S. Supreme Court opin-ion lambasted expert witnesses for being as "effective in producing obscurity and error as in the elucidation of truth."[7] By the end of the nineteenth century, legal scholars, practitioners, and journalistic commentators had raised issues about the effectiveness of expert testimony, from their allegedly biased ser-vice as "hired guns" to their specialized knowledge appearing to do more to confuse jurors than aid them. As one contemporaneous commentator wrote, "if there is any kind of testimony that is not only of no value, but even worse than that, it is . . . that of . . . experts,"[8] regardless of specialty. Another critic claimed that expert testimony "is the subject of everybody's sneer, and the object of everybody's derision. It has become a newspaper jest. The public has no confidence in expert testimony."[9]

Critics of expert witnesses identified witness partiality as "probably the most frequent complaint of all against the expert witness."[10] By virtue of being retained by one party or the other, intentional or unintentional partial-ity on the part of expert witnesses often impacted the content of evidence they presented. While some commentators recognized that there could be legitimate differences of expert opinion due to differing methods and inter-pretations, there was still the possibility that such disagreements resulted from the expert's ethical and financial allegiance to the party that retained them. As nineteenth-century commentators noted, courts were all too often "entertained with the sad spectacle of two sets of experts giving solemn testimony in direct contradiction to each other."[11] Beyond contradictory testimony, other commentators pointed toward the "loose way in which the trial court admit[ted]"[12] witnesses as experts as well as the hypothetical questions attorneys often posed to expert witnesses.[13] Despite increasing skepticism surrounding their contributions over the nineteenth century, these specialized witnesses grew entrenched into court proceedings. Especially for music copyright cases, they provided pertinent technical knowledge to legal proceedings and attempted to answer questions that ordinary factfinders seemed otherwise ill-equipped to understand.

MUSICAL EXPERTS PERFORM LIVE IN THE COURTROOM

One of the earliest functions that musical expert witnesses fulfilled was performative. Initially, experts were retained principally to sing, or play, in the courtroom so that factfinders might aurally compare the music at issue. While these witnesses did little to control the final decision in each case, they carried the heavy burden of performance decisions that had an implicit influence on the ways in which the court heard the music at issue. In the absence of readily available recordings, these live courtroom performances were the only means outside of sheet music examination that courts at this time could use to conduct musical comparisons.

While not the first of its kind to address music,[14] one of the first cases to include a musical performance at trial was *Reed v. Carusi*, which was decided in 1845 by presiding circuit Judge Roger Taney.[15] The *Reed* court struggled to establish a method for conducting a legal investigation of music copyright infringement claims and for determining damages in the event infringement was identified. Although not recorded in extant court documents, at least one musical performer was said to have been introduced as a witness to offer a performance of the songs in the courtroom.

This case hinged on competing claims over the rights to piano-vocal sheet music settings of the popular English poem, "The Old Arm Chair." The litigation process revealed a web of poets, composers, and bandleaders over nearly a decade of interaction. Eliza Cook composed the poem in 1838, and it was first set to music by composer Henry Russell the following year. Russell's setting has been said to be the most popular American setting of the sentimental song, likely due in part to his undertaking of a U.S. tour. In December 1842, Boston publishers Oakes and Swan obtained the copyright to the song, which was ultimately assigned to George P. Reed, the plaintiff.

Legal problems arose because Marine Band leader Samuel Carusi, the defendant, had already obtained copyright for his setting of Cook's poem to the music of the song, "New England," two months earlier, in October 1842. Although it would seem that Carusi's predated copyright registration gave him the legal upper-hand, it was Reed who filed the complaint in 1844. The fact that Reed, rather than Carusi, filed suit, coupled with the fact that one of Carusi's compositions appeared in Reed's 1840 publication catalog, suggests that the case might have been a strategic attempt to begin refining the contours of federal copyright law pertaining to music, or at least a direct attempt at market control by Reed.[16]

Although the motivation for initiating the lawsuit remains unclear, litigation commenced in 1844 under Section 7 of the 1831 Copyright Act, with Reed alleging that Carusi published against Reed's copyright "with varying design" and "with intent to evade the law."[17] Reed sought $2,000 in damages based on the "one-copy, one-dollar" statutory damages formula established in the 1831 Act. Carusi replied by claiming that Reed's version was unoriginal, instead being based on earlier airs, and that the two pieces at bar were ultimately different. The jury awarded Reed only $200, to be divided evenly between Reed and the federal government.[18]

The final judicial opinion made no reference to musical experts, nor did it show any explicit influence from their testimony, and extant records do not include any sheet music or written comparisons conducted by experts. Likewise, the opinion offers no explicit musical analysis or comparison. Extant sources, nonetheless, indicate that musical experts participated in the trial. In his memoir, defense attorney William Frederick Frick noted that there was "a great deal of learned musical testimony and forensic discussion."[19] Frick's association of forensic evaluations with musical analysis suggests a contemporaneous assumption regarding the scientific or objective nature of expert testimony and reveals forensic musicology as a nascent discipline forming alongside music copyright litigation practices.

Among these experts was John Cole, described as a professional singer as well as a music publisher, who was introduced by Reed and required to sing the two songs to the jury so that they could judge whether the songs were similar or not. Although the particulars of Cole's performance were not preserved, the court likely heard two songs that beyond the lyrics were by no means identical, but that bore a certain amount of musical congruence. While Reed (Russell)'s version is in E-flat and in common time and Carusi's is in D-major and in 2/4, the two melodies follow similar trajectories in pitch, rhythm, and phrasing. Likewise, the accompaniments both feature simple, slurred broken chords featuring similarly voiced triadic harmonies. Even without these particulars, the performance was allegedly

made "in the gravest manner, under direction of the Chief Justice, to
intone the two songs successively in open court."[20] Frick described the
performance:[21]

> the appearance of the singer, the lamentable monotonous cadence of both airs,
> the pathos of the words . . . together with the singular and varied expressions
> of pleasure or disapprobation on the faces of the musical dilettanti present,
> produced by Mr. Cole's emphatic rendering of the songs, would, under any
> other circumstances, have created in the crowd of bystanders irresistible laugh-
> ter and confusion. But the Chief Justice, with that power peculiarly his own,
> of restraining almost by a glance the slightest breach of decorum in his Court,
> overawed and repressed every demonstration of disrespect by the placid and
> dignified attention which he bestowed throughout upon Mr. Cole's musical
> efforts.

At the time of performance, Frick claimed that he objected to this evidence
on grounds that it violated courtroom decorum. Judge Taney supposedly
overruled the objection, finding the performance to be a "novel species of
evidence."[22] Frick nonetheless expressed concern that such a performance
could not have occurred "in any other Court without inducing some, at
least, of the listeners to forget and violate the customary rules of judicial
decorum."[23]

The validity of Frick's interpretation of the *gravitas* by which Cole's
performance was treated in court is impossible to confirm, but his concern
regarding music performances in the courtroom and the novelty of the evidence are significant. By extending copyright to protect this new category
of expressive works, courts were faced with finding new ways to determine
similarity between works of music, made more challenging by the specialized literacy required to examine sheet music and the intangible nature
of music itself. Judge Taney's admission and allegedly serious interest
in the evidence suggests at least that expert witnesses had an important
role in music copyright infringement cases. The extent to which the
performance influenced the decisions of the jurors, however, remains
undetermined.

Despite limited extant records indicating the role of experts, *Reed* established a pattern of employing experts early in the history of music copyright
litigation that continues into the present day. In particular, the practice of
experts like Cole performing music in court to aid aural comparison has
continued even through the rise of mechanical recording. Even with the
introduction of recorded excerpts for demonstrations, courtroom aural performances would endure as one of the central functions of forensic musical
expertise.

FORENSIC SIMILARITY ANALYSIS IN
THE NINETEENTH CENTURY

Live performance in the courtroom provided a practical means for factfinders to compare the music at issue, especially for those who could not read western music notation. Experts' own detailed analyses of the sheet music, however, would provide specialized comparisons that reached levels of depth not necessarily perceptible by musical nonexperts. In addition to performance of the music at issue, arguably the central function of expert witnesses within copyright litigation was established in these earliest cases: conducting analytical comparisons between the pieces of music at issue to advise the court in determining infringement.

A few years after *Reed*, in 1850, the court in *Jollie v. Jaques* reinforced the establishment of similarity as the core legal inquiry for copyright infringement cases. The court described similarity between two works as the "basis for inquiry,"[24] evaluated according to a substantiality standard to distinguish lawful commonality from unlawful appropriation established by a similar case involving books.[25] The *Reed* lawsuit involved a pair of competing arrangements, only this time for a popular German dance song. George Loder, the musical director of Burton's Theater, had arranged "Röschen Polka" for piano with the title, "The Serious Family Polka," and then granted copyright for the song to music publisher and instrument seller, Samuel Jollie. This simple piano sheet music featured 2/4 meter and "oom-pah" accompaniment typical of polka style with a charming melody.

Upon finding a competing piece of sheet music, Jollie sued John and James Jaques for arranging and publishing the same polka under the same title. The brothers claimed that their arrangement was an original, protectable adaptation of the polka. Moreover, they denied Jollie's copyright claim, instead arguing that his version was unoriginal and merely a reproduction of the "Röschen Polka." While the case raised procedural issues regarding the delivery of copies as a prerequisite for copyright, the substantive issue was whether "The Serious Family Polka" could even be considered an original musical composition, such that it was eligible for federal copyright protection.[26]

To make its decision, the court relied on the analysis from at least three expert witnesses whose party affiliation, if any, is not confirmed in extant records. Among existing expert depositions, or out-of-court sworn testimony, one witness addressed the cultural history of the music at issue; the other two gave depositions that compared the melodies and instrumentation of the two versions. The comparative analysis presented by these latter two experts, who located similarity through identification of musical congruences, proved to be most significant to the court.

According to expert witness Johann Munck, who served as a teacher, composer, and band leader in New York City:[27]

> Loder's Polka is a substantial copy of a piece of music by a German composer called the "Röschen Polka," which has been played by various bands in the City of New York for some time antecedent to Mr. Loder's production thereof and deponent has himself seen the same in a book belonging to Mr. Weise a leader of a Band German Musicians, and that the said Loder has made no change in the melody whatever and had added no original matter to the Composition and had made no new combination of the materials of said original air but has merely adapted the old melody to the piano-forte.

Without outlining any of his analytical method or specific points of musical similarity, Munck's deposition, only presented his summary conclusions regarding the extent of similarity between the two songs at issue. He couched his discussion in his awareness of contemporary German band music repertory instead of detailed theoretical analysis.

In contrast, Charles H. Dibble, who served as a clerk at William Hall and Son music publisher, offered more specific analytical discussion. The court reporter noted that Dibble was "acquainted with music practically and theoretically"[28] and that he had "examined the several polkas published by Samuel E. Jollie"[29] involved in the case. Dibble's analysis was then summarized as describing the polkas being "different in their arrangement and that the one published by the above defendants [the Jaques brothers] contains several bars of matter not contained in that published by the above plaintiff [Jollie]."[30]

This formal introduction and analytical summary, which served to establish Dibble's credibility, was also used in music teacher George H. Curtis's deposition, likely for the same purpose. Curtis's deposition, however, included a bar-by-bar explanation of where the two songs differed. His deposition, focused mostly on musical congruence according to melodic pitch, which he referred to as "notes," and overarching harmonic relationships, while not addressing their relationship to rhythm and meter:[31]

> [the one] published by the defendants is written in the key of A Major, the plaintiff being written in the Key of G Major; the first, third, fourth, the first half of the fifth, seventh, and sixteenth bars of the said Editions differ in the arrangement of the treble and bass notes of each bar as may be seen by inspection.

> That in the second part the first third and fifth bars differ in the arrangement of the bass notes and the second fourth and sixth bars differ in the arrangement of the treble notes and the Seventh has of the same part differ in the arrangement of both treble and bass notes.

And deponent further says that the portion marked Trio in the Edition published by defendants containing Eight bars is different in every respect from the same part of the Polka published by complainant [the plaintiff, Jollie].

And deponent further says that he finds an examination that to the finalie of the Polka in question published by defendants are added Eight bars of original music not found in any portion of the Polka published by complainant. That the new music bears no similarity or affinity to the melody of the preceding part & differs entirely in arrangement therefrom.

And deponent further says that he has compared the Polka published by complainant with a piece of music known as the Roschen Polka & that by such comparison the former appears to have been *substantially* copied in melody from the later: the only difference being that in the piece of music deponent saw was arranged for the clarionet while the same melody appears in the Polka published by complainant arranged for the Piano forte: which change is not attended with the slighted difficulty and is susceptible of being accomplished by any person able to transpose music in a very short space of time.[*sic*]

Unlike other available expert testimony, Curtis's analysis appears almost verbatim in the court's decision.

After a recitation of the contours of the new copyright provisions and the procedural issues in the case, the court summarized both Jollie and the Jaques brothers' arguments, and then introduced Curtis's analysis:[32]

It is further shown by an expert, who had examined and compared the two pieces of music, that the one published by the defendants is not only written in a different key, but that the first, third, fourth, fifth, seventh and sixteenth bars of the first part of the two editions, differ in the arrangement of the treble and bass notes of each bar; that in the second part, the first, third and fifth bars differ in the arrangement of the bass notes, the second, fourth and sixth bars in the arrangement of the treble notes, and the seventh bar in the arrangement of both treble and bass notes; that the portion marked trio in the defendant's edition, containing eight bars, is different in all respects from the same part of the polka published by the plaintiff; that to the finale of the defendants' polka are added eight bars of original matter not found in any portion of the plaintiff's edition; that the music of his edition is, in the melody, taken substantially from the "Roschen Polka," the only difference being that the latter was arranged for the clarionet, and the former, by Loder, for the piano-forte; and that the adaptation to one instrument of the music composed for another, requires but an inferior degree of skill, and can be readily accomplished by any person practised in the transfer of music.[*sic*]

Through this reasoning, the court determined the Jaques brothers did not infringe because the two arrangements appeared to be similar according to a standard of substantiality likely borrowed from Curtis.

In its reliance on experts, the *Jollie* court demonstrated the significant role that musical experts had played in the litigation process. By providing their technical analysis, expert witnesses contextualized musical comparisons at issue in the case according to congruence revelatory of copying rather than stylistic commonality or resemblance. The analytical techniques they applied emphasized pitch comparisons. As the court explained, "[t]he original air requires genius for its construction; but a mere mechanic in music, it is said, can make the adaptation or accompaniment."[33] Here, the court relied on melody, or "the original air," as the central source of copyright-protectable material to determine whether the alleged copy rose to the conceptual level of legal infringement. The court avoided the experts' discussions of style and originality in the context of polka music, choosing instead to focus on the two melodies as the "genius" behind the music, with minimal judicial treatment of the accompaniment, or "bass notes," that "a mere mechanic" could have allegedly provided.

The legal process outlined in the *Jollie* decision, which relied heavily on expert witness evaluations, laid a foundation for detailed forensic similarity analysis in subsequent cases as the purview of musical experts, whose contributions were intended to inform the court before any final legal determinations were made. After this landmark case, however, the next published music copyright decision did not appear in historical records for nearly thirty years. It is likely that other copyright claims were raised during this period whose decisions were either unpublished or settled out of court, as many such claims are treated still today.

BLUME V. SPEAR

By 1878, the case of *Blume v. Spear* was decided, which revealed an expansion in reliance on expert witnesses as well as in their analytical techniques.[34] With an issue and fact pattern similar to the cases that preceded it, the *Blume* court dealt with competing claims to rights control over a popular domestic song. Building on precedent set by the *Jollie* decision and other copyright cases, the main issue in *Blume* regarded the degree of similarity necessary to constitute infringement. In this case, songwriter Fannie Beane composed "My Own Sweet Darling, Colleen Dhas Machree" and granted the copyright to publisher Frederick Blume. In 1877, Blume claimed that defendant Frederick Spear stole the song and retitled it "Call Me Back Again." As part of the defendant's argument, he introduced another song, "Sweet Spirit Hear My Prayer," to argue that Blume's "My Own Sweet Darling" was based on prior compositions.

To support their arguments, both parties relied on a surprisingly large number of expert witnesses for nineteenth-century copyright lawsuits. Most notably, Blume introduced music professor Sigismond Lasar, who taught at the Packer Collegiate Institute in Brooklyn. In his deposition, Lasar claimed that he had examined a number of melodies "in the line of discovering plagiarisms,"[35] offering what appears to be one of the earliest references to serving as a professional expert witness, or a kind of proto-forensic musicologist. Lasar's deposition addressed issues of melodic similarity primarily during direct examination, using similar analytical techniques to those used by experts in *Jollie*. Treating musical similarity as a function of musical congruence, Lasar indicated which measures were "identical" or "nearly so."[36] He also discussed issues of rhythmic similarity and nonchord tones in the melody during cross-examination, first between the songs at issue and then between "My Own Sweet Darling" and "Sweet Spirit."[37]

To demonstrate visually his analysis and explanatory testimony, Lasar's deposition included a comparison chart, shown in figure 1.1. In this chart, the three melodies were removed from their formal contexts, transposed to the same key and then aligned in tandem. Unique features of each melody were written smaller and in red—appearing gray in the figure—while overlapping pitches were notated in black. The chart served as a representation of Lasar's discussion of melody, harmony, and rhythm. Its graphic depiction exploited the color contrast by also including song titles, measure numbers, and lyrics minimally relevant to the comparison in red ink. Thus, the more black ink a viewer saw, the more similarity it was assumed that they could perceive.

Even setting aside Lasar's apparently partisan strategy, the coloration of the notation provided a striking visual marker of similarities in melodic pitch and rhythm. Yet it does not seem to account for other similarities, such as harmony or form. Thus, the chart might have been deceiving to nonexpert viewers.

Extending his analysis beyond the music as it appeared in notation, Lasar drew attention to a melodic figure in the second measure of "Sweet Spirit," and "Colleen," which Lasar identified as being of "Scottish derivation":[38]

A. the four notes proper in the second measure of the song of Sweet Spirit, & C. [*sic*]

Q. Can you tell us anything about these four notes as they appear in musical compositions?

A. They are usually known as a peculiar Scottish derivation. . . . appearing everywhere in ordinary street or minstrel songs, and they have no special identity.

As a result, Lasar argued, the overlap in this four-note figure should have been considered insignificant or insubstantial, not because of the quantity of notes, but because it was common to Scottish music, and therefore unoriginal and

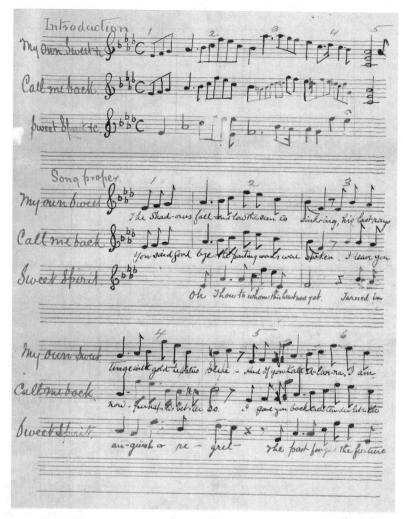

Figure 1.1 *Blume v. Spear*, **Comparison Chart, Sigismond Lasar.** Record Group 21; National Archives and Records Administration Philadelphia; Record Entry NY-213; National Archives ID 749265; Circuit Court Southern District of New York; Equity Case Files 1876–1907, Box #400; "Blume v. Spear." Credit: National Archives and Records Administration Philadelphia.

legally unprotectable. This portion of the analysis, although critical to determinations of infringement, required expert knowledge regarding style, musical borrowing, and compositional process not readily apparent in the sheet music.

Blume also introduced composer, arranger, and accompanist Charles Pratt, who applied many of the same analytical techniques as Lasar and the experts in *Jollie*. Pratt had previously corrected the printer's copy of Blume's song, so by the time of trial, he was "very familiar with it."[39] It is possible that Pratt's familiarity with the plaintiff's song created at least some partisan bias in his analysis, but there is no record of the court pursuing this concern.

Like Lasar's deposition, Pratt's deposition included a black-and-red melodic comparison chart, shown in figure 1.2. The smaller red notes—appearing

Figure 1.2 *Blume v. Spear,* **Comparison Chart, Charles Pratt.** Record Group 21; National Archives and Records Administration Philadelphia; Record Entry NY-213; National Archives ID 749265; Circuit Court Southern District of New York; Equity Case Files 1876–1907, Box #400; "Blume v. Spear." Credit: National Archives and Records Administration Philadelphia.

gray in the figure—highlighted points of dissimilarity and red lines—also appearing gray in the figure—were drawn between offset similarities in pitch. Pratt seems to have used this chart for his analysis to conclude that not only were the two songs "substantially identical" but also that "the former [Call Me Back Again] was either copied from the latter [Colleen Dhas Machree], or was more likely carried in the memory of some person."[40]

In addition to Pratt's analysis, extant court records include a series of nearly identical affidavits, or written statements, from music experts, mostly composers and teachers, all agreeing with Pratt. The list includes documents signed by J. Hazen Ross, James J. Freeman, James O'Neil, Joseph P. Skelley, Charles Puemer, Anthony Baris, and Charles Cappa.[41] These affidavits lent credibility to Pratt's work, but they offer little in the way of independent analysis. None of the expert documents outline the witnesses' analytical techniques, but it is likely that the similarity they identified referred more to pitch than harmony or rhythm.

In opposition, Defendant Spear called Harrison Milliard, a composer "thoroughly versed in the knowledge of music and harmony."[42] Unsurprisingly given his party affiliation, Milliard arrived at the opposite conclusion of Blume's experts. Milliard did not explicitly outline his comparative analysis in prose or shown graphically in a chart. Instead, he emphasized the relationship of the music at issue to prior compositions, thereby arguing that the similarities were not significant to infringement decisions:[43]

> I find that the music of ["Call Me Back Again"]—which in some respects is similar as far as portions of the melody go, differs materially and substantially from the music and melody of the other two, especially as to the arrangement of the accompaniment.

> The prelude for the piano is entirely different in composition and such resemblances as may be found are only in a few bars of the melody which are repeated several times during the composition.

> This similarity of idea is a thing which is of almost daily occurrence and it is difficult to determine who originates any given musical phrase, as even the bars of music claimed as identical by the several musicians whose affidavits I have read in connection with plaintiffs papers are almost identical with "Sweet Spirit Hear My Prayer," written by Wallace and made popular in 1861.

> I often find musical phrases which I believe have been originated by me and first used in some of my popular songs introduced and used in other songs by

musical composers, but I do not think they in any way detract from the merit of my songs or in any way inspire them if the songs are sold under different titles and subjects, differing from those which I have originally published.

According to Milliard, the similarities that Blume's experts identified were irrelevant to finding infringement because such similarity reflected musical borrowing that was, in his opinion, common to the compositional process. As a result, that material would be considered not legally protectable. This discussion also recast Lasar's dismissal of the similarity based on the material "of Scottish derivation," as being more relevant to the comparison. Millard's deposition also presented a critique of Lasar and Pratt's analytical technique, which emphasized melodic pitch similarity out of the context of the rest of the music and over a comparison of the accompaniment.

The defense introduced additional testimony from composer Clark Evans and a generalized "expert on music," Paul Steinhagen. Both expert witnesses presented similar findings to Milliard, giving nearly identical depositions. Evans and Steinhagen reinforced Milliard's argument by stating that the similarities between the songs appear in well-known published songs, therefore, the similarity should constitute legally acceptable borrowing, not illegal infringement. "A few bars of the melody in each resemble each other but these bars are almost identical with bars found in the well-known song published more than twenty years ago, 'Sweet Spirit, Hear My Prayer.'"[44] Although melody was the main focus of their depositions, Evans and Steinhagen also addressed differences in the arrangement and accompaniment of the songs, without specifying what musical relationships they meant. They both "compared the two pieces of music hereto annexed called 'My Own Sweet Darling Coleen Dhas Machree' marked 'B' and 'Call Me Back Again,' marked 'C'—and [the experts found] that they differ materially in the prelude for the piano and in the arrangement of the accompaniment and in other respects."[45] The records remain unclear as to other musical "respects," but it could have referred to harmonic or rhythmic comparisons.

The partisan strategy behind these expert contributions seems apparent. Given that Milliard, Evans, and Steinhagen were retained by Spear, their affiliation with the defendant likely motivated them to cast the inherent melodic similarities as unoriginal prior art, and then to draw attention to differences in other parts of the song, most notably the arrangement and accompaniment. The argument also presented a new dimension to the infringement analysis based on assessments of originality that separated similarity from misappropriation, foreshadowing future legal divisions. According to the defendant and his experts, similarity did not demonstrate infringement automatically; rather, similarity had to be specific to protectable elements of the plaintiff's music.

The defendants' strategy ultimately proved to be unsuccessful. The most legally significant reasoning in the opinion, however, was the court's reinforcement of the point at which similarities between two pieces of music were relevant and "substantial" enough to constitute infringement. As the court noted:[46]

> Upon the question of infringement there is not much room for doubt. The theme or melody of the music is substantially the same in the copyrighted and the alleged infringing pieces. The measure of the former is followed in the latter, and is somewhat peculiar. When played by a competent musician, they appear to be really the same. There are variations, but they are so placed as to indicate that the former was taken deliberately, rather than that the latter was a new piece.

The decision also began to account for unlawful appropriation without introducing it as a separate legal inquiry from similarity. The court did make an oblique reference to examining "variations" of the melody as presented and discussed by the expert witnesses, which were "so placed as to indicate that the former was taken deliberately, rather than that the latter was a new piece."[47] This "deliberate" copying introduced an intent to infringe as opposed to similarity resulting from common compositional process within the stylistic idiom. But the court formalistically interpreted similarity as the central legal inquiry without introducing its own practical approach given the facts of the lawsuit and the nature of each party's argument. The presence of musical expert witnesses nonetheless highlights period conceptions of musical similarity as fact-specific, and their disagreements point toward the subjectivity of interpreting it in a legal context.

Despite its legal insights, the *Blume* decision offered little historical guidance regarding the influence that expert witnesses had on judges' decisions or the precise role that they played in litigation. Without an explicit reference to experts, or even a correlation between their reports and the court's decision, it is unclear the extent to which the court relied on expert witnesses or made its own comparisons in reaching the final outcome of the case. It is also unclear how the quantity experts, particularly on the plaintiff's behalf, impacted the court's decision. Extant records nevertheless offer a glimpse into the ways that experts did serve the court by lending their specialized skill and knowledge to the arguments of both parties.

Unlike *Jollie*, where the court explicitly examined pieces of sheet music rather than performances of them, the opinion from *Blume* offered no such musical analysis. In so doing, the opinion obscured the detailed comparative analytical process conducted by expert witnesses as preserved in extant court records. It likewise did not address the disagreements between experts for opposing parties or the large quantity of experts hired for the case. The *Blume* decision did suggest, however, that courts considered comparative analysis of the songs and prior compositions where applicable to be the appropriate method for determining infringement and claimed that the method was applied to some extent. Thus, although the court did not explicitly outline the context of musical similarity in its opinion, that similarity was nonetheless contextualized by musical expert witnesses.

While the *Jollie* and *Blume* decisions did little to define the role of experts, available court records suggest that they played an essential role. To varying extents, experts conducted close analyses of musical similarity, moving note by note in search of musical congruences. Their comparisons were primarily focused on melody, with rhythm and harmony serving as secondary considerations; only some experts provided even limited discussions of style, originality, and musical borrowing not immediately apparent in the sheet music. These analyses led to conclusions regarding similarity, but expert witnesses occasionally used these conclusions to extrapolate regarding the ultimate issue of infringement in each case. Whether cited directly or merely contributing on the court's reasoning, experts played an essential role by informing the judge's final decision.

TOWARD THE TWENTIETH CENTURY

The foundations of American music copyright litigation can be found in formalistic legal procedure established during the nineteenth century that centered on substantial similarity analysis. By the end of this century, courts seeking to establish fundamental principles interpreted from federal statutory copyright law had turned to other issues relevant to copyright protection, such as prior art and the scope of federal copyright protection. Seemingly more pressing for the role of musical expert witnesses during this period, the court defined infringement by substantial similarity between two expressive works as the relevant legal standard. Nineteenth-century courts lacked a practical process for making such determinations, however, which had the effect of precluding any consistency of judicial decision-making between one case and another. As music copyright cases demonstrated, finding substantial similarity in order to determine infringement was indeed a fact-specific endeavor.

Among the missing elements to this legal procedure were guidelines for the role of expert witnesses and their analyses. Despite legal commentary that critiqued the contributions of expert witnesses across areas of law, they had few, if any, constraints on the scope of those contributions. In court, musical experts could apply their analyses to comment on similarity, but they could also comment on ultimate determinations regarding infringement. Their analyses, although treated with a sense of forensic impartiality, could just as soon serve the competitive ends of the hiring party. In some cases, the court quoted directly from expert reports; in other cases, the court could have just as easily ignored expert analysis entirely. Despite a lack of procedure guiding them, the participation of expert witnesses in early music copyright litigation appears to have been routine and significant. The extent to which those expert contributions could, or should, impact the outcome of each case, however, was left for future courts to determine.

NOTES

1. *Copyright Act of 1790*, 1 Statutes at Large 124 § 1 (1790).
2. *An Act to Amend the Several Acts Respecting Copyrights*, 4 Stat. 436 (1831) (amended 1870).
3. Learned Hand, "Historical and Practical Considerations Regarding Expert Testimony," *Harvard Law Review* 15 (May 1902): 40.
4. David Bernstein, David H. Kaye, and Jennifer L. Mnookin, *The New Wigmore Treatise on Evidence: Expert Evidence* (Austin, TX: Aspen, 2011) § 1.3, 8 [hereinafter Wigmore]; Hand, "Historical and Practical Considerations," 42–43.
5. Wigmore, § 1.3, 8; see also Hand, "Historical and Practical Considerations," 40–43.
6. See Wigmore, § 1.3, 9–10; Jennifer L. Mnookin, "Idealizing Science and Demonizing Experts: An Intellectual History of Expert," *Villanova Law Review* 52 (2007): 767–68.
7. *McCormick v. Talcott*, 61 U.S. 402, 409 (1857).
8. Wigmore, § 1.3 at 11.
9. See Mnookin, "Idealizing Science," 771 (citing Henry Wollman, "Physicians-Expert Witnesses: Some Reforms," *Medico-Legal Journal* 17 (1899): 20).
10. William L. Foster, "Expert Testimony: Prevalent Complaints and Proposed Remedies," *Harvard Law Review* 11 (October 1897): 171.
11. See Mnookin, "Idealizing Science," 775 (citing O. W. Wight, "What Is Expert Testimony? And Who Are Experts?" *Medico-Legal Journal* 1 (1889): 146).
12. Mnookin, "Idealizing Science," 779 (citing Conway W. Noble, "The Relative Position of the Judge and the Expert Medical Witness, and Their Respective Duties," *Medico-Legal Journal* 11 (1893): 306).
13. Mnookin, "Idealizing Science," 780–81.
14. See *Millett v. Snowden*, 17 F.Cas. 374, No. 9600 (Cir. Ct. S.D. New York, NY, 1844).
15. *Reed v. Carusi*, 20 F.Cas. 431 (C.C.Md. 1845).
16. McCormick, *George P. Reed v. Samuel Carusi*, 5.
17. *Reed*, 20 F. Cas. at 431.

18. McCormick, *George P. Reed v. Samuel Carusi*, 13 (citing William Frederick Frick). In 1846, however, then-President James K. Polk pardoned Carusi's debt to the government.

19. McCormick, *George P. Reed v. Samuel Carusi*, 12–13.

20. McCormick, *George P. Reed v. Samuel Carusi*, 13 (quoting William Frederick Frick).

21. McCormick, *George P. Reed v. Samuel Carusi*, 13 (quoting William Frederick Frick).

22. McCormick, *George P. Reed v. Samuel Carusi*, 13.

23. McCormick, *George P. Reed v. Samuel Carusi*, 13 (quoting William Frederick Frick).

24. *Jollie v. Jaques*, 13 F. Cas. 910 (C.C.S.D.N.Y. 1850). In between *Reed* and *Jollie* was *Ferrett v. Atwill*, 8 F. Cas. 1161 (S.D.N.Y. 1846).

25. See *Emerson v. Davies*, 8 F. Cas. 615, 622 (C.C.D. Mass. 1845).

26. *Jollie*, 13 F. Cas. at 910.

27. *Jollie v. Jaques*, Munck Deposition, 1–3. Record Group 21; Record Entry NY-213; National Archives ID 749265; Circuit Court Southern District of New York; Equity Case Files 1846–1877, Box #5; National Archives and Records Administration, Philadelphia, PA.

28. *Jollie v. Jaques*, Dibble Deposition, 1. Record Group 21; Record Entry NY-213; National Archives ID 749265; Circuit Court Southern District of New York; Equity Case Files 1846–1877, Box #5; National Archives and Records Administration, Philadelphia, PA.

29. *Jollie v. Jaques*, Dibble Deposition, 1.

30. *Jollie v. Jaques*, Dibble Deposition, 1–2. Dibble also claimed that Munck performed the Jaques brothers' polka two weeks before Jollie's polka was published.

31. *Jollie v. Jaques*, Curtis Deposition, 1–3 (emphasis added). Record Group 21; Record Entry NY-213; National Archives ID 749265; Circuit Court Southern District of New York; Equity Case Files 1846–1877, Box #5; National Archives and Records Administration, Philadelphia, PA.

32. *Jollie*, 13 F. Cas. at 910 (emphasis added).

33. *Jollie*, 13 F. Cas. at 910.

34. *Blume v. Spear*, 30 F. 629 (C.C.S.D.N.Y. 1878).

35. *Blume v. Spear*, Lasar Deposition, 1. Record Group 21; Record Entry NY-213; National Archives ID 749265; Circuit Court Southern District of New York; Equity Case Files 1876–1907, Box #400; National Archives and Records Administration Philadelphia, PA.

36. *Blume v. Spear*, Lasar Deposition, 3–4.

37. *Blume v. Spear*, Lasar Deposition, 5–6.

38. *Blume v. Spear*, Lasar Deposition, 4–5.

39. *Blume v. Spear*, Pratt Deposition, 2. Record Group 21; Record Entry NY-213; National Archives ID 749265; Circuit Court Southern District of New York; Equity Case Files 1876–1907, Box #400; National Archives and Records Administration Philadelphia, PA.

40. *Blume v. Spear*, Pratt Deposition, 5.

41. *Blume v. Spear*, J. Hazen Ross Affidavit, 1; James J. Freeman Affidavit, 1; James O'Neil Affidavit, 1; Joseph P. Skelley Affidavit, 1; Joseph P. Skelley Affidavit, 1; Charles Puemer Affidavit, 1; Anthony Baris Affidavit, 1; Charles Cappa Affidavit, 1. The list reflects the order in which the documents appear in the case file. See Record Group 21; Record Entry NY-213; National Archives ID 749265; Circuit Court Southern District of New York; Equity Case Files 1876–1907, Box #400; National Archives and Records Administration, Philadelphia, PA.

42. *Blume v. Spear*, Milliard Deposition, 1. Record Group 21; Record Entry NY-213; National Archives ID 749265; Circuit Court Southern District of New York; Equity Case Files 1876–1907, Box #400; National Archives and Records Administration, Philadelphia, PA.

43. *Blume v. Spear*, Milliard Deposition, 2–3.

44. *Blume v. Spear*, Steinhagen Deposition, 1–2; Evans Deposition, 1–2. Record Group 21; Record Entry NY-213; National Archives ID 749265; Circuit Court Southern District of New York; Equity Case Files 1876–1907, Box #400; National Archives and Records Administration, Philadelphia, PA.

45. *Blume v. Spear*, Steinhagen Deposition, 1–2; Evans Deposition, 1–2.

46. *Blume*, 30 F. at 628.

47. *Blume*, 30 F. at 628.

Chapter 2

Judges, Experts, and
Ordinary Listeners

Since the earliest federal music copyright infringement cases heard in the United States, judges have sought to devise legal strategies intended to produce consistent, equitable results across cases and copyrightable media, from books and maps to music.[1] Nineteenth-century judges first developed formal models for legal evaluations of similarity, but when they were applied to music, judges found themselves often relying on "forensic discussion" from musical expert witnesses hired by either plaintiffs or defendants. Usually composers or band leaders by trade, these expert witnesses provided courtroom performances and analytical comparisons that primarily identified melodic congruences indicated through strategic marking of note-by-note comparisons on sheet music. In so doing, their analyses contextualized the nature of each lawsuit and the boundaries of each implicated song according to what were believed to be defining musical features.

Expert witnesses in the first half of the twentieth century continued to negotiate these contested musical spaces in similar ways. Increases in the frequency of music copyright litigation nationwide at this time were due in no small part to the meteoric rise of sound recordings and Tin Pan Alley composers churning out song after song in hopes of achieving, and maintaining, commercial success in the burgeoning popular music market. This legal climate brought about increased opportunities for musical experts, with most cases featuring at least one expert witness, and for some to be hired across multiple cases. Experts, including famous radio "Tune Detective" Sigmund Spaeth, began to produce increasingly sophisticated analyses tailored to distinguish commonality from copying, which integrated comparisons of pitch, rhythm, and form in the context of style. These analyses did as much to increase the precision of demarcating boundaries between music as to establish routine analytical techniques applied across

33

cases. Yet as reliance on musical expert witnesses increased for both plaintiffs and defendants, jurisprudential shifts toward legal realism motivated
judicial skepticism toward expert witnesses and the evidentiary role of
forensic similarity analysis. Beyond determining quantitative and qualitative thresholds for infringement, judges framed cases involving music
according to legal questions regarding the individuals best-equipped to
evaluate similarity.

STATUTORY OVERHAUL

By the turn of the twentieth century, the United States was poised for another
major overhaul of federal copyright law. The Supreme Court's 1908 decision
in *White-Smith Music Publishing Co. v. Apollo Co.*, the case that famously
resulted in a finding that player piano rolls were not protectable because they
were not legible to the human eye, served as one of a few catalysts to reconsider the nature of music as intellectual property and the legal requirements
for federal copyright.[2] Congress enacted the third major revision of federal
copyright statutes the following year, in 1909, which notably shifted from
listing specific types of protectable works to more generalized categories of
them. Additionally, the new regime introduced categories of unpublished
works accepted for registration, the statutory term for which was established
at the time of publication. In order for a creator to receive protection, the 1909
Act required compliance with a system of registration formalities, including
publication, notice, registration, and deposit.[3]

At least partially in response to lobbying efforts from recording companies and music industry professionals, the 1909 Act marginally attempted to
account for new technologies that allowed music to be reliably reproduced in
radically new ways. The new Act notably introduced a compulsory license
system that permitted use of a copyrighted work by someone other than
the copyright holder provided that the user paid a modest fee. Compulsory
licensing was especially important because it allowed musicians to make
recordings of copyrighted works without the holder's explicit consent. This
new scheme extended a modicum of legal protection to sheet music composers over recording artists, and subsequently the venues that played their
recordings, thereby ensuring the continued creation of new music. It did not,
however, provide protection to recording artists.

Although these revisions had significant implications for the federal copyright system, they did very little to impact the process by which infringement
claims were evaluated or to codify the role of expert witnesses. These issues
were instead managed by common law set forth in judicial opinions as to
the outcome of each case. As a result, early twentieth-century federal judges

defined precedential thresholds for similarity, the processes by which it was to be evaluated, and by whom.

FEDERAL MUSIC COPYRIGHT LITIGATION

While the 1909 Act did not necessarily stimulate a rise in music copyright litigation, early twentieth-century courts heard an increasing number of federal copyright claims, particularly in the Southern District of New York and its appellate court, the Second Circuit, whose jurisdiction, or binding legal purview, extended over much of the music industry in New York City. During this period, shifts in legal theory motivated judges to begin seeking functional procedures for determining infringement, and specifically for understanding the legal contours of similarity. Legal concerns about the applicability of judicial opinions in later federal copyright cases motivated judges to refine the similarity inquiry in ways that emphasized fact-driven, and seemingly objective, legal analysis that fulfilled the underlying purposes of copyright law.

In their reasoning, presiding judges over such cases attempted to reconcile competing factors. On the one hand, the economic policy at the core of U.S. copyright law, namely, the protection of artists' market control over their creations, encouraged greater legal consideration for so-called "average" or "ordinary" consumer perceptions. On the other hand, the "music appreciation" movement,[4] emerging hand-in-hand with institutions and pedagogies of "classical" music nationwide, encouraged a contrary argument: namely, that "the processes of music are so subtle and the meaning is so indefinite as compared to that of the other arts,"[5] that some kind of musical training would be necessary for a full comprehension of music—one that, over time, a growing population of listeners was supposed to achieve. But judges were skeptical of the highly detailed, and often detectably partisan, analyses proffered by experts, which the judges themselves could only partly understand. They questioned whether, and how, such sophisticated analyses should be brought into play, given that nonexpert listeners might lack the musical acuity to interpret them.

THE ROLE OF EXPERTS ACCORDING
TO JUDGE LEARNED HAND

Although most courts in the first half of the twentieth century relied on musical experts to provide analytical comparisons, some judges with sufficient musical training preferred to conduct forensic similarity analysis on their own. The notable example is then-district court Judge Learned Hand, who completed his own analyses following many of the same analytical techniques as the expert witnesses themselves. Judge L. Hand still not only received expert analytical evidence presented at trial but also conducted his own analyses, which served as a powerful check on the ways in which experts could strategically frame musical similarity.

Judge L. Hand's early music copyright opinions offer a glimpse at a nascent legal distinction between categories of listeners based on the Judge's own ideas about musical training. "Music meant a great deal"[6] to Judge L. Hand, and he supposedly enjoyed writing copyright decisions, in part because of his interest in musical creativity and in part due to the "intellectual challenges" that such cases presented. The Judge was known to be an avocational performer, and his opinions align with perceptions of an allegedly increasing divide between trained musicians and so-called "average" listeners believed to be unable to engage in "true listening."[7]

Judge L. Hand's opinions reflected his realist jurisprudence, including suspicion toward the seemingly academic rigor of evidence introduced by expert witnesses, which he found to be as obfuscating and partial as it could be informative.[8] In his objections to the use of expert witnesses, Judge L. Hand argued that "the fatal difficulty . . . lies in the logical fulfillment of the expert's position, as witness and not as adviser of the jury. The result is that the ordinary means successful to aid the jury in getting at the fact is, aid, instead of that, in confusing them."[9] He also presented a solution to these problems by advocating for neutral, court-appointed experts to serve as a kind of "advisory tribunal,"[10] harkening back to older court practices. This way, expert witnesses could present "those general truths, applicable to the issue, which they may treat as final and decisive,"[11] presumably with little hindrance from adversarial party bias.

HEIN V. HARRIS

The first district-court copyright case Judge L. Hand heard shortly after joining the bench was *Hein v. Harris*. In this case, the plaintiff-composer of the music theater show, *The Boys and Betty*, Silvio Hein, along with Marie Cahill, the assignee of rights from lyricist Daniel Arthur, sued publisher Charles K. Harris to enforce their rights for the song, "Marie Cahill's The Arab Love Song," the chorus melody from which they claimed Harris had violated with his song, "I Think I Hear a Woodpecker Knocking at My Family Tree," which was featured in the show, *The Golden Girl*. In response, Harris alleged that the chorus melody imitated a variety of similar songs, not simply the plaintiffs' song.[12] While extant court records include piano-vocal sheet music for both songs and indicate the participation of expert witnesses in this case, there are only summaries of witness comparisons and generalized stylistic discussions of ragtime and other contemporary popular music. No preserved trial transcript reflects more detailed musical discourse.

The plaintiffs relied on a comparison chart prepared by Silvio Hein, shown in figure 2.1. Similar to charts used in previous cases, Hein's comparison chart isolated and aligned the two melodies at issue, transposed them into the same key—E-flat Major—and then represented them using black and red ink on separate staves. Unlike earlier charts, coloration did not indicate similarity, or a lack thereof, but simply appeared to differentiate between the two songs. While the red ink, which appears gray in the figure, may not have

Figure 2.1 *Hein v. Harris,* **Comparison Chart.** Hein v. Harris. Record Group 21; National Archives and Records Administration Kansas City; U.S.D.C. Southern District of New York; Equity Case Files, Box #137, No. 5-77; "Hein v. Harris." Credit: Author.

conveyed the same information regarding similarity, it could have played off normative expectations that red signaled points of musical congruence to warp perceptions of similarity in the plaintiff's favor.

Even disregarding coloration, the alignment of melodies highlights significant pitch and rhythmic overlap, as well as the distinctive chromatic passing tones in "Arab Love Song" only partly included in "I Think I Hear a Woodpecker."

Conversely, the defendants employed Stephen Jones, a "specialist in 'ragtime' music," who compared the two songs according to his assessment of their musical style. Based on the sheet music at issue in the case, both songs seem to be at the periphery of ragtime style, containing simple meter but only minimal notated syncopation, plus few instances of chromaticism in "Arab Love Song." Jones, nevertheless, found that they had[13]

> nothing but the commonest kind of jingle strung together, and both of such poor composition even as "rag-time" music that it would be foolish to claim for either of them any unique, peculiar or extraordinary merit as musical compositions; that poor as both songs are in the opinion of the deponent that they are unlike in theme, melody, arrangement, and construction, and except for a few notes placed here and there, no resemblance or similarity exists such as appears in other "rag-time" compositions. That they are like many other songs on the market in which any old kind of music is published for the sale of the lyrics.

Jones's analysis emphasized "theme, melody, arrangement, and construction," which contextualized melodic congruence in more integrated, and thus compelling, ways to demonstrate similarity. His comparison was framed according to the songs' underlying originality according to contemporary notions of ragtime style. In so doing, Jones provided evidence that called into question the copyrightability of the plaintiff's song and the validity of their claim in court.

Expert musicians Charles Hirst, Harry De Costa, Thomas Clark, and Frank Saddler, each identified as composers, arrangers, and performers, followed this common defense strategy that recast musical congruence as reflecting unoriginal musical resemblance rather than illegal copying. These expert witnesses confirmed Jones's analysis that the two songs were similar, but concluded that neither song was protectable because of their close resemblance to each other and to prior popular music compositions. To that end, DeCosta notably classified ragtime as possessing "nothing original, unique, extraordinary or original in this trashy stuff, which no real musician recognizes as real music."[14] Hirst not only reinforced Jones's analysis but also drew comparisons between "Arab Love Song" and "Bon Bon Buddy," "The Glow-Worm," "The Mobile Prance," and finally to a more pejorative and dismissive combination of "other coon songs almost innumerable,"[15] to suggest that the songs lacked originality. The other expert witnesses reinforced this opinion, making similar disparaging value statements regarding ragtime and a perceived lack of originality across songs that the experts afforded to it.

Instead of focusing solely on the stylistic idioms and perceived aesthetic value of ragtime like other expert witnesses, Saddler's deposition contextualized discussion of stylistic comparisons with theoretical discussion of compositional techniques. He argued that the commonality between the two songs reached broadly to "all popular songs," of which there were "but four or five different styles."[16] Even without offering greater explanation as to these "four or five different styles," Saddler's deposition contributed a music-theoretical understanding that disqualified certain kinds of musical congruence, such as key or stylistic convention, as nonindicative of similarity for legal purposes. Together, the defendant's expert witnesses emphasized their genre classification of the songs as indicative of common stylistic idiom and relationship to prior compositions, not to mention the alleged lack of musical value which would have been irrelevant to, yet likely influential on, the court.

In his decision, however, Judge L. Hand conducted his own comparison of "Arab Love Song," and "I Think I Hear a Woodpecker Knocking at My Family Tree":[17]

I have no difficulty in finding that the defendant's song is an infringement of the complainant's. They are written in the same measure, called "common time," and each is in the minor mode[sic]. It is true that the keys are different; *but this is a distinction which is of no consequence to the ears of all but those especially skilled in music*, and, indeed, even among persons skilled in music the power to distinguish two keys when they are not played in immediate juxtaposition is by no means universal. If the melody of the defendant's chorus be transposed into the key of three flats, it exhibits an almost exact reproduction of the complainant's melody. Each consists of 17 bars, of which the first, second, third, fourth, and fifth are alike, almost note for note. The quantity of the notes is not precisely similar; but when they are played in succession it would take the ear of a person skilled in music to distinguish between them. The sixth bar of the defendant's melody is unlike that of the complainant's; but even this difference is not great, and justifies an inference that the change may have been colorable. The seventh bars are likewise unlike. The eighth and ninth, upon the other hand, have a striking similarity. The tenth, eleventh, and twelfth in each melody are repetitions of the second, third, and fourth, and are therefore duplicates. The fourteenth, fifteenth, sixteenth, and seventeenth are quite dissimilar. Therefore, out of a total of 17 bars, the first 13 are substantially the same in each song; and whether or not the defendant, as he alleges, had never heard the complainant's

song, when he wrote his chorus, the chorus certainly is an infringement, and the
complainant under his copyright is entitled to protection.

His own analysis relied on melodic congruence and eschewed differences in key as seemingly superficial "red-herrings" of musical similarity.
Transposition of the melodies into the same key reflected the increasing
sophistication of analytical techniques used by expert witnesses at the time,
which emphasized intervallic relationships in a melody as more representative of musical originality than pitch determined by key. This analysis led
Judge L. Hand to a decision in favor of the plaintiffs with seemingly less
reliance on musical experts. It is likely that their contributions nevertheless
offered at least some influence on the Judge's own musical analysis, if not his
legal analysis and decision in the case.

More significant for the future trajectory of music copyright, Judge L.
Hand characterized the legal evaluation of similarities and differences
according to musical training. "If the choruses be transposed into the same
key and played in the same time, their similarities become at once apparent.
In certain of the bars, *only a trained ear can distinguish them.*"[18] The judge
suggested that the perception of similarity for copyright purposes depended
on musical skill, or a lack thereof: "when [some of the melodies at issue]
are played in succession *it would take the ear of a person skilled in music
to distinguish between them.*"[19] Instead, Judge L. Hand reasoned that "only
when the similarity is substantially a copy, *so that to the ear of the average
person* the two melodies sound to be the same,"[20] would there be copyright
infringement. According to him, similarity was to be evaluated based on
the assumed judgment of a hypothetical average listener. This decision
would be affirmed on appeal to the Second Circuit, with the three-judge
panel offering no additional discussion regarding Judge L. Hand's legal
approach.[21]

The model for a so-called "average" listener in *Hein* is reminiscent of the
average or ordinary "reasonable person," a legal fiction predicated on notions
of an ideal representative of the lowest common denominator within a diversity of individuals impacted by a law, or simply how "most people" might
think or behave. Although legally binding definitions of what average musical training entailed are absent from the *Hein* opinion, Judge L. Hand created
a correlation between "untrained" and "average" as distinguishable from
"musically skilled." His discourse established that musical skill separated
groups of listeners and favored the comparisons of so-called "average listeners" over those of musical experts in the courtroom. To make his decision for
the purposes of *Hein*, however, Judge L. Hand relied on his own evaluation
of similarity, as perhaps a self-identified average listener, or at least a skeptic
of all witness testimony, to reach his finding of infringement.

HAAS V. LEO FEIST

The case of *Haas v. Leo Feist*, which Judge L. Hand decided six years later, involved a similar analytical process but revealed a surprisingly more prominent role for musical expert witnesses. Similar to other music copyright cases, this case involved composer Harry Haas suing the Leo Feist Company over his song, "You Will Never Know How Much I Really Cared."[22] Haas alleged that the defendant's widely popular anti-interventionist song, "I Didn't Raise My Boy to be a Soldier," attributed to Al Piantadosi, was similar.[23] In 1914, Harry Haas composed "You Will Never Know How Much I Really Cared," which was transcribed by Rouch with lyrics by Cahalin. The song was copyrighted by the Haas and Cahalin Music Company, a trade-name for Adolph Deutsch, who paid the songwriting team provided he received a one-third interest in profits. Months later, in November 1914, Cahalin allegedly gave a copy of the song to cabaret singer, Samuel Smith, who at the time was working with Leo Feist, and specifically, Al Piantadosi. Leo Feist claimed Piantadosi composed "I Didn't Raise My Boy To Be a Soldier" the month before, in October 1914, and it was registered for copyright in December that year.

Extant records for the case include an unattributed comparison chart that continues the analytical techniques used by expert witnesses in earlier cases. The chart, shown in figure 2.2, features the melodies aligned on separate staves, drawing attention to shared melodic trajectories. It also employed yet another manifestation of the two-color format in its strategic use of red—shown as gray in the figure—to mark both note-for-note pitch congruences as well as uncontroversial information, such as title and measure numbers.

The chart is accompanied by an unusual "Detailed Comparison of Two Songs" document, which identified "Complainant's song designated as 'A,' Defendant's song designated as 'B'" and outlined in brief statements which measures are similar. For example, "1st bar of 'B' similar to 1st half of 'A.'/2nd, 3rd, 4th, and 5th bars of 'B' similar to 2nd and 3rd bars of 'A.'"[24] The chart used vocabulary such as "exactly the same," "practically the same," "exactly like," "exactly similar," "identical," and "similar," to note congruences, and "different," "dissimilar," "entirely dissimilar," to refer to generic and specific musical differences between the songs. For all these distinctions, the comparison document rarely indicates the musical dimension to which each statement referred, that is, it almost never distinguishes melody as opposed to harmony or rhythm. The exceptions are where comparison statements identify "notes," which presumably refer to melody, and where "progression" is used, the statement presumably refers to harmony.[25] Overall, the language of this document added complexity to the comparison chart by introducing degrees of similarity, from entirely dissimilar to identical, for what amounts to melodic congruence. The underlying purpose of this document is not explained in extant records, but it likely served to negotiate verbally commonality from copying.

At trial, the defendants introduced the comparison chart in figure 2.2 and showed it to a composer and routine expert witness, Lee Orean Smith.

Figure 2.2   *Haas v. Leo Feist*, Comparison Chart. Record Group 21; National Archives and Records Administration Kansas City; U.S.D.C. Southern District of New York; Equity Case Files, Box # 446; "Haas v. Leo Feist." Credit: Author.

During his testimony, Smith reiterated that he did not prepare the chart, but that he would use it to explain putative similarities for the court.[26] Although prompted to provide a close comparative analysis by defense attorney Nathan Burkan, Judge L. Hand stopped Smith's bar-by-bar close examination of the songs, instead wanting him to focus on simultaneous performances of the two melodies on piano, played by Smith, and on violin, played by another unnamed witness. Only after this performance did Smith's direct examination delve into discussions of melodic similarities, and only during cross examination did Smith address matters of rhythm and meter.

The defendants also called Abner Greenberg, a performer in "music houses" who later chose to become a lawyer. Greenberg's examination did not emphasize his forensic qualifications, and he instead presented analysis typical of any other contemporary musical expert. During his examination, Greenberg confirmed that he had "made a comparison of the two songs bar by bar with a view of ascertaining points of similarity and points of dissimilarity."[27] In keeping with Smith's discussion of meter, Greenberg then offered the following explanation:[28]

> I find upon examination of these two songs that the A song ["You Never Can Tell How Much I Really Cared"] is a chorus in 16 bars. I find upon examination of B ["I Never Wanted My Boy To Be A Soldier"] that that is a chorus of 32 bars. The B is written in what is called 2/4 time, double time. The A is written in common time, so that if we play the chorus of A in double time we should have substantially the same length as the B.

Here, Greenberg established metrical difference as superficial to evaluating similarity. As he would later explain, "[a]s to the ear there would be absolutely no difference [between the songs]. It would be the same progression as it was before, but only as to the time it would make it sort of a dancing two-step 2/4 melody; that is all."[29] His discussion continued to the melody and accompaniment, offering comparisons that emphasized melodic congruence that were reinforced through a live demonstration at the piano.

Unlike his decision in *Hein v. Harris*, Judge L. Hand's opinion outlined less of his own analysis, although it did mention conclusions he drew about the music. "[R]ely[ing] upon such musical sense as [he had],"[30] it is likely that Judge L. Hand used many of the same techniques, however, including a melocentric approach and a standard for similarity based on his own notions of musical skill. Judge L. Hand identified "between the two choruses in question there is a parallelism which seems to my ear to pass the bounds of mere accident. If the choruses be transposed into the same key and played in the same time, their similarities become at once apparent. In certain of the bars, *only a trained ear* can distinguish them, and their form and rhythm is quite the same."[31] The Judge contextualized this analysis based on notions of musical originality and, according to him, Piantadosi's reputation for borrowing musical content:[32]

> It is said that such similarities are of constant occurrence in music, and that little inference is permissible. Perhaps I should not take them as enough without the opportunity proved, the habits of Piantadosi shown in other instances, and the serious question of his credibility; but it would be absurd not to regard them as evidence of the most impressive character in combination with the rest. The case is not of the mere suggestion of a bar common to each, but of a continuously suggestive melodic parallelism, except at the end.

Although the decision ultimately hinged on damage allocation rather than similarity analysis, Judge L. Hand's introductory statement regarding infringement is revealing. Not only did it show the judge relying on his own "musical sense" to conduct his own comparisons, but it also reflected a cumulating understanding among expert witnesses and the judge that key and meter were nonindicative of similarity for legal purposes. As applied to the case, although the two songs appeared different on the sheet music, synchronizing their meter and transposing to the same key revealed remarkably similar choruses.

In these early twentieth-century decisions, Judge L. Hand's opinions reflect a judge-centered approach to copyright infringement inquiries. Yet despite claiming to rely on his own musical sense, it is doubtful that the judge's reasoning was entirely unaffected by musical expert witnesses introduced by both parties in each lawsuit. Distinctions in the relevance of certain similarities to finding infringement, such as matters of melody and rhythm from key and meter, are reflected in both Judge L. Hand's own analyses. Perhaps more significantly for these cases, however, Judge L. Hand propelled legal skepticism surrounding the subtle, and at times unperceivable, similarities and differences between pieces of music identifiable by expert witnesses as irrelevant to the court's decisions.

Although Judge L. Hand's questions permeated the Second Circuit Appellate Court, principally in the Southern District of New York, not every judge shared the same skepticism. Contemporaneous cases heard by other judges dealt with many of the same legal similarity issues as in the lower court. In *Edward B. Marks v. Leo Feist*, for example, expert witnesses had a strong influence on the court's final infringement decisions. This case involved two rival publishing companies, with Marks seeking an injunction against Leo Feist from publishing and selling "Wedding Dance Waltz," composed by Paul Linke. Marks alleged that Linke's composition infringed on "Swanee River Moon."[33] While the legal ramifications of the case served mostly to reinforce existing procedures for assessing similarity, it is the discussion of forensic similarity analysis that is more significant.

Both songs are notated in triple meter with waltz-style accompaniments, but there are few further similarities. The expert witness, who is unnamed but directly referenced by the court in its opinion, identified similarities between the melodies of the two songs: "A similarity of tone succession with respect to 5 or 6 bars, but [said] the rhythm and accent are entirely different."[34] In their contributions, the expert witness criticized the common analytical technique of separating musical elements before comparison, noting that focusing on any one dimension of music to the exclusion of the totalizing musical context provided by the other dimensions could create false similarities. "If any one plays the notes, not as they are written, but gives these notes equal values, suppressing the real effect that should be given to the base[*sic*] accompaniments, he will produce a result of similarity."[35] Thus, the identification of musical congruence based primarily on pitch, without accounting for rhythm or harmonic structure, could result in finding false similarities because they inadequately represented the music at issue.

Despite the expert witness's critique of common analytical techniques that he believed were contextualizing similarity in ways that disserved the music at issue, their statements did not stop the court from continuing to rely on techniques that isolated musical elements. Presiding Judge Rogers took a different approach to evaluating similarity predicated on quantitative, as well as qualitative, thresholds for similarity, likely drawing from expert contributions to determine that "appellant's composition comprises 450 bars of music. . . . 6 bars of this are [allegedly] infringed by the appellee's composition."[36] In their finding of no infringement, the *Marks* decision reinforced the threshold standard for similarity constituting infringement as "substantial." This term, which had roots in nineteenth-century copyright precedent, indicated that copyright infringement could not be proven by merely a few points of congruence. Although the distinction between substantial and insubstantial congruence remained the subjective determination of the presiding judge, in *Marks* at least, quantitative measures of similar melodic material in the context of the totality of dissimilar material indicated a lack of infringement.

Like his colleagues, Judge Rogers contextualized his evaluation according to notions of a hypothetical ordinary listener with limited musical training presumed to be the audience for popular music. Based on this reasoning, Judge Rogers concluded that popular music is necessarily simplistic in order to be accessible, and thus commercially viable:[37]

Musical signs available for combinations are about 13 in number. . . . It is called the chromatic scale. In a popular song, the composer must write a composition arranging combinations of these tones limited by the range of the ordinary voice and by the skill of the ordinary player. To be successful, it must be a combination of tones that can be played as well as sung by almost any one. Necessarily, within these limits, there will be found some similarity of tone succession.

As a result of these limitations, Judge Rogers made an assertion common to music copyright: that there are only so many combinations of tones, therefore, there will necessarily be some similarity between pieces of the same style. The case was ultimately resolved in favor of the defendant, Leo Feist, and reinforced mounting precedent within the Second Circuit regarding the role of experts and nonexperts.

THE LEGAL CONTOURS OF MUSICAL EXPERT TESTIMONY

Cases heard by Judge L. Hand and others contributed to a gradual accumulation of custom for introducing expert witnesses in federal copyright infringement cases. Questions surrounding the limits of expert testimony were widespread, however, extending to seemingly unrelated, yet precedent-setting, areas of law. In a case unrelated to music heard around the same time, the Supreme Court codified judicial criteria for the admissibility of expert witnesses and their testimony in *Frye v. United States*. The ruling, which was specific to scientific testimony most commonly given by physicians and forensic scientists, required "general acceptance" of the expert's method in order for the testimony to be admissible:[38]

> Just when a scientific principle or discovery crosses the line between the experimental and demonstrative stages is difficult to define. Somewhere in this twilight zone the evidential force of the principle must be recognized, and while courts will go a long way in admitting expert testimony deduced from a well-recognized scientific principle or discovery, the thing from the deduction is made *must be sufficiently established to have gained general acceptance in the field in which it belongs.*

For all that courts applied this test, they did not offer a method for determining the boundary between "experimental" and "demonstrative" stages of the method. Instead, it relied on the determinations within the relevant field for determining expertise; that is, generally accepted by other experts.[39] Regardless of its pitfalls, the *Frye* test became a rarely cited, yet influential, standard for managing expert testimony.[40] The breadth of its precedent presented as both a strength and a weakness for courts, permitting a wide variety of individuals and skills to be available as the evidence of each case required.

Despite recognizing the importance of experts in litigation, contemporaneous copyright treatises afforded little space to outlining the practicalities of working with expert witnesses. Instead, these treatises seemed to rely implicitly on their readers' knowledge of evidence law, which itself remained imprecise, and emphasized only the problems and limits of expert testimony within the court based on developing principles in this broader area of law. Two treatises in particular, however, reflect the suspicion introduced by Judge L. Hand and others by emphasizing the limited scope of expert testimony in copyright infringement cases. Both establish the ultimate issue "as not a question of whether persons skilled in the arts can differentiate the two works . . . but of whether the ordinary reasonable man would do so."[41]

Binding common law and advisory treatises shaped the ways that evidence, specifically contributions from expert witnesses, could be introduced and assessed in any federal case, including those involving copyright. The Supreme Court's decision in *Frye* generated a legal climate that emphasized "generally accepted" analytical methods among experts over idiosyncratic methods specific to the evidence in a particular case. This requirement, coupled with increasing judicial reliance on evaluations according to a hypothetical ordinary person, contributed to a growing number of legal controls on the role of musical expert witnesses.

IRA ARNSTEIN AND THE ROLE OF MUSICAL EXPERTS

By the 1930s, courts under jurisdiction of the Second Circuit had had decades to interpret the copyright similarity standard and to settle on a consideration of the persons best suited to conduct comparisons. The court was poised to set new precedent when it began receiving infringement complaints filed by Ira Arnstein. A Russian immigrant to New York, Arnstein emerged amidst the increasingly competitive, and increasingly litigious, commercial music industry in the early twentieth century. His career trajectory was unusual, with greater fame as a belligerent litigant than as a marginal composer. His lawsuits against more notable Tin Pan Alley composers and publishing companies constitute a collection of at least five separate lawsuits, in which over fifty defendants and over sixty songs were named under nearly the same complaint: that his music was stolen by another, usually more successful, composer.

Arnstein became known for outlandish presentations and live music demonstrations in court, as well as antics that pushed the boundaries of courtroom etiquette and unbiased evidence.[42] As Sigmund Spaeth, who was called routinely as a musical expert witness in these cases, explained, "[t]he king of musical litigants is unquestionably Ira B. Arnstein, who has spent the greater part of his adult life in trying to prove that most of the hit songs of modern times have been stolen from him, attacking the biggest names in popular music and timing his activities with rare commercial perspicacity."[43] The evidence and decisions from the Arnstein cases reveal changes in attorney strategy and legal procedure for music copyright litigation, with significant implications for the role that musical expert witnesses played. When considered together, the legal impact of these cases challenged courts to consider the nature of musical expertise and the kinds of analyses that should, rather than could, be produced as evidence of alleged copying.

By the time of his second lawsuit, which was filed against publisher Edward B. Marks, Arnstein had already encountered now-appellate Judge L. Hand, who had joined the Second Circuit bench in 1924. As would become common across Arnstein's lawsuits, his claims would be found unsuccessful, but the lawsuit provided an opportunity for the court to continue considering the contours of legal similarity analysis and the individuals best-suited to evaluate it. In his cases against Marks, Arnstein claimed that his copyrighted song, "The Russian Gypsy Valse," later retitled "I Love You Madly," was allegedly copied by Emery Deutsch and Arthur Altman, employees of Edward B. Marks Music Corporation, in their control of Jack Lawrence's "Play, Fiddle, Play."[44] Although the defendants acknowledged that another employee, L. Wolfe Gilbert, saw a version of Arnstein's song as it was submitted to the publisher, they denied receiving a copy of it.

At trial, Arnstein had requested Leonard Liebling, then-editor of the *Musical Courier* journal, to serve as his expert witness, but Liebling refused due to contractual obligations. Instead, Arnstein presented his own analysis at trial, aided by two violinists, Aaron Fastobsky and Simon Mogilanisky. Unlike Cole's "grave" performance of each song in the nineteenth-century case of *Reed v. Carusi*, Arnstein directed the violinists to play selections from each song with little regard to faithful performance of the sheet music. The violinists, for example, played the principal melody of "I Love You Madly" blended with parts of its accompaniment against the principal melody of "Play, Fiddle, Play" to create a nine-note sequence of identical pitches.[45] Arnstein also called two more experts, New York synagogue organist-composer Melchiorre Mauro-Cottone and associated cantor Isidore Weinstock, who likewise performed selected phrases from both songs to demonstrate their similarity.[46]

In contrast, the defendants introduced Sigmund Spaeth, emphasizing his forensic credibility based on his academic training and public reputation on radio as the "Tune Detective" for identifying musical commonalities. During his direct examination, Spaeth responded to Arnstein's violin demonstration and manipulation of the music at issue, testifying that musical similarity involved more than note-for-note comparisons:[47]

Q: Doctor, let me ask you this: Is it musicianly to take broken bars, irrespective of the musical content or the completeness of the theme or phrase, and compare them note for note to determine whether there is similarity?

A: That is not a fair way of making comparisons. Music runs phrases.

Thus, Spaeth described his analytical technique as determining "a melodic parallel through an absolute sequence of tones. By an absolute sequence I mean note for note and identity of at least we will say five, six, eight or nine notes in a row."[48] Although this technique continued a growing common practice of quantifying melodic congruence, Spaeth sought to extend analysis in ways that emphasized the relevance of phrasing and formal structure to melocentric comparisons. Nonetheless, when he was recalled, Spaeth was prompted to provide a more simplistic analysis for the court that identified rhythmic and melodic congruence in both songs, thereby deviating from his proposed technique that incorporated matters of musical form.[49]

Spaeth also fielded questions regarding the difference between the similarities as they appeared on the sheet music, and thus protected by copyright, and similarities that could be perceived when the songs were heard live or on record. These questions called on Spaeth to distinguish not only manifestations of music as intellectual property but also musical similarities as they could be perceived by either experts or nonexperts seemingly ill-equipped to read western music notation. On both direct and cross-examination, Spaeth noted that musical similarity could be heard, but he did not clarify by whom. As he explained, "[i]t all depends on the ear."[50] To this end, Spaeth demonstrated comparisons of musical phrases in court, drawing both from the songs being compared as well as other songs with similar melodic phrasing.

The court also heard testimony from composer Albert G. Robyn, who reinforced concepts of "stock phrases" and other common musical gestures as not indicative of copying, as well as musical "design," by which he likely meant musical form. Robyn's testimony bolstered Spaeth's formal analysis by explaining that it contextualized the melodic comparisons that dominated discussions of musical similarity. Together, the analyses provided by the two expert witnesses hired by the defendants served to undermine Arnstein's analysis by imposing formal context on his cobbled together comparisons of pitch sequences. While these techniques may reflect Robyn and Spaeth's partisan affiliations, their calls for a multidimensional, and perhaps even integrated, approach to analysis arguably offered a more forensic, or precise, comparison of the music as it was printed.

The district court, with Judge Foster Symes presiding, found the evidence overwhelmingly in favor of the defendants.[51] Judge L. Hand affirmed the decision on appeal to the Second Circuit, at which time he unsurprisingly presented his own analysis like one expected to have been provided by a musical expert. Rather than dwelling on note-by-note comparisons, Judge L. Hand presented his own hierarchical approach to forensic similarity analysis that emphasized phrasing:[52]

> The first phrase of the infringing chorus consists of the same four notes as the first phrase of the copyrighted song; that particular sequence can be found in several earlier musical pieces and its spontaneous reproduction should be no cause for suspicion. The second phrase of the chorus has no resemblance whatever to the next phrase of the song, but if one takes some notes of the treble in the accompaniment, moves them to the melody, raises them an octave, and cuts short the resulting melodic phrase, an identity can be made to appear. When the two songs are played the phrases show no resemblance, at least to the untrained ear. To a mind already set to find piracy, this of course seems proof strong as Holy Writ, but it is really of no significance. A plagiarist might of course work in that way, seizing a sequence from the middle of a phrase in an accompaniment as a happy theme; but Altman was scarcely the man for that; his gifts were very limited, and to attribute to him the ingenuity and penetration so to truncate and modify, and thus really to create a melody out of other elements, is harder than to suppose that the extremely simple theme should have occurred to him out of his own mind. . . . These songs were both written in the key of B-flat; the seven notes available do not admit of so many agreeable permutations that we need be amazed at the re-appearance of old themes, even though the identity extend through a sequence of twelve notes. The rest of the chorus follows a very simple and well-known pattern, and is derived for the most part from the two phrases we have just discussed, which account for the first four measures. The first sixteen measures, all substantially alike, are followed by eight measures, concededly original, and the chorus concludes with a repetition of the first eight. The verse follows the chorus closely enough not to require any separate discussion.

Judge L. Hand's emphasis on melodic phrasing, despite quantitative pitch comparisons, reinforced his judicial push away from what had come to be regarded as simplistic melodic congruence to considering music more holistically, as well as a likely influence from Spaeth's testimony. Although Judge L. Hand still relied on such elements, there is a greater emphasis in this opinion on large-scale compositional construction and integration of musical elements.

Beyond analytical techniques, Judge L. Hand's decision in *Arnstein v. Edward B. Marks* was legally significant because it reflected a trend toward including access as an element of copyright infringement analysis distinct from, but influential on, similarity. Whether the defendant came into contact with the plaintiff's allegedly infringed composition allowed courts to begin distinguishing between similarity caused by copying and similarity caused by coincidental "independent reproduction,"[53] or what would later become known as subconscious copying.[54]

ARNSTEIN AND THE JUDGES HAND

Arnstein next took on Broadcast Music, Incorporated (BMI), alleging infringement of eight separate songs whose copyright was assigned to BMI by their composers.[55] Embracing the growing legal tension between expert and lay listener, one of Arnstein's arguments was to suggest that Arnstein's claim that Dominguez's song, "Frenesi," pitted against Arnstein's "Soldiers of Zion," would sound identical to an expert despite the songs sounding different to nonexpert listeners.[56] Composers, Arnstein claimed, "always add two notes or three notes in order to cover up"[57] whether they had copied.

Although the court rendered Arnstein's complaints unsuccessful, Judge Augustus Hand—cousin to Learned—rendered a decision that called into question the techniques by which similarity should be determined. In his attempt to find copying based on Arnstein's allegations, Judge A. Hand noted that "similarities between these songs cannot be readily detected by the lay ear, nor by the effect of the composition as a whole, [it] can only be discovered by what Judge Hough aptly called 'dissection.'"[58] In this context, dissection referred to the comparative analysis usually conducted by experts that seemed to split music apart. Like his cousin, Judge A. Hand challenged the application of such "[t]echnical analysis," finding it to be "not the proper approach to a solution; it must be more ingenuous, more like that of a spectator, who would rely upon the complex of his impressions,"[59] to decide if whole songs were similar enough to constitute infringement.

Judge A. Hand thus offered clarification for the extent of musical skill or training possessed by a nonexpert and framed what would become the foundational question for the legal similarity inquiry: whether infringement should be based on totalizing, synthesizing, intuitive, or impressionistic perceptions of a hypothetical "ordinary," nonexpert listener that would be essentially untranslatable into exacting terms, or instead the detailed comparisons conducted by expert witnesses, which depended on the precise application of technical musical concepts and terminology not readily understood by nonexpert listeners. While this question may have seemed to turn on jurisprudence and public policy regarding copyright, it had implications for the analytical techniques applied by expert witnesses and, more broadly, their future role in the legal decision-making process. Although for nearly a century, previous courts had relied heavily on the role of expert witnesses in this respect, Judge A. Hand followed the example set by his cousin to draw significant attention to ordinary listeners, which for him should be juxtaposed against expert witnesses.

Arnstein's following lawsuit against Twentieth Century Fox Film Corporation was decided in August of the same year. Compared to some of Arnstein's other cases, *Arnstein v. Twentieth Century Fox Film Corp.* seemed routine: Arnstein sued titans of the popular music and film industry with a flimsy case that his compositional genius and copyright registration had been exploited. Nonetheless, the case contributes to a broader musical-legal climate of the time. In *Arnstein v. Twentieth Century Fox Film Corp.*, Arnstein alleged that his song, "Kalamazoo," was infringed on by Harry Warren's hit song, "I Got a Gal in Kalamazoo," as featured in the movie, *Orchestra Wives*. In an unusual strategic effort, Arnstein requested a jury trial, but the defendants' motion for a nonjury trial transfer was granted. At the bench trial, Arnstein argued that similarity between the songs extended to the title, lyrics, and music of his song. Finding a lack of proof for access or similarity, the district court dismissed the complaint. In particular, the opinion focused on Arnstein, serving as his own expert witness in this case, who presented an "ingenious manipulation of his composition."[60] From moving melodic figures between voices to swapping phrases into a new order, Arnstein tried to prove that the songs were musically similar. As the court reaffirmed its own precedent, "similarity cannot be established in this manner."[61] Arnstein remained undeterred, however, and would continue developing further music copyright claims.

THE CHANGING ROLE OF MUSICAL
EXPERTS NATIONWIDE

In the wake of Arnstein's cases against BMI and Twentieth Century Fox, courts nationwide labored to establish the extent to which comparisons according to experts and nonexperts should influence the court's final decision. With little, if any, apparent citation to research on listening practices or musical training, a judicial dichotomy between the so-called "expert" and "average" or "ordinary" listener nevertheless emerged. Judges, both in and beyond the Second Circuit, raised questions regarding the roles each group should play in the infringement inquiry. Some courts continued to rely exclusively on the musical-theoretical analyses of expert witnesses, while others considered nonexpert listener evaluations more indicative of the economic harm caused by alleged copyright infringement, preferring instead to rely on such listeners for dispositive legal evaluations.

The burgeoning film industry in California, within jurisdiction of the Ninth Circuit, generated a second locus for copyright infringement claims involving music, many of which overlapped with important cases heard in the Second

Circuit. In *Hirsch v. Paramount Pictures*, for example, plaintiff Hortense Hirsch sued defendant Paramount Pictures for its alleged infringement of eight measures of the popular love ballad, "Lady of Love," by Hortense Hirsch, in the film, *Two for Twilight*, appearing under the new title, "Without a Word of Warning," as composed by Harry Revel with lyrics by Mack Gordon.[62] The court ultimately decided in favor of the defendant corporation based on relationship to prior compositions, access, and similarity grounds, thus deciding that the two songs were different enough not to constitute infringement.

The *Hirsch* opinion relied heavily on the example set by the Second Circuit regarding an "average hearer" standard for similarity as well as the advice of expert witnesses presented by both parties, including prominent art-music composer, Sigmund Romberg. The opinion included a rare notated musical example to demonstrate the difference between the two melodies at issue, stating "[i]t is difficult to describe by words similarities or differences in musical compositions. They can be best illustrated by the music itself. There is, therefore, attached here, by way of illustration, one of the exhibits demonstrating the similarity between the eight bars in the plaintiff's song and the others referred to in the opinion."[63] Presiding Judge Leon Yankwich also noted earlier in his opinion that the two songs were heard "both in recorded form and on the piano in the courtroom,"[64] clarifying that during the live performance, the two songs "were played in the same key and tempo."[65] Here, the court addressed, and then dismissed, discernable differences created by live performance as irrelevant to legal evaluations of musical similarity. Despite the court's effort to dispel concerns of stylistic flexibility, any perceived differences could have afforded an advantage to the party who presented the witness.

Later courts emphasized the importance of nonexpert listeners, especially when the differences between pieces of music were purportedly obvious. In *Carew v. R.K.O. Radio Pictures*, for example, plaintiff Evelyn Carew sued defendant composer Jerome Brainan, along with music industry corporations responsible for publishing and distributing the song, for infringing on her copyright of the "lyrics, music, musical theme"[66] of her "Chatterbox" with his own by the same name. Brainan prevailed on a pretrial motion to dismiss the claim without trial based on the facts of the case, with the court indicating that the only similarity between the two pieces of music was the title.[67] In another opinion drafted by Judge Yankwich, the court relied on precedent to establish legally that Carew failed to prove similarity.[68]

Beyond the shared title and lyric "chatterbox," Carew's argument was undermined by the testimony of two expert witnesses who stated that the two pieces shared a common melodic motive, including testimony from Albert Sirmay, a musical editor and advisor for Chappell and Company who had assisted in arranging Brainan's song for piano. In addition to offering explanations of the relationship to melody, Sirmay responded to questions comparing the two songs note-by-note both melodically and rhythmically, finding similarity only in three shared pitches. Sirmay even indicated that the songs were mostly dissimilar, responding to the question "[h]ave you found any similarity in melody between these two compositions?" with "[n]ot the slightest."[69] Extant records do not indicate that Sirmay prepared any comparison chart, instead offering his "written opinion" that outlined in prose a lack of similarity between the pieces.

The court recognized the same dissimilarity, but instead of basing its reasoning on expert analyses, the court turned to the ordinary listener standard to evaluate Carew's claim:[70]

> [e]ven if it be conceded that there is a similarity in the motive, that in itself would not be sufficient to warrant a finding of infringement. As to that, however, I may say that the playing of the particular motive carried no idea of similarity to my ear. And one of the experts admitted that the only similarity lay in the use of two of the three notes, in reverse order. The ordinary words of the English language, used by the average person, amount to ordinary speech. The same words, woven into poetic speech by a Keats or Shelley, or any other great poet, sound like the most poetic words in the English language. Certainly, before we find plagiarism in a song, *we should be able to find some substantial part in it, which can be traced to and discerned by the ordinary listener* in the composition which it is claimed to infringe.

The court continued to emphasize "the ordinary listener" as presenting a more significant opinion regarding similarity to that of the expert. "[I]t is not the dissection to which a musical composition might be submitted under the microscopic eye of a musician which is the criterion of similarity, but the impression which the pirated song or phrase would carry to the average ear."[71] *Carew* revealed a court outside the Second Circuit raised similar concerns regarding the role of musical experts in determining infringement, highlighting nationwide concerns regarding listener skill and underlying copyright policy.

THE JUDICIAL PROBLEM WITH EXPERTS
AND ORDINARY LISTENERS

By the 1940s, courts raised more functionalist jurisprudential questions about the role of expert witnesses in the litigation process on their own and in relation to nonexpert, or so-called "average" or "ordinary" observers. At the same time, musical expert witnesses in particular offered testimony based on increasingly sophisticated analytical techniques. Rather than melocentric bar-by-bar comparisons that could be manipulated through the use of colored ink to maximize the appearance of similarity, expert witnesses began to integrate phrasing, formal structure, and style to contextualize musical congruences that might be indicative of unlawful copying rather than simply stylistic commonality. To that end, they problematized transposition, metrical shifts, and arbitrary musical connections as not indicative of legal similarity.

In some cases, these statements proved influential on judges and the opinions that resolved each case, but not always. By the mid-twentieth century, an increasing number of opinions cast expert testimony as alienating or unhelpful to the ultimate determination of copyright infringement, which was characterized as having an "intricate" and "conflicting" nature. Although many previous judges had relied on expert witnesses, mid-century judges had become more concerned about the perceptions of nonexpert listeners as ordinary observers and representatives of the commercial market intended to be reserved for the copyright holder. With an open legal question regarding the individuals best-equipped to determine infringement, some judges instead relied on their own sensibilities regarding music, often irrespective of analyses produced by musical expert witnesses.

Early-twentieth-century music copyright opinions served to construct a contested legal space between musical experts and nonexperts based on judicial assumptions about listener acuity and the fundamental economic purposes of copyright. While some musical expert witnesses sought to refine their analyses to the task of more precise identification of similarity, judges simultaneously sought to limit these same analyses, which they classified as unrecognizable for nonexperts soon to become the final legal arbiters of music copyright infringement. The notably partial analytical tactics introduced by some parties caused further damage by undermining presumptions of forensic objectivity in experts' similarity analyses. By the mid-twentieth century, the Second Circuit, with Judge L. Hand at its helm, was poised to codify new procedures for determining copyright infringement that promised to narrow the role of musical expert witnesses.

NOTES

1. Portions of this chapter were previously published in, or are adapted from, Katherine Leo, "Musical Expertise and the 'Ordinary' Listener in Federal Copyright Law," *Music and Politics* 13, no. 1 (Winter 2019): ISSN 1938-7687.

2. *White-Smith Pub. Co. v. Apollo Co.*, 209 U.S. 1 (1908).

3. *Copyright Act of 1909*, 35 Stat. 1075 (amended 1976).

4. Stewart Macpherson identified "for want of a better term, [what] has been called the Appreciation movement both [in France, referring to E. Jaques-Dalcroze] and in America," the "inauguration" for which was isolated to 1908. Stewart Macpherson, *The Appreciation, or Listening, Class* (London: Joseph Williams Limited, 1936), 1–3.

5. Clarence G. Hamilton, *Music Appreciation: Based upon Methods of Literary Criticism* (New York, NY: Oliver Ditson, 1920), 9.

6. Gerald Gunther, *Learned Hand: The Man and the Judge* (Oxford: Oxford University, 2011), 37.

7. Stewart Macpherson, *Music and Its Appreciation or The Foundations of True Listening* (London: Joseph William, 1910), 4 (outlining "points necessary in true listening" that only musically trained listeners could address, including the "nature of the composition," instrumentations, date, melodic identification, development, form, and harmony).

8. Hand, "Historical and Practical Considerations," 52.

9. Hand, "Historical and Practical Considerations," 52.

10. Hand, "Historical and Practical Considerations," 56.

11. Hand, "Historical and Practical Considerations," 55.

12. *Hein v. Harris*, 175 F.875, 875 (C.C.S.D.N.Y. 1910).

13. *Hein v. Harris*, Jones Deposition, 1. Record Group 21; National Archives and Records Administration, Kansas City; U.S.D.C. Southern District of New York, Equity Case Files, Box #137, No. 5–77, "Hein v. Harris."

14. *Hein v. Harris*, DeCosta Deposition, 1. Record Group 21; National Archives and Records Administration, Kansas City; U.S.D.C. Southern District of New York, Equity Case Files, Box #137, No. 5–77, "Hein v. Harris."

15. *Hein v. Harris*, Hirst Deposition, 1. Record Group 21; National Archives and Records Administration, Kansas City, MO; U.S.D.C. Southern District of New York, Equity Case Files, Box #137, No. 5–77, "Hein v. Harris." *Hein*, 184 F. at 875.

16. *Hein v. Harris*, Saddler Deposition, 1–2. Record Group 21; National Archives and Records Administration, Kansas City; U.S.D.C. Southern District of New York, Equity Case Files, Box #137, No. 5–77, "Hein v. Harris."

17. *Hein*, 175 Fed. at 875.

18. *Hein*, 175 F. at 875 (emphasis added).

19. *Hein*, 175 F. at 875 (emphasis added).

20. *Hein*, 175 F. at 875 (emphasis added).

21. *Hein v. Harris*, 183 Fed. 107 (2d Cir. 1923).

22. *Haas v. Leo Feist*, 234 F. 105 (S.D.N.Y. 1916).

23. *Haas*, 234 F. at 106.

24. *Haas v. Leo Feist*, Detailed Comparison of Two Songs, Record Group 21; National Archives and Records Administration, Kansas City; U.S.D.C. Southern District of New York; Equity Case Files, Box # 446; "Haas v. Leo Feist."

25. *Haas v. Leo Feist*, Detailed Comparison of Two Songs.

26. *Haas v. Leo Feist*, Transcript, 173 (Smith). Record Group 21; National Archives and Records Administration, Kansas City; U.S.D.C. Southern District of New York; Equity Case Files, Box # 446; "Haas v. Leo Feist." During cross-examination, Smith

indicated that he did not create the chart. See *Haas v. Leo Feist*, Transcript, 180 (Smith).

27. *Haas v. Leo Feist*, Transcript, 60 (Greenberg).

28. *Haas v. Leo Feist*, Transcript, 60 (Greenberg).

29. *Haas v. Leo Feist*, Transcript, 62 (Greenberg).

30. *Haas v. Leo Feist*, 234 F. 105, 107 (S.D.N.Y. 1916) (emphasis added).

31. *Haas*, 234 F. at 107.

32. *Haas*, 234 F. at 107.

33. *Edward B. Marks v. Leo Feist*, 290 F.959, 959 (2d. Cir. 1923).

34. *Marks*, 290 F. at 960.

35. *Marks*, 290 F. at 960.

36. *Marks*, 290 F. at 959.

37. *Marks*, at 960.

38. *Frye v. United States*, 293 F. 1013, 1014 (D.C. Cir. 1923) (emphasis added).

39. See also Mnookin, "Idealizing Science," 764.

40. Susan Haack, "The Expert Witness: Lessons from the U.S. Experience," *Humana Mente Journal of Philosophical Studies* 28 (2015): 48.

41. See, for example, Arthur W. Weil, *American Copyright Law: With Special Reference to the Present United States Copyright Act, with Appendices Containing Forms from Adjudicated Cases, and the Copyright Laws of England, Canada, Australia, Germany, and France* (Chicago, IL: Callaghan, 1917), § 1201, 458; Leon H. Amdur, *Copyright Law and Practice* (New York, NY: Clark, Boardman, 1936), § 18, 1075.

42. Gary Rosen, *Unfair to Genius* (Oxford: Oxford University, 2012), 127–36.

43. Rosen, *Unfair to Genius*, 119 (quoting Spaeth).

44. *Arnstein v. Edward B. Marks Music Corp.*, 11 F. Supp. 535, 535 (S.D.N.Y. 1935).

45. Rosen, *Unfair to Genius*, 127–29.

46. *Arnstein v. Edward B. Marks*, Joint Appendix, 195–219. Record Group 21; National Archives and Records Administration, Kansas City; U.S.D.C. Southern District of New York; Equity Case Files, Box # 3489; "Arnsein v. Edward B. Marks."

47. *Arnstein v. Edward B. Marks*, Joint Appendix, 149.

48. *Arnstein V. Edward B. Marks*, Joint Appendix, 143.

49. *Arnstein V. Edward B. Marks*, Joint Appendix, 269.

50. *Arnstein v. Edward B. Marks*, Joint Appendix, 168.

51. *Arnstein v. Edward B. Marks Music Corp.*, 11 F. Supp. 535, 535 (S.D.N.Y. 1935).

52. *Arnstein v. Edward B. Marks Music Corp.*, 82 F.2d 275, 277 (2d Cir. 1936).

53. *Arnstein v. Edward B. Marks Music Corp.*, 82 F.2d 275, 275 (2d Cir. 1936).

54. *Arnstein v. Edward B. Marks Music Corp.*, 82 F.3d 275, 276 (2d Cir. 1936). The issue of access had been addressed by courts in the Second Circuit as early as *Simonton v. Gordon*, 12 F.2d 116 (S.D.N.Y. 1925).

55. *Arnstein v. Broadcast Music, Inc.*, 137 F.3d 410 (2d. Cir. 1943) [hereinafter *BMI*]. Arnstein had submitted eleven songs to BMI, eight of which became the objects of the lawsuit. Rosen, *Unfair to Genius*, 207.

56. *BMI*, 137 F. at 410.

57. *BMI*, Arnstein Deposition, 42–43. Record Group 21; National Archives and Records Administration, Kansas City; U.S.D.C. Southern District of New York; Equity Case Files, Box # 446; "Arnstein v. Broadcast Music, Inc."

58. *BMI*, 137 F.3d at 412.

59. *BMI*, 137 F.3d at 412 (citation omitted).

60. *Arnstein v. Twentieth Century Fox Film*, 52 F. Supp. 144, 115 (SDNY 1943) [hereinafter *Twentieth Century Fox*].

61. *Twentieth Century Fox*, 52 F. Supp. at 115.

62. *Hirsch v. Paramount Pictures*, 17 F. Supp. 816 (S.D. Cal. 1937).

63. *Hirsch*, 17 F. Supp. at 818–19.

64. *Hirsch*, 17 F. Supp. at 818.

65. *Hirsch*, 17 F. Supp. at 818.

66. *Carew v. R.K.O. Radio Pictures*, Complaint, 5. Record Group 21; National Archives and Records Administration, Kansas City; U.S.D.C. Southern District of New York; Equity Case Files, Boxes # 160–61; "Carew v. R.K.O. Radio Pictures."

67. *Carew*, 43 F. Supp. at 200.

68. *Carew*, 43 F. Supp. 199, 201 (S.D. Cal. 1942).

69. *Carew v. R.K.O. Radio Pictures*, Sirmay Deposition, 11. Record Group 21; National Archives and Records Administration, Kansas City; U.S.D.C. Southern District of New York; Equity Case Files, Boxes # 160–61; "Carew v. R.K.O. Radio Pictures." For note-by-note comparison, see Sirmay Deposition, 7–9.

70. *Carew*, 43 F. Supp. 199 at 202 (emphasis added).

71. *Carew*, 43 F. Supp. 199 at 200–01.

Chapter 3

Arnstein, Krofft, and the Narrowing Role of Expertise

Ira Arnstein's many lawsuits against Tin Pan Alley, carried out between 1928 and 1946, pressured courts under Second Circuit jurisdiction to develop a practical, systematic legal process for assessing copyright infringement claims. By his final lawsuit, which was filed against Cole Porter, the Second Circuit was poised to codify a functional legal procedure for finding similarity that disaggregated copying from improper, and thus unlawful, appropriation. In recasting what was treated as a question of law—to be decided by judges—now as a question of fact—to be decided by a jury—the *Arnstein v. Porter* court would bring about major changes in federal copyright litigation, with specific consequences for the roles of expert witnesses. By 1977, in *Sid and Marty Krofft Television Productions, Inc. v. McDonald's Corp.*, however, the Ninth Circuit had introduced a second legal test that, in seeking to refine the one established in *Arnstein*, superimposed new criteria on existing copying and improper appropriation inquiries. These new legal tests constrained expert analyses to the production of analytical "dissections" of the music at issue and prevented them from commenting on dispositive matters of improper appropriation.

These legal structures had the effect of narrowing the scope of influence that expert witnesses could have on a given case. Despite the legal changes, expert analytical techniques continued early-twentieth-century trends toward sophistication during this time, with growing emphasis on formal structure situating melocentric comparisons, which had two main results. On the one hand, these techniques responded to the call in the new legal tests for analysis that "dissected" music; on the other, as expert witnesses reached new levels of technical sophistication, their analyses undoubtedly grew increasingly mystifying to nonexpert factfinders.

Chapter 3

ARNSTEIN'S LAST STAND

In early 1945, on the heels of lawsuits against BMI (Broadcast Music, Incorporated) and Twentieth Century Fox, Arnstein filed his final copyright lawsuit.[1] This time, Arnstein sued Cole Porter, accusing the famed composer of infringing Arnstein's copyright with some of Porter's most famous songs, including "Night and Day," "What Is This Thing Called Love?," "Begin the Beguine," "I Love You," "You'd Be So Nice to Come Home To," "My Heart Belongs to Daddy," and "Don't Fence Me In."[2] Matching each one of Porter's songs with one of his own, Arnstein strategically demanded a jury trial, instead of a bench trial, and damages of $1 million from Porter in compensation for his alleged violations.

Both parties' strategies embraced legal emphasis in the Second Circuit on a defendant's purported access to a plaintiff's work as a critical element of copyright infringement. According to Arnstein, Porter's commercial success was a result of "wholesale pirating"[3] of Arnstein's music, with dubious accusations as to Porter's access. In his deposition, Arnstein alleged that Porter "'had stooges right along to follow me, watch me, and live in the same apartment with me,' and that [Arnstein's] room had been ransacked on several occasions."[4] In response, Porter did not deny Arnstein's earlier copyright claims or the similarities between the claimed songs. Instead, he focused on his purported lack of any access to Arnstein's songs, which would have precluded Porter's ability to copy, and thus defend against any infringement claims. After a trial and appeal process that lived up to Arnstein's reputation by late 1946, Porter had prevailed and the decision-making process for infringement would be revolutionized.

At trial, both parties called musical expert witnesses to comment on similarity and their understanding of nonexpert listener perceptions of it, as well as whether such similarity could evince copying.[5] The expert witnesses presented a dynamic discussion of musical composition and theoretical analysis of it, using disposable visual charts placed on an easel for all present to view, verbal explanations of music theory and composition, and aural demonstrations of phrases and themes from the songs at issue. The explicit influence of their contributions on the court, however, would seem to be overshadowed by the courts' frustration with Arnstein's arguments and courtroom antics.

As plaintiff, Arnstein relied primarily on retired organ professor Samuel A. Baldwin to serve as expert. In his protracted examination, Baldwin chose analytical techniques to show that despite an apparent lack of melodic congruence between each set of paired songs, these dissimilarities were inconsequential when compared to the underlying harmonic and formal similarities he had located to make each song pair seem alike. For example, Baldwin drew attention to the similarity in "the chord line,"[6] or harmonic progression, between Arnstein's claimed "Modern Messiah" and Porter's "Don't

Fence Me In." From this similar harmonic progression, Baldwin was able to analytically remove what he called "changing notes,"[7] thereby analytically reducing the music to what he called the "theme."[8] Without these ornaments, the remaining theme appeared to be generic, being one "which is practically identical that a thousand composers could invent. We find such similarities always."[9] To demonstrate his point, Baldwin explained a series of comparison charts to the court, pointing at each nonchord tone and each note of the theme: "Here (indicating), you see, he doesn't go directly to A. Mr. Arnstein, he has [an] A. Then he has to fill that in there, and he needs the notes. Here we have a similarity (indicating). That is a very characteristic theme—a portion of his melody and here it is (indicating). Don't you see?"[10] In his comparisons, Baldwin excluded ornamental nonchord tones, treating these as embellishments on the main theme that did little more than purportedly disguise it.

Baldwin's demonstration was aided by a Mr. Sapiro, who performed excerpts from the sheet music exhibits and Baldwin's charts.[11] "I hope I can make you hear, but you see what I mean,"[12] he promised, relying on live performance to direct the court's attention to the particular musical elements Baldwin wanted it to see in the charts. By focusing on a reduced, structural melodic line, Baldwin supported Arnstein's argument that apparent dissimilarities were merely a way of concealing musical material that was substantially similar enough to indicate copying. Upon a question regarding nonexpert listeners detecting similarity that he pointed out, Baldwin responded that he couldn't "account for the average listener, because there are lots of them who listen but do not hear music."[13] For the same question of detecting similarity by musically trained listeners, he responded "oh yes, of course . . . the eye sees the similarity as well as the ear hearing it. Any musician would pick it up."[14]

As they argued, these similarities showed that Porter copied the theme and then "disguise[d] it" through melodic, as well as rhythmic, variation:[15]

> I could sit down and play you a dozen different ways of developing that theme and not use Mr. Porter's at all, but I won't take the time. Then, again, if one were disposed to copy a piece, he could disguise it absolutely by a change of rhythm—by rhythm we mean the relationship of tones with respect to duration, that is long or short. Here is the rhythm which you will all know (pounding on table). That is the tune . . . I could play you a theme that you all know, and you would not recognize it, by changing the rhythm.

During cross-examination, defense attorneys challenged Baldwin's analysis by systematically drawing attention to deficiencies in his arguments according to the melodic, harmonic, rhythmic, and metrical construction of the themes in question. This line of questioning was predicated on analysis that integrated musical elements and placed them in the broader context of musical form, in this case, the "popular song idiom" and 32-bar AABA song form.[16] This questioning served to undermine Baldwin's analysis and his credibility by exposing biased analytical manipulations of Porter's music.

Baldwin also contended that the similarities he found were not merely a matter of common compositional models, which he described using AABA 32-bar song form and repetition in compositions by Robert Schumann as examples, but rather because of deliberate copying:[17]

> a thousand composers can get the same idea like that (indicating), that first part of it. But in composition it makes an expansion of a musical idea; you go from one to the other. You may write two measures, then you write two more, then you write four more, then you may write eight more. Now, no two composers would ever, not in the history of the art as I know it . . . precisely the same for four measures. In the next four it would be different.

Over the course of his testimony, Baldwin explained a notion of creative process where composers could use up to four similar measures with another composer's music before "coming under suspicion" of copying, because "you have a limited number of notes, but there are millions of combinations."[18] As he attempted to demonstrate, the putative similarities between Arnstein's and Porter's songs amounted to more than the allegedly permissible four measures.

Conversely, the defendant called Spaeth, alongside music critic Deems Taylor and Albert Sirmay, who were by then being brought to court routinely as music expert witnesses in copyright infringement cases. Although records of Spaeth's testimony are incomplete, his cross-examination clarified the relationship between melody and harmony according to abstract music theory, and the extent of musical variation possible based on a series of up to eight notes.[19] Spaeth hypothesized that there were as many as "478 million and some thousand,"[20] possible combinations of the twelve notes in the chromatic scale. This testimony highlighted the melocentric emphasis on pitch comparisons typical of expert analyses during this time, but it also pushed for a more contextualized approach to such comparisons. His testimony undoubtedly applied these theoretical concepts to each set of paired songs at issue in the case.

For the majority of Spaeth's cross-examination, the plaintiff's attorneys attempted to impeach him not because of unsound testimony, but rather by constructing a reputation of him as "a fraud, a musical trickster and a cheat,"[21] based on Arnstein's accusations and a separately settled defamation lawsuit brought by Spaeth against Warner Brothers for producing a movie with a crooked character allegedly based on Spaeth's "Tune Detective" persona.[22]

Following the techniques used by expert witnesses before him, Taylor's analysis began by demonstrating a lack of melodic congruence,[23] and then analogized differences between Arnstein's and Porter's songs to prior compositions:[24]

> The only striking similarity occurs in the first two measures of both songs in which both employ the device of a leap downward. In Mr. Arnstein's case it is a leap of an octave and in Mr. Porter's case it is a leap down of a major seventh. It is a device commonly used. Wagner in his 'Tristan and Isolde' and Tschaikovsky's song "None But The Lonely Heart" have exactly the same interval.

Although Taylor would later revise his discussion of melodic leaps, the analogy to western art music served to undermine Baldwin's analysis by casting such leaps as unoriginal, and therefore, not protectable and irrelevant to copyright infringement.[25]

Taylor's redirect and recross-examination also included a line of questioning that addressed his ethical motivation for serving an expert witness. Taylor indicated that, as then-president of the American Society of Composers, Authors, and Publishers (ASCAP), he needed to contribute his opinion regarding "a completely baseless attack on a very talented composer and one which if successful could be brought against practically every successful composer, publisher or author in this country."[26] Taylor's goal was to protect "Cole Porter in particular,"[27] but also composers more generally, by offering his expertise in hope of influencing a result that he found favorable. In one of the only explicit statements regarding the ethical duties of a musical expert witness, Taylor recognized the impact that his expertise could make on the court, its decision, and future copyright litigation.

For all that the musical expert witnesses seemed to offer a critical dialogue to the case, the district court paid no expressed attention. Instead, presiding Judge Caffey relied on Arnstein's litigious reputation to present an opinion that summarily outlined the issues, forms of relief, and then determined:[28]

> If time were available, I would deal with all the phases concerning each kind of relief sought. But my work growing out of the recent motion term is too pressing and voluminous to permit me to go further now. I have gathered all the files in five cases tried in this court wherein plaintiff sued for judgment in an action relating to music or copyrights on musical compositions. The size of the files warns me that several weeks would be needed in order to go through all the details. I feel bound to go to other cases in which decisions have been reserved.

Without wanting "to go further," the judge dispensed with assessing musical similarity to dispose of the case swiftly.[29] Instead, in a legal gesture that would bring about change in the legal decision-making process for infringement, Judge Caffey granted summary judgement in favor of Porter to dismiss the action.

THE *ARNSTEIN* TEST

On appeal, the Second Circuit remanded Judge Caffey's decision based on improper decision-making. The issue before the three-judge panel, consisting of famed Judges Frank, L. Hand, and Clark, was whether there was the "slightest doubt" as to the facts applied in the district court opinion, which legally framed the appeal around questions of fact.[30] This emphasis on factual inquiries, coupled with the court's skepticism regarding evidentiary inquiries and disapproval of Judge Caffey's seemingly cursory decision against Arnstein, drove the opinion.[31] Contemporaneous jurisprudence regarding the roles of experts and nonexperts, most notably discussed in previous opinions written by Judge L. Hand, along with his growing skepticism toward expert witnesses in general, also undoubtedly impacted the decision.

Writing for the majority, Judge Frank, with Judge L. Hand in concurrence, remanded the case back to the district court. The opinion codified a functional process for deciding infringement intended for application by the district court that was based on separate, yet seemingly repetitive, and even redundant, evaluations of similarity conducted first according to expert evaluation and then by nonexperts. The new, two-step process galvanized the fact-driven approach and considered the role that experts and nonexperts, or what he called "ordinary lay hearers,"[32] would play in the inquiry.

With the new legal decision-making process, or "test," a court should follow a two-step process. First, a court should identify valid copyright registration.[33] The first step would prove to be relatively straightforward; it is the second step where listening skill began to matter. Next, a court should determine improper appropriation, which involved its own two-prong process that disaggregated copying into two separate inquiries: "(a) that defendant copied from plaintiff's copyrighted work and (b) that the copying (assuming it to be proved) went to [sic] far as to constitute improper appropriation."[34] To prove prong (a), a plaintiff might present direct evidence of copying through the defendant's own admission, or they might present circumstantial evidence, "usually evidence of access—from which the trier of the facts may reasonably infer copying,"[35] plus evidence of similarity based on close comparison of the works at issue. "If there is evidence of access and similarities exist,"[36] only then should a court move to prong (b), whether the copying was sufficient to be considered improper appropriation. Only where there is reasonable evidence of copying can the second step be resolved, that is, to evaluate whether the copying was sufficient to be considered improper appropriation or infringement. This determination, which turned on witness credibility and lay perceptions, would henceforth be the province of the jury.[37]

The legal disaggregation of what was simply "similarity" into copying and improper appropriation invited contributions from both nonexpert listeners and musical experts, each serving a different function:[38]

> analysis ("dissection") is relevant, and the testimony of experts may be received to aid the trier of the facts. If evidence of access is absent, the similarities must be so striking as to preclude the possibility that plaintiff and defendant independently arrived at the same result. If copying is established, then only does there arise the second issue, that of illicit copying (unlawful appropriation). On that issue . . . the test is the response of the ordinary lay hearer; accordingly, on that issue, "dissection" and expert testimony are irrelevant.

Here, the court established that expert witnesses could only contribute analytical dissection to the issue of copying while nonexpert listeners would determine whether that copying was sufficient to be considered infringement based on their perception of an ordinary listener. Experts could no longer comment on the issue of whether the similarity amounted to improper appropriation, or evaluate the legal extent of any congruence they identified. Instead, they could only contribute what has been called "probative similarity," or the evaluation of similarity based on close comparisons.[39] The court remained silent, however, on matters of analytical technique or the role that originality or stylistic commonality should play in such evaluations.

The qualifications for expertise, however, were left undefined. Instead, the "ordinary lay hearer," whose hypothetical perceptions were to be ascertained, or in practice represented, by a jury itself made up of such nonexpert listeners, would have the final determination regarding misappropriation. Because of the new test, the *Arnstein* court shifted what had been a question of law, or an issue to be decided by a judge through the application of legal principles, to a question of fact, or an issue regarding facts and evidence to be decided by a jury.

THE RELATIONSHIP BETWEEN EXPERT AND ORDINARY LISTENERS

The new test handed down by the *Arnstein* court, particularly its binary division between expert and nonexpert, seemed to resolve competing factors underlying music copyright infringement and to address case-specific problems with the hurried district court judge and the repeat plaintiff. However, the judges' solution was oriented idiomatically around music and reflected decades of music copyright case opinions that emphasized the perceptions of an abstract "ordinary listener," undoubtedly influenced in no small part by concurring Judge L. Hand. By setting forth the new test, Judge Frank created a division between categories of not just observers, but "auditors," continuing a discussion that had been brewing in the Second Circuit:[40]

> At the trial, plaintiff may play, or cause to be played, the pieces in such manner that they may seem to a jury to be inexcusably alike, in terms of the way in which lay listeners of such music would be likely to react. The plaintiff may call witnesses whose testimony may aid the jury in reaching its conclusion as to the responses of such audiences. Expert testimony of musicians may also be received, but it will in no way be controlling on the issue of illicit copying, and should be utilized only to assist in determining the reactions of lay auditors. The impression made on the refined ears of musical experts or their views as to the musical excellence of plaintiff's or defendant's works are utterly immaterial on the issue of misappropriation; for the views of such persons are caviar to the general—and plaintiff's and defendant's compositions are not caviar.

The roles that experts and nonexperts would play in future cases were specifically constructed according to music and notions of a listening disparity between "lay auditors" and the "refined" ears of experts. The caviar metaphor implied a kind of stratification to listening and the popular status of the songs at issue, as well as the rarity of an acquired understanding believed to be necessary for the courtroom luxury of musical analysis. This idea followed throughout Judge Frank's opinion, which explicitly pointed to economic issues as a motivator for the distinction between expert and nonexpert. The opinion explicitly pointed to economic rationales driving federal copyright to justify the distinction, which highlighted an apparent need to constrain experts:[41]

> The proper criterion on [the issue of improper appropriation] is not an analytic or other comparison of the respective musical compositions as they appear on paper or in the judgment of trained musicians. The plaintiff's legally protected interest is not, as such, his reputation as a musician but his interest in the potential financial returns from his compositions which derive from the lay public's approbation of his efforts. The question, therefore, is whether defendant took from plaintiff's works so much of what is pleasing to the ears of lay listeners, who comprise the audience for whom such popular music is composed, that defendant wrongfully appropriated something which belongs to the plaintiff.

According to the majority, because copyright protects "financial returns" received by the copyright holder for the protected work, it was necessary to consider the perceptions of the primarily nonexpert, or lay, listener audience likely to provide those returns. In this way, the distinctions drawn by experts between two musical works could, or could not, be relevant to the economic status of song sales, and profits, as well as the perceptions of nonexpert lay listeners who composed the work's paying audience. While those distinctions may be perceptible by such listeners, it is equally plausible that they would be only perceptible to trained eyes and ears, thereby having comparatively little economic effect.

Judge Frank's decision was undoubtedly influenced by previous cases, concerns for establishing functional procedures, and evidentiary skepticism, all of which can be traced as closely to Judge L. Hand's concurring guidance as to Judge Frank's own ideas about musical structure and training. In an article written two years after the opinion, Judge Frank analogized the decisions made by judges and music performers.[42] He used the example of a hypothetical melody as a metaphor in his argument regarding intuitive "hunches" that could not be broken down into analytical perceptions:[43]

> The gestaltist's favorite illustration is a melody: a melody does not result from the summation of its parts; thus to analyze a melody is to destroy it. It is a basic, primary unit. The melody, a pattern, determines the function of the notes, its parts; the notes, the parts, do not determine the melody.

Judge Frank's metaphor revealed the perspective regarding music from which he likely approached the *Arnstein* decision, and provided a clue to his perspective underlying the role of musical expert witnesses. If a melody must be perceived as a whole, then expert "dissection" could not be the sole, or even decisive, evidence for determining copyright infringement. Instead, the ultimate decision regarding infringement was one that "a [non-expert] jury is peculiarly fitted to determine."[44]

The majority's new test ultimately relied on comparative perceptions of an ordinary listener, but it paradoxically guaranteed that musical experts at least could, and commonly would, contribute to the discussion. The inclusion of expert comparisons may in hindsight seem to have been superfluous, given the predominant role of the nonexpert jury whose perceptions were easily inserted as representatives of the ordinary or average listener. But the persistence of expert witnesses can be traced to what by that time had become a common litigation strategy in music copyright infringement cases. This tradition undoubtedly stemmed from the high regard in which musical training was held, particularly the ability to read and compare analytically the sheet music considered to represent materially copyright-protected musical works. Given their skepticism about the nature of musical evidence as a whole, however, the judges' reduplication of similarity evaluations in the *Arnstein* test resulted in a process complex enough to give the appearance of promoting objectivity, preventing partiality, overcoming discrepancies of opinions resulting from diverse levels in music skill, and accounting for the marketplace and critical reception of musical works.

THE DISSENT AND PROBLEMS WITH EXPERTS AND NONEXPERTS

Judge Clark's dissenting opinion likewise focused on judicially perceived peculiarities to musical analysis, albeit with a rare citation to a contemporaneous music appreciation text. He found greater fault in the new test and reasoning than with the outcome of the appeal, characterizing the majority's limitations on expert testimony as having an "anti-intellectual and book-burning nature."[45] The dissent railed against the majority opinion's reliance on nonexperts. It presented the division of similarity from improper appropriation as one of the fundamental problems with the new legal test:[46]

> I find nowhere any suggestion of two steps in adjudication of this issue, one of finding copyright which may be approached with musical intelligence and assistance of experts, and another that of illicit copying which must be approached with complete ignorance; nor do I see how rationally there can be any such difference, even if a jury—the now chosen instrument of musical detection—could be expected to separate those issues and the evidence accordingly.

Using thematic turns of phrase that played on Porter's evocative lyrics, the dissenting Judge Clark also found problems with limiting experts and ultimately relying on nonexpert jurors, which the dissent found to have suspect qualifications: "the judicial eardrum may be peculiarly insensitive after long years of listening to the 'beat, beat, beat' (I find myself plagiarizing from defendant and thus in danger of my brothers' doom) of sound upon it, though perhaps no more so than the ordinary citizen juror—even if tone deafness is made a disqualification for jury service."[47] The core of the dissent's concern, however, was more a matter of the balance between lay and expert evidence. Relying on Stewart Macpherson's contemporaneously published *Form in Music* as a learned treatise to justify the application of "the intellect," referring to expert dissection, "as well as the emotions," referring to lay listener perception, the dissenting opinion noted that both are necessary for "a just appreciation of music."[48] While Judge Clark did not elaborate on what such appreciation entailed, it was likely intended to be synonymous with ideas about musical training. Regardless of this imprecision, if jurors were to disregard expert dissection when making their decision, as the new test required, then this balance would be disturbed.

The Second Circuit remanded the case and sent its newly minted process for identifying copyright infringement back to the district court. With Porter's "Night and Day" set to be released only a few months later, Porter's attorneys pushed to expedite the trial on remand.[49] The remand trial itself lived up to the reputation of other Arnstein cases that came before it as a result of Arnstein's unusual, "far-fetched and abstruse"[50] litigation strategy. After only two hours of deliberation, the jury unsurprisingly decided in favor of Porter.

Matters of listener acuity and balance aside, both the *Arnstein* majority and its dissent expressed a need for detailed analyses of copyrighted works, which in practice would be produced by expert witnesses, alongside the totalizing evaluations of nonexperts. For the three judges involved in *Arnstein*, the distinction between categories of listeners appeared mutually exclusive, based on an assumption that average listeners could not perceive musical detail and that expert analyses would not offer an accurate representation of average listener comparisons. On the one hand, experts producing "dissections" of musical works were understood to approach music with a theoretical and analytical mindset focused on musical structure and compositional subtlety. On the other hand, the more holistic—and the dissent might suggest emotional— approach presumptively taken by the nonexpert listener, or the jurors likely to insert themselves as representatives, were believed to present an accurate representation of the market impact from any alleged similarity. The retention of both expert and nonexpert seemed simultaneously to generate a less partial, more evidence-driven decision-making process based on analytical facts while remaining responsive to foundational copyright policies.

Perhaps in an effort to construct what would be construed by later courts as a broadly applicable infringement test across all copyrightable media, or perhaps due to judicial assumptions about commonly understood definitions of expert witness and lay-listener as equivalent to the hypothetical average reasonable person, neither opinion dwelled on matters of musical genre or style, let alone the diversity of listener acuity that could blur divisions between expert and nonexpert. By establishing a functionalist approach to the evaluation of copyright infringement, the *Arnstein* case nevertheless served as a legal pivot in the ways that judges approached similarity analysis in copyright infringement litigation. This change of perspective was not simply a product of the judges' jurisprudence or a practical response to the conditions of case. Rather, the language of the appellate opinions suggests that the three judges were concerned specifically with the challenges of musical analysis and nationwide disparities in musical training and skill.

Chapter 3

APPLYING *ARNSTEIN V. PORTER*

After *Arnstein*, a plaintiff would state their infringement case by proving three elements: ownership of a valid copyright, that the defendant copied, and that the copying occurred to an extent that it could be considered illegal. District courts, particularly the Southern District of New York, soon after discovered the challenges of applying the new test. Despite the radical changes it had on legal similarity analysis, the practical functions of musical expert witnesses in litigation appeared initially to have changed little, apart from being no longer able to comment directly on matters of infringement. Their analyses continued to privilege melody and pitch comparisons, in the increasingly sophisticated context of interwoven harmony, rhythm, and formal structure. They continued to reinforce these musical dimensions as more indicative of musical similarity than key, tempo, meter, and ornamentation. During this period, however, there is a rise in testimony regarding prior composition and musical style that correlates with the codification of access and threshold questions of copyrightability.

Although the *Arnstein* decision has come to be known for introducing what is generically referred to as "substantial similarity" analysis, the term derived not from *Arnstein*, but from previous cases traceable to the nineteenth century, as well as another music copyright case decided by the same panel of judges less than a week later. In that case, *Heim v. Universal Pictures*, they applied the new procedure for evaluating similarity.[51] The case dealt with Hungarian composer Heim's copyright infringement claim against Universal Pictures, alleging that the chorus of his song, "*Ma Este Meg Boldog Vagyok*," was infringed by a verse of the song, "Perhaps," as it appeared in the movie, *Nice Girl*. To meet the access requirement, Heim claimed that Universal had access to his song because it was used in a Hungarian movie. Universal rebutted the argument by demonstrating that both works drew on Antonin Dvořák's piano cycle, *Humoresque*.[52]

The district court found in favor of Universal on grounds that Heim's evidence of access was "contradictory and untrustworthy,"[53] despite applying the newly minted *Arnstein* test and a finding that the works were indeed similar. The Second Circuit, represented by the same three-panel court as in *Arnstein*, affirmed that decision. Writing for the majority again, Judge Frank's reasoning was that Heim's music lacked originality. Judge Frank referred to expert witnesses detecting "substantial similarity" between the two pieces, which is said to be the genesis of the combined term as it is used in subsequent opinions and scholarship to refer to the inquiry established in the previous *Arnstein* case. Yet there was no mention on appeal as to the lack of a jury, which Judge Frank justified later only as the court not needing to reach the final step in the *Arnstein* test.[54]

Two years after *Arnstein* and *Heim*, the Southern District of New York grappled with the alleged infringement of calypso songs carried into the popular music market. In *Baron v. Leo Feist*, plaintiff Maurice Baron sued publisher Leo Feist, Paul Baron, Jeri Sullavan, and Morey Amsterdam claiming that their hit calypso-inflected song, "Rum and Coca-Cola," infringed on his composition, "*L'Année Passée*," one of twelve songs in his collection, "Calypso Songs of the West Indies."[55] In 1941, publisher Maurice Baron claimed that famed calypso musician Lionel Belasco and professional singer Massie Patterson approached him to make a sheet music collection of Belasco's music. In late 1942, professional Calypso singer Rupert Westmore Grant claimed he wrote the lyrics to "Rum and Coca-Cola" based on a melody he had recently learned from one of Belasco's cousins, Cyril Monrose— the melody for which was called "*L'Année Passée*." Belasco claimed that the melody was composed as early as 1906. Baron transcribed and arranged the songs, including "*L'Année Passée*," and the song was copyrighted as part of the collection.[56]

Conversely, defendant Paul Baron claimed that his song came from two preexisting Spanish melodies that he allegedly had heard many times while in Spain but had never seen notated on sheet music.[57] Entertainer Morey Amsterdam alleged that he heard the lyrics, "rum and coca-cola kill the yankee soldier"[58] once during a month-long visit to Trinidad. He subsequently brought the lyrics to Jeri Sullavan, a New York night club performer, to be sung to the well-known tune, "It Ain't Gonna Rain No More." Sullavan, in turn, brought the lyrics to Paul Baron, who set them to music.[59] Although the plaintiff's song was copyrighted, the defendants claimed that the song was an unprotected folk tune and therefore the scope of federal copyright protection for it was limited to Baron's arguably original arrangement of the melody.

Twenty-eight witnesses were called at trial, including Norman Lockwood and Sigmund Spaeth to serve as experts.[60] Composer and popular music arranger Lockwood, called on behalf of the plaintiff, presented a comparison chart not retained in extant court records, but that was said to have placed the two melodies in tandem on it, with red lines connecting similarities and blue lines marking differences.[61] In his testimony, Lockwood drew attention to a repeated weak suspension and chromatic harmony that appeared in both songs, associating these musical features with calypso style.[62] As he explained, both songs had repeated use of weak suspensions typical of calypso, and similarly uncommon resolutions of chromatic harmonies, which he contended were unusual and therefore indicative of "Rum and Coca Cola" being copied. He also provided the court with a quantitative summary of the amount of similarity according to melodic, harmonic, and rhythmic congruences.[63]

In the course of his examination, Lockwood also introduced a solfège-based chart, which Spaeth challenged for neglecting rhythmic duration and confusing nonexpert lay listeners present in ways that other notational charts would not.[64] Although the chart itself was not retained with the court records, it was described in Spaeth's critique of its detail:[65]

> there are actual mistakes in it, mistakes in putting down the two tunes in the sol-lah-fah system[*sic*], and also because the use of the sol-fah[*sic*] system in this case does not in any way represent the actual tunes. It is a picture, and a picture would impress anyone who cannot read notes with an apparent similarity, a very considerable similarity. However, since there is no indication whatever, first of all, of key which—these happen to be the same—but there is no indication of what the key is, and if I were asked to sing every one of these from the chart I could sing this one in one key and this in another key . . . And there is no indication of the length of any notes. So there is no indication whatever of the length of the notes; there is no indication of the actual pitch of the notes.

More than describing the chart, Spaeth also highlighted its shortcomings: the lack of key or rhythmic indication to distinguish a set of pitches as a particular melody.[66] It is likely that the chart format was strategic on Lockwood's part to focus the court's attention on obvious melodic similarities by abstracting pitch information into an easily perceptible format for nonexperts. Regardless of motive, the solfège-melody-only format that strayed from general practice of black-and-red notation. As a result, the expert witnesses and the parties engaged in a bitter confrontation regarding the validity of each expert's technique and conclusions.[67] In his discussion of his own analysis for the defendants, visually summarized in a no-longer-extant comparison chart that supposedly used red lines to mark parallels between the two songs,[68] Spaeth focused on the melodic structure of the two songs, in terms of pitch, rhythm, and phrasing. The majority of his testimony, however, was directed toward rebutting Lockwood's analysis for the plaintiff.

Both parties called additional musical expert witnesses whose backgrounds were diverse but relevant to establishing admissible expertise. Experts included John Tasker Howard, then head librarian of the New York Public Library American Music Collection, and physician Walter Merrick, who had studied music with Belasco and who had considered himself to be an avocational "expert on calypso music."[69] In an unusual legal strateggym, plaintiff Maurice Baron was also admitted at trial as his own expert witness to present his own comparison of the songs and explanation of his compositional model.[70] Despite the partiality of this strategic move, the plaintiff explained both his compositional process and demonstrated the similarity between the two songs through charts and live demonstration at the piano.

The depth of musical-theoretical discussion concerned presiding Judge Simon Rifkind, who complained at trial that "we are going much further into the theory of the structure of music than most of the cases I am familiar with in this field pretend to go. However, I am wondering whether we are beginning an innovation—which may be useful—which is beyond the confines of previous adjudication."[71] While the abstract discussion of music theory between Spaeth and Lockwood effectively dissected the music at issue and challenged the credibility of each other's analyses to avoid such confusion, this discussion occurred at the risk of alienating the nonexpert legal fact-finder. In his opinion, Judge Rifkind suggested that there might be a limit to the contributions of expert witnesses and their analyses, which Spaeth and Lockwood had crossed, but that implication, along with notions of innovation in their forensic musical analyses, was not fully realized.[72]

Despite the court's problems with expert testimony, its approach to making the final decision relied on the *Arnstein* test, particularly in its limited influence from expert witnesses. The court first considered Maurice Baron's valid copyright registration, then took into account Baron, Sullavan, and Amsterdam's access as well as expert testimony that identified the high level of similarity between the two songs. Although the experts' analyses, no matter how confusing, supported a finding of unlawful appropriation, it was "lay analysis and evaluation"[73] that determined infringement.

The court ultimately decided in favor of Maurice Baron on grounds that his copyright registration was valid and that there was close similarity—a decision that was later affirmed by the Second Circuit.[74] The district court opinion explicitly addressed the issue of expert partiality, thereby challenging the value of their contributions: "experts for each side demonstrated, in their *zealous partisanship*, the doubtful function of the expert as an aid to the court in this class of litigation. . . the differing qualities of the testimony made the resolution of most of the issues of fact comparatively easy. The music itself lent itself quite readily to lay analysis and evaluation."[75] The "zealous partisanship" to which the court referred likely resulted not simply from disagreements about similarity, but from a more theoretically sophisticated discourse over comparison charts not retained in the court records. The juxtaposition of the manner in which the court approached expert and nonexpert evaluations, from the confusion and suspicion with which it viewed experts and the trust with which it viewed nonexpert listeners, revealed the problems courts faced in applying the *Arnstein* test and balancing the perceived divide between experts and nonexperts.

In *Jones v. Supreme Music, Corporation*, decided only three years after *Baron*, Selina Jones claimed that her song, "Just an Old Fashioned Mother and Dad" was infringed by Francis Craig's song, "Near You," which was published by Supreme Music Corporation.[76] Jones had submitted the song for copyright registration and publication, for which 1,500 regular copies and 500 artists' copies were produced, but the song was never widely disseminated and no copies were sold.[77] Yet even after establishing that Craig could not have had access to Jones's song, the court nevertheless conducted similarity analysis before resolving the case in favor of the defendant.

To conduct its analysis, the court relied on its own consideration of the songs to determine improper appropriation,[78] but took into consideration the similarity identified by the experts, including now-routine expert witnesses Deems Taylor and John Tasker Howard.[79] In particular, Taylor's analysis proceeded phrase-by-phrase to show a lack of melodic and harmonic resemblance according to contour, rather than a lack of note-for-note consecutive congruence.[80] His testimony also served to explain music-theoretical concepts for the court, specifically focusing on the lack of indication of musical difference that tempo and embellishment had in contrast to structural melodies and repetition.[81] Like earlier decisions, the opinion replicated a detailed dissection of the songs that drew directly on expert analysis but also considered the aural perceptions of nonexpert listeners.[82]

Northern Music Corp. v. King Records Distributing likewise followed the *Arnstein* test as binding legal authority, but read the decision as creating two separate approaches to addressing similarity to compare rather than as a two-step process.[83] The case arose out of an infringement claim made by Northern Music Corporation, a subsidiary of Decca Records and the assignee for "Tonight He Sailed Again," against King Records Distributing for creating and distributing records and sheet music for "I Love You, Yes I Do."[84] This claim dealt specifically with the chorus of the two songs, rather than the songs in their entirety.

Musical expert witnesses involved in this case included John Howard, big band arranger Joseph Xavier Burke, and BMI editor and defense attorney Milton Rettenberg. In particular, Burke's analysis included a comparison of the music at issue by "type," or style, of which he explained that "songs are typified according to whether they are rhythm songs, blues songs, ballads, waltzes, polkas, romantic ballads, historical ballads, [or] outright jazz tunes."[85] Identifying the songs at issue as love ballads, Burke then compared the music based on formal structure, melody, and rhythm. Burke also sought to demonstrate his comparison, which the court found concerning because it "had no way of perpetuating it for the purposes of the record."[86] Despite the court's astute anxiety that sheet music could not capture the musical elements that Burke would demonstrate, he permitted the performance to continue. Serving as an expert witness, Rettenberg presented a recording of his performance of the music for comparison,[87] which the court "endured on trial 'with patience and fortitude.'"[88] While the recording seemed to resolve the court's short-term concerns, it was not retained in the court records.

The opinion is revealing both for expert analyses as well as for the court's interpretation of *Arnstein*. The court's decision cast doubt on expert analysis, instead of relying exclusively on its own perception of resemblance as a nonexpert: "Expert testimony has been offered by both sides. Much of it is in conflict. While it has been of some help, we rely on the only other test available to a judge, who is a musical layman, namely—whether there is a resemblance noticeable to the average hearer."[89] Despite this reasoning, the decision still included an extensive discussion of formal, rhythmic, and melodic comparison of the music at issue to contextualize the nature of the conflict.[90] As the court explained, "[t]echnically analyzed, a musical composition is made up of rhythm, harmony and melody,"[91] from which originality can be ascertained primarily through melodic comparison. "It is in the arrangement or succession of musical notes, which are the fingerprints of the composition, and establish its identity."[92] This model of musical composition contributed to a growing legal approach to musical infringement that principally considered these four musical dimensions, and primarily melody, to analyze and locate similarity and originality.

BEYOND THE SECOND CIRCUIT: SEVENTH CIRCUIT

As music copyright infringement cases swept the nation, other appellate court panels looked to the Second Circuit and its *Arnstein* test for persuasive authority to resolve the challenges of determining copyright infringement, only to discover that the test was problematic. In 1958, for example, the Seventh Circuit heard one of its first cases to address issues of access and substantial similarity. In *Cholvin v. B&F Music Co.*, a lack of direct evidence of copying led plaintiffs Homer Cholvin and Norman Stade to sue defendant Kaczmarek. They alleged that Kaczmarek infringed on the melody of their then-popular song, "When the Sun Bids the Sky Goodnight," with his own song, "While We Dream," the rights for which were acquired by B&F Music in 1953.[93] While Kaczmarek regularly listened to the radio, and thus may have had access, he could not read music, therefore it would have been impossible for Cholvin and Strade to prove that Kaczmarek directly copied from their sheet music.

At trial, the court received testimony from expert witnesses hired by the plaintiffs: John Bach, an arranger; James Baumann, a teacher and organist at the Milwaukee Art Institute[94]; and Harold Barlow, identified as a "music plagiarism expert"[95] but also a noted writer about music. Barlow's testimony in particular explicitly described the comparison chart he used to graphically represent his analysis, shown in figure 3.1, and what it should convey to the court: "A comparison chart is a chart I make showing note for note a visual comparison of the songs in question, usually by signifying notes in duplication for the lay eye in red, so that these duplications may easily be seen. . . . Therefore the redder the page looks to the lay eye, it is to be presumed the

Figure 3.1 *Cholvin v. B&F Music,* **Comparison Chart, Harold Barlow.** Records Group 21 National Archives and Records Administration Chicago; U.S.D.C. Chicago, Civil Transcripts Case 55C771, Box C-236 "Cholvin v. B&F Music." Credit: Author.

more similar are the two songs in question."[96] While Barlow prepared the chart, all three experts relied on it to make their comparisons in court indicating the similarity of the two songs. No complaint regarding its format, which showed Barlow's retention of the original meter and rhythm but spaced the two songs so that similar pitches aligned, was recorded in the court records.

Although the chart served to direct the attention of the court as to what Barlow intended them to see, and presumably hear, the fact that the other musical expert witnesses accepted the chart sheds light on the potential for collegial relationships between the individual witnesses retained, at least in this case. Unlike in previous cases, where experts contested one another's charts and analytical techniques, these expert witnesses presumably evaluated Barlow's chart and found it to be an equitable representation of the music, which outweighed any benefit to creating additional, and potentially partial, analytical diagrams.

Much of the expert testimony in this case involved a search for melodic congruences as they appeared in the sheet music, but Barlow's discussion extended beyond this analytical technique. During his examination, Barlow outlined his procedure for conducting a reductive theoretical analysis that eliminated nonessential musical material before comparing structural melodies and harmonies. As he described: "[i]n the problem of associating one song with another, one should reduce the song to its skeleton without the folderol,"[97] by which he probably meant ornamentation. This analytical technique continued a trend among experts of to focus on musical elements indicative of similarity to the exclusion of nonindicative features of legal-musical similarity, including key, tempo, meter, and ornamental nonchord tones.

Despite testimony that the songs were similar, the trial court determined that B&F, and specifically Kaczmarek, did not infringe on Cholvin's song. On appeal, the Seventh Circuit affirmed. While the appellate decision hinged on the plaintiffs' "latitude" during cross-examination regarding royalties and fees rather than on the similarity inquiry, the Seventh Circuit court also reviewed the trial court's consideration of access and similarity evidence. With regard to the expert testimony received, the appellate court applied precedent directly quoted from *Arnstein* to conclude that the expert testimony heard was not clearly erroneous.[98]

Unlike the Second Circuit, which appeared to take a more qualitative approach to applying expert testimony, the Seventh Circuit quantitatively distilled testimony from expert witnesses to percentages of shared musical material. In *Cholvin*, for example, the appellate court noted that "Plaintiffs' expert testified that fifty percent of the defendants' composition was exactly like the one claimed by the plaintiffs. The defendants' expert testified that the works were alike a shade less than fifty percent."[99] In another case, *Withol v. Wells*, the court introduced similar percentage evidence regarding the extent of similarity between two works: "Plaintiff contends, apparently without dispute, 'taking note for note, the soprano scores reckon 80.95% identical, the alto scores 69.84% identical and the bass scores 59.96% identical.' Plaintiff does not claim that defendant copied the tenor score of the copyrighted work."[100] Although this approach to expert testimony presented a plausible interpretation of *Arnstein*, it introduced another layer of interpretation regarding what expert dissection entailed. For this court, quantitative summaries seemed to provide an even more precise, seemingly forensic or objective, formula for distinguishing between similarity and illegal copying than merely qualitative descriptions, despite the values deriving from what were fundamentally nonobjective expert analyses.

Through the middle of twentieth century, the Seventh Circuit maintained its restraint on expert testimony, but did not universally apply the percentages interpretation. In *Packson v. Jobete Music*, for example, Packson Music Publishing, headed by Lorenzo Pack, sued Motown Record Corporation and Jobete Music Company. Pack alleged that the first two measures of his unpublished "I'm Afraid" were infringed by Motown's hit, "Baby Love," made popular by the Supremes. Although the presiding judge did not explicitly cite to *Arnstein*, the court's method for evaluating the complaint reflected a bifurcated approach to similarity that incorporated evaluations by both experts and nonexperts.

In his affidavit, music publishing mogul Robert Silverman separately analyzed each element of "I'm Afraid" and "Baby Love," including the melody,[101] formal structure and harmony,[102] as well as tempo and lyrics.[103] To support his conclusion that there was "no correlation" between the two songs in any of these respects, Silverman prepared a comparison chart, shown in figure 3.2, containing the first few bars of "Baby Love," "I'm Afraid," "Till The End of Time," as well as the original on which it was based, Chopin's "Polonaise 6," plus two more popular songs, "Dancing Cheek to Cheek," and "It Might As Well Be Spring." In the chart, each melody was transposed into the same key and into duple meter to aid comparison. Appearing to dispense with color-based differentiations used in earlier charts, Silverman's chart used circles and a variety of arrows to direct viewers' attention to similarities. In addition to comparing the two songs at issue, Silverman included below other songs with similar motivic structures with the effect of arguing that the melodic similarity was unoriginal, or as the court wrote, "common to music literature."[104] While perhaps not as visually striking, the arrows convey a similar idea even to viewers who could not read music that there was allegedly a fair amount of similarity. Likely due in part to these contributions, the case was ultimately dismissed on summary judgment.

After review that likely incorporated this chart as evidence, the court reasoned in granting the motion that "the two compositions have an entirely different structure, melodic line, accompaniment and lyric. The two compositions do not sound alike upon a playing of the melody lines alone, the melody lines with the respective accompaniments as written or in vocal rendition."[105] No mention appears to have been made to quantitative, or percentage-based, evaluations.

Figure 3.2 *Bright Tunes Music Corp. v. Harrisongs Music, Ltd.*, Expert Report, David Greitzer. Records Group 21; National Archives and Records Administration Chicago; U.S.D.C. Chicago, Civil Transcripts Cases 1966, Box 28687, "Packson v. Jobete." Credit: Author.

BEYOND *ARNSTEIN*: THE NINTH CIRCUIT

Other circuits responded similarly as more copyright cases arose regarding music, looking closely to the Second Circuit's *Arnstein* approach for guidance. Courts in the Ninth Circuit initially applied the *Arnstein* test and relied on expert witnesses to offer facts without commenting on their application to ultimate issues in each case. In *Overman v. Loesser*, for example, Robert E. Overman sued Frank Loesser over his commercially successful song, "On a Slow Boat to China," which Overman claimed infringed on his song, "Wonderful You." Overman claimed that he and lyricist Betty Hawes secured copyright on "Wonderful You" in 1947, a year before Loesser did the same for "On a Slow Boat to China."[106] While Overman attempted to prove access based on this timeline, as well as limited claims to melodic similarity between the two songs, Loesser explained that he composed "Slow Boat" in 1945 and merely sought copyright and publication later. Although the trial court, proceeding without a jury, found infringement based on both access and similarity, Loesser ultimately prevailed on appeal due to a difference of evidentiary standard.[107]

On appeal, the court reinforced the limits of expert testimony to discrete facts, excluding opinions on the significance of these facts to findings of unlawful appropriation. Overman challenged a question raised at trial to his musical expert witness, whose identity remains anonymous in court records, regarding the possibility of independent composition of the two songs. Loesser's attorney objected on grounds that the question "call[ed] for the opinion of the witness on a matter not the subject of expert testimony, [that it is] argumentative and invades the province of the court,"[108] and the court sustained. The Ninth Circuit panel ultimately agreed with the trial court's decision, stating that "[i]t was a matter of the court's discretion and we think it took the more desirable course by confining the expert's opinion to definite facts in the case, rather than receiving his application of them."[109] In so doing, the court sought to "confine" expert testimony in ways that may have seemed more systematic and analytical, thus ostensibly more objective and less prone to partiality. Far from offering an opinion regarding infringement, experts served only to locate the similarities, and dissimilarities, between pieces of music.

KROFFT AND THE NINTH CIRCUIT'S "NEW DIMENSION"

For much of the mid-twentieth century, music copyright cases heard nationwide relied directly on the *Arnstein* test for its disaggregation of copying from improper appropriation and in its bifurcated factual approach to similarity that involved both expert and nonexpert evaluations. But in the 1970s, the Ninth Circuit introduced its own methods. Copyright cases heard in the Ninth Circuit at that time gave rise to new formulations of infringement analysis, leading to the codification of two separate tests. Neither case directly involved music as a medium for copyright, but the legal analyses would apply to future music copyright litigation.

The first legal approach, commonly called the "total concept and feel test," originated in a case involving the verbal sentiments and images printed on greeting cards.[110] Decided in 1970 on appeal, the Ninth Circuit found judicially evaluated similarity in the "total concept and feel" of the greeting cards, despite differences in the images and the sentiments that were considered to be fundamentally not protectable. The court defined this process as referring to the "combination of the art work conveying a particular mood with a particular message."[111] This test diverged from prevailing practices across jurisdictions derived from *Arnstein*, practically removing reliance on expert witness evaluations.

Yet seven years later, in 1977, the Ninth Circuit presented another legal test claiming to refine the *Arnstein* procedure that, in effect, diverged into a new test. In *Sid & Marty Krofft Television Productions Inc. v. McDonald's Corp.*, the creators of the children's television show, "H.R. Pufnstuf," Sid and Marty Krofft, sued fast-food giant McDonald's for allegedly infringing on copyrighted episodes, characters, and merchandising as it appeared in the "McDonaldland" advertising campaign. Although Krofft licensed the use of its H.R. Pufnstuf characters for toys and other merchandise, it had not extended a license to McDonald's, and Krofft sued despite the Corporation's request. The district court found in favor of Krofft and granted a jury award for damages, which McDonald's appealed.[112]

On appeal, the Ninth Circuit reviewed the process for determining infringement and redefined the parameters of substantial similarity analysis, not according to the total concept and feel test, but instead based on their interpretation of *Arnstein*.[113] Concerned that its combination of ownership, access, and similarity might impermissibly broaden copyright protections, the *Krofft* court superimposed "the classic distinction between an 'idea' and the 'expression' of that idea,"[114] onto similarity analysis, giving the test what it called "a new dimension." Relying on over a century of copyright jurisprudence regarding the limits of copyright protection to the expression of more ineffable ideas, the *Krofft* court read the *Arnstein* court's concept of copying as separate from improper appropriation as "not itself an infringement," thus they "must be suggesting copying merely of the work's idea, which is not protected by copyright."[115] Therefore, according to the *Krofft* court, "[t]he real task in a copyright infringement action . . . is to determine whether there has been copying of the expression of an idea rather than just the idea itself,"[116] reaching the level of unlawful appropriation. Although the court claimed it was "not resurrecting the *Arnstein* approach," in effect, the court introduced a familiar two-prong inquiry that retained a divide between experts and nonexperts.

The majority opinion introduced what has come to be known as the "extrinsic-intrinsic" test, in which similarity must be found "not only of the general ideas but of the expressions of those ideas as well."[117] This required a two-step process, with the first step being the establishment of valid copyright registration. Second, to prove similarity, the court would follow a two-prong evaluation: first, an "extrinsic test" would be conducted based on "specific criteria which can be listed and analyzed [including] the type of artwork involved, the materials used, the subject matter and the setting for the subject."[118] This inquiry would be conducted through analytic dissection familiar and "appropriate" to expert witnesses. The second prong, the "intrinsic test," evaluated substantial similarity of the expression of ideas, which was considered "necessarily more subtle and complex," was to be made *ad hoc* based on "the response of the ordinary reasonable person."[119] This test "is intrinsic because it does not depend on the type of external criteria and analysis which marks the extrinsic test."[120] Without this two-prong finding of similarity and then improper appropriation, no amount of proof of access could lead to an infringement finding.

In the context of the *Krofft* case, because McDonald's admitted to having copied H.R. Pufnstuf in so far as it was a "fantasy land with diverse and fanciful characters in action,"[121] the extrinsic test did not apply. As a result, experts were not consulted and McDonald's attempt to distinguish individual characters through a kind of dissection was not considered. Instead, the court emphasized the intrinsic, holistic perceptions of average viewers on which the district court had relied. Ultimately, the *Krofft* court affirmed the infringement finding.[122] The new "extrinsic-intrinsic" test it introduced, however, complicated legal decision-making processes redefined relationships between experts and nonexperts as well as between expert and courts.

THE LEGACY OF *ARNSTEIN* AND *KROFFT*

Far from achieving its goal, *Krofft* instead introduced new layers of complexity to the *Arnstein* test through its overlay of an idea-expression divide on substantial similarity analysis. In so doing, *Krofft* adapted the *Arnstein* test, but conflated analysis of fundamental ideas with *Arnstein's* access-plus-similarity, on the one hand, and analysis of expression with improper appropriation, on the other. In its arguably flawed interpretation of *Arnstein*, *Krofft* thus created a qualitative distinction between legal and illegal copying based on the aspects of the expressive work that should be considered.[123] In contrast, *Arnstein* had settled on a matter of degree, or the point at which the line between lawful commonality and unlawful appropriation had been metaphorically crossed.

The *Arnstein* and *Krofft* decisions together ensured the continued presence of expert witnesses and revealed ongoing judicial skepticism toward their contributions. The result of these decisions was to constrain the role of expert witnesses and privilege that of nonexpert jurors instead. In theory, experts employed under either test should contribute to decisions regarding copying, but not the subsequent decisions regarding improper appropriation. In practice, however, this limitation did more to create questions regarding the role of expert witnesses, and their relationship to nonexpert listeners, than to answer them. Both the *Arnstein* and *Krofft* tests redirected the final determination of infringement from judges to jurors. This legal shift recast the similarity inquiry as a question of fact, thereby reinforcing the fact-specific nature of each case that had challenged courts since the nineteenth century. It likewise ensured that the decisions would continue to be unpredictable, due in large part to the jury-centric nature of the decision, as well as inconsistent, due to differing legal tests across circuits and the specific nature of comparisons between the works at issue.

In their newly constrained role, experts could do little to assist in resolving these issues. Despite legal limitations on the questions to which experts may contribute, neither decision commented on musical matters, such as experts' analytical techniques and their reliance on earlier copyrighted works, nor did they offer recommendations for analytical criteria in assessing similarity. This silence prudently left musical analysis to the expert witnesses themselves, but it also did very little to reduce opportunities for partisanship. It likewise did little to reduce the influence or confusion from sophisticated, abstract analyses about which courts were growing suspicious.

NOTES

1. Portions of analysis for *Arnstein v. Porter* were previously published in, or are adapted from, Leo, "Musical Expertise."

2. *Arnstein v. Porter*, 154 F.2d 464, 467 (2d Cir. 1946) [hereinafter *Arnstein*].

3. *Arnstein*, Complaint, 62–63. Records Group 21; National Archives and Records Administration, Kansas City; U.S.D.C. Southern District of New York, Equity Case Files, Box 5977, "Arnstein v. Porter."

4. *Arnstein*, 154 F.2d at 467.

5. See *Arnstein*, Transcript, 12, 18, 79 (Baldwin); *Arnstein*, Transcript, 2 (Taylor), Records Group 21; National Archives and Records Administration, Kansas City; U.S.D.C. Southern District of New York, Equity Case Files, Box 5977, "Arnstein v. Porter."

6. *Arnstein*, Transcript, 3–4 (Baldwin).

7. *Arnstein*, Transcript, 4 (Baldwin). Based on his later definition, Baldwin appears to use "changing note" to refer to neighbor tone: "By a changing note we mean a note which leaves the regular note of the harmony of the chord and comes back again. Some call it an appoggiatura . . . it is nothing but an ornament." During later cross–examination, Spaeth railed against the term "changing notes." See *Arnstein*, Transcript 3–5, 11–12 (Spaeth).

8. *Arnstein*, Transcript, 4 (Baldwin). See also n.13 (citing *Arnstein*, Transcript 3–5, 11–12 (Spaeth)).

9. *Arnstein*, Transcript, 5 (Baldwin).

10. *Arnstein*, Transcript, 5 (Baldwin).

11. *Arnstein*, Transcript, 8–9 (Baldwin).

12. *Arnstein*, Transcript, 6 (Baldwin).

13. *Arnstein*, Transcript, 12 (Baldwin).

14. *Arnstein*, Transcript, 13 (Baldwin).

15. *Arnstein*, Transcript, 11 (Baldwin).

16. See, e.g., *Arnstein*, Transcript, 38–63 (Baldwin).

17. *Arnstein*, Transcript, 10–11 (Baldwin).

18. *Arnstein*, Transcript, 19 (Baldwin).

19. See, e.g., *Arnstein*, Transcript, 18 (Spaeth). Records Group 21; National Archives and Records Administration, Kansas City; U.S.D.C. Southern District of New York, Equity Case Files, Box 5977, "Arnstein v. Porter."

20. *Arnstein*, Transcript, 8 (Spaeth).

21. *Arnstein*, Transcript, 24 (Spaeth).

22. *Arnstein*, Transcript, 24–39 (Spaeth).

23. *Arnstein*, Transcript, 3 (Taylor).

24. *Arnstein*, Transcript, 3 (Taylor).

25. *Arnstein*, Transcript, 6–7 (Taylor).

26. *Arnstein*, Transcript, 19 (Taylor).

27. *Arnstein*, Transcript 18–19 (Taylor).

28. *Arnstein v. Porter*, 1945 WL 6897 (S.D.N.Y. 1945).

29. See also Shyamkrishna Balganesh, "The Questionable Origins of Copyright Infringement Analysis," *Stanford Law Review* 68 (April 2016): 791–862.

30. See Balganesh, "Questionable Origins," 14.

31. See also Balganesh, "Questionable Origins," 15–19.

32. *Arnstein v. Porter*, 154 F.2d 465, 468 (2d Cir. 1946).

33. *Arnstein v. Porter*, 154 F.2d 465, 468 (2d Cir. 1946).

34. *Arnstein*, 154 F.2d at 468.

35. *Arnstein*, 154 F.2d at 468.

36. *Arnstein*, 154 F.2d at 468.

37. *Arnstein*, 154 F.2d at 468–69.

38. *Arnstein*, 154 F.2d at 468 (citations omitted).

39. See generally Alan Latman, "Probative Similarity as Proof of Copying: Toward Dispelling Some Myths in Copyright Infringement," *Columbia Law Review* 90 (1990): 1187–222.

40. *Arnstein*, 154 F.2d at 473 (citations omitted).

41. *Arnstein*, 154 F.2d at 473 (citations omitted).

42. Jerome N. Frank, "Say It with Music," *Harvard Law Review* 61 (June 1948): 928–92.

43. Frank, "Say It with Music," 929.

44. *Arnstein*, 154 F.2d at 473.

45. *Arnstein*, 154 F.2d at 478 (Clark, J., dissenting).

46. *Arnstein*, 154 F.2d at 476 n.1 (Clark, J., dissenting).

47. *Arnstein*, 154 F.2d at 476 (Clark, J., dissenting). Clark's reference is to the opening lyrics to Porter's "Night and Day" ("Like the beat, beat, beat of the tom tom/ When the jungle shadows fall").

48. *Arnstein*, 154 F.2d at 476 (Clark, J., dissenting) (citing Stewart Macpherson, *Form in Music* (London: J. Williams, 1930), 1–2).

49. See Rosen, *Unfair to Genius*, 231.

50. Rosen, *Unfair to Genius*, 231.

51. 154 F.2d 480, 484 (2d Cir. 1946).

52. *Heim*, 154 F.2d at 482–84.

53. *Heim v. Universal Pictures Corp.*, 51 F. Supp. 233, 233–34 (S.D.N.Y. 1943).

54. Letter from Jerome N. Frank to Charles E. Clark regarding *Heim v. Universal*, February 2, 1946 (referenced in Balganesh, "The Questionable Origins," 57).

55. *Baron v. Leo Feist, Inc.*, 78 F. Supp. 686, 686 (S.D.N.Y. 1948).

56. *Baron*, 78 F. Supp. at 688.

57. *Baron*, 78 F. Supp. at 688–89. The two songs were "*Si Formas Tuvieran Mis Pensamientos*" and "King Jaja."

58. *Baron*, 78 F. Supp. at 688.

59. *Baron v. Leo Feist, Inc.*, 78 F. Supp. 686, 688 (S.D.N.Y. 1948).

60. Louis Nizer, *My Life in Court* (Garden City, NY: Doubleday, 1961), 235 (Nizer served as Plaintiff's attorney in *Baron v. Leo Fiest*).

61. Nizer, *My Life*, 258.

62. *Baron v. Leo Feist*, Transcript, 538–40 (Lockwood). Records Group 21; National Archives and Records Administration, Kansas City; U.S.D.C. Southern District of New York, Equity Case Files, Box 6272, "Baron v. Leo Feist." Spaeth addressed the same point regarding rhythm in *Baron v. Leo Feist*, Transcript, 794–95 (Spaeth).

63. Nizer, *My Life*, 259.

64. *Baron v. Leo Feist*, Transcript, 738–39 (Spaeth), Records Group 21; National Archives and Records Administration, Kansas City; U.S.D.C. Southern District of New York, Equity Case Files, Box 6272, "Baron v. Leo Feist."

65. *Baron v. Leo Feist*, Transcript, 738 (Spaeth).

66. See, e.g., *Baron v. Leo Feist*, Transcript, 760–74 (Spaeth).

67. See also Nizer, *My Life*, 248–49.

68. *Baron v. Leo Feist*, Transcript, 747 (Spaeth).

69. *Baron*, 78 F. Supp. at 690; Nizer, *My Life*, 258.

70. Nizer, *My Life*, 247–48.

71. Nizer, *My Life*, 236 (quoting Rifkind, J.).

72. *Baron v. Leo Feist*, 78 F. Supp. 686, 687–88 (S.D.N.Y. 1948).

73. *Baron*, 78 F. Supp. at 687.

74. *Baron v. Leo Feist*, 173 F.2d 288 (2d Cir. 1949).

75. *Baron*, 78 F. Supp. at 686–87 (emphasis added).

76. *Jones v. Supreme Music Corp.*, 101 F. Supp. 989, 989–90 (S.D.N.Y. 1951).

77. *Jones*, 101 F. Supp. at 990.

78. *Jones*, 101 F. Supp. at 992.

79. *Jones*, 101 F. Supp. 991–92. For Howard's qualifications, see *Jones v. Supreme Music, Corp.*, Transcript, 2 (Howard). Records Group 21; National Archives and Records Administration, Kansas City; U.S.D.C. Southern District of New York, Equity Case Files, Box 701049, "Jones v. Supreme Music Corp."

80. *Jones v. Supreme Music Corp.*, Transcript, 9–16 (Taylor).

81. *Jones v. Supreme Music Corp.*, Transcript, 46–55 (Taylor).

82. *Jones*, 101 F. Supp. 991–92.

83. *N. Music Corp. v. King Record Distrib. Co.*, 105 F. Supp. 393, 393 (S.D.N.Y. 1952).

84. *N. Music*, 105 F. Supp. at 393.

85. *N. Music Corp. v. King Record Distrib. Co.*, Transcript, 154 (Burke). Records Group 21; National Archives and Records Administration, Kansas City; U.S.D.C. Southern District of New York, Equity Case Files, Box 700835, "N. Music Corp. v. King Record Distrib. Co."

86. *N. Music Corp. v. King Record Distrib. Co.*, Transcript, 162 (Burke).

87. *N. Music Corp. v. King Record Distrib. Co.*, Transcript, 277 (Rettenberg).

88. *N. Music Corp. v. King Record Distrib. Co.*, 105 F. Supp. 393, 398 (S.D.N.Y. 1952).

89. *N. Music Corp.*, 105 F. Supp. at 397 (citing *Hirsch* (outlining the "average hearer" test that relies on lay listeners rather than experts)).

90. *N. Music Corp.*, 105 F. Supp. at 397–98.

91. *N. Music Corp.*, 105 F. Supp. at 400.

92. *N. Music Corp.*, 105 F. Supp. at 400.

93. *Cholvin v. B&F Music Co.*, 253 F.2d 102 (7th Cir. 1958).

94. *Cholvin v. B&F Music Co.*, Transcript, 121. Records Group 21; National Archives and Records Administration Chicago; U.S.D.C. Chicago, Civil Transcripts Case 55C771, Box C-236, "Cholvin v B&F Music Co."

95. *Cholvin v. B&F Music Co.*, Transcript, 83 (Barlow) (identifying and establishing credibility of Harold Barlow).

96. *Cholvin v. B&F Music Co.*, Transcript, 83–85 (Barlow).

97. *Cholvin v. B&F Music Co.*, Transcript, 89 (Barlow).

98. See *Cholvin v. B&F Music*, 253 F.2d 102, 103 (7th Cir. 1958).

99. *Cholvin*, 253 F.2d at 103.

100. *Wihtol v. Wells*, 231 F.2d 550, 552 (7th Cir. 1956).

101. *Packson v. Jobete Music*, Silverman Affidavit, 2–4. Records Group 21; National Archives and Records Administration Chicago; U.S.D.C. Chicago, Civil Transcripts Cases 1966, Box 28687, "Packson v. Jobete."

102. *Packson v. Jobete Music*, Silverman Affidavit, 4.

103. *Packson v. Jobete Music*, Silverman Affidavit, 5.

104. *Packson v. Jobete*, Music Findings of Fact, 2. Records Group 21; National Archives and Records Administration Chicago; U.S.D.C. Chicago, Civil Transcripts Cases 1966, Box 28687, "Packson v. Jobete."

105. *Packson v. Jobete*, Findings of Fact, 2.

106. *Overman v. Loesser*, 205 F.2d 521, 521 (9th Cir. 1953).

107. *Overman,* 205 F.2d at 522–23.

108. *Overman*, 205 F.2d at 524.

109. *Overman*, 205 F.2d at 524.

110. *Roth Greeting Cards v. United Card Co.*, 429 F.2d 1106 (9th Cir. 1970).

111. *Roth*, 429 F.2d at 1110.

112. *Sid & Marty Krofft Television Product., Inc. v. McDonald's Corp.*, 562 F.2d 1157, 1161 (9th Cir. 1977).

113. *Roth*, 429 F.2d at 1106.

114. See *Krofft*, 562 F.2d at 1162–64.

115. *Krofft*, 562 F.2d at 1165.

116. *Krofft*, 562 F.2d at 1163.
117. *Krofft*, 562 F.2d at 1163.
118. *Krofft*, 562 F.2d at 1163.
119. *Krofft*, 562 F.2d at 1165.
120. *Krofft*, 562 F.2d at 1164.
121. *Krofft*, 562 F.2d at 1165.
122. *Krofft*, 562 F.2d at 1165.
123. Manuelian, "The Role of the Expert Witness," 136–38.

Chapter 4

The Problems with *Arnstein* and *Krofft*

After the *Arnstein–Krofft* circuit split, courts across the United States struggled to apply legal tests designed to assess allegations of copyright infringement, especially for music. Problems manifested not only in the judicial interpretation of these precedents but also in the divide between expert witnesses and nonexpert factfinders as well as the role each one played. This divide in effect reduced the scope of expert contributions by retaining their presence in the fact-driven process for evaluating similarity while removing their ability to expound on the legal implications of their assessments. Ongoing legal reliance on expert "dissection," however, undoubtedly influenced an increase in abstract analytical techniques and conclusions produced by expert witnesses.

Legal strategies surrounding the introduction of more theoretical musical analyses, coupled with the enactment of the 1976 Copyright Act and the Federal Rules of Evidence (FRE), led to a rise in witnesses qualified as experts according to academic credentials as much as professional music industry experience. These credentials not only met new standards of admissibility for expert witnesses more concretely but also correlated with forensic analytical trends toward academic sophistication. Yet for all that experts introduced more abstract musical comparisons, with variable effects, the legal purpose of their analyses remained relatively unchanged. As a result, late-twentieth and early-twenty-first-century music copyright cases reflect a consistent presence of musical experts despite legal constraints and judicial skepticism.

During this period, other appellate jurisdictions continued looking to the *Arnstein* and *Krofft* decisions for guidance, but soon discovered problems with the decision-making processes outlined in both opinions. While some courts still adopted *Krofft* or *Arnstein* in their totality, others tried to resolve apparent, and emergent, issues. These refinements attempted to manage the subjectivity and unpredictability of the existing legal tests, but they did little to resolve underlying problems with the legal similarity inquiry itself or to rebalance the influence that experts might have on the outcome of each case. These cases instead did more to reveal issues surrounding the application, or even misapplication, of musical expert testimony to evaluations of similarity and in balance with access in ultimate assessments of putative infringement. They furthermore galvanized long-standing questions surrounding the role of musical expert witnesses, from suspicions of witness partiality to perceptions of disparities in listener skill and acuity.

STATUTORY REFORMS

The contemporaneous passage of the FRE and two major revisions in statutory copyright law presented a new legal landscape in which federal copyright litigation existed. Perhaps more essential to copyright protection for music, Congress extended federal copyright laws in the 1971 Sound Recording Act to include sound recordings as fixed "writings" distinct from sheet music.[1] Five years later, Congress enacted the 1976 Copyright Act, which overhauled the federal copyright system enforced since 1909. The new Act notably extended the duration of copyright protection from twenty-eight years plus a twenty-eight-year extension to much longer durations, depending on the type of author and conditions of the work's creation.[2] It altered the system for categorizing expressive works into nonexclusive categories, which included a new, separate copyright for sound recordings.[3] The Act also revised the conditions that activated federal protection for works copyrighted after January 1, 1978, notably replacing "publication," which for music referred to notated sheet music, with the requirement of "fixation" in a tangible medium, which now included sound recordings. For works copyrighted after 1978, copyright registration became voluntary; however, copyright holders would need to register and deposit copies of the work before filing an infringement suit in federal court.[4] This legal distinction between musical compositions and recordings would over time muddy the terrain for mapping music as intellectual property and comparisons of music in federal copyright litigation.

　　The 1976 Act, furthermore, enacted the long-standing common law principle of "fair use" as an affirmative defense. This new doctrine permitted use of copyright-protected material, published or unpublished, under certain conditions.[5] To determine whether use could be deemed fair, a court would now have to balance four factors traceable to nineteenth-century common law:[6] (1) The purpose and character of the use; (2) the nature of the copyrighted work; (3) the amount and substantiality of the portion used in relation to the copyrighted work; (4) the effect of the use upon the potential market.[7]

Congress left courts to interpret and balance these factors in the context of each case, however.

Although Congress had the opportunity to resolve the circuit split between *Arnstein* and *Krofft* among the sweeping changes it introduced in the 1976 Copyright Act, it remained silent as to legal contours of similarity. This lack of legislative action left courts, and parties employing expert witnesses in each case, to interpret and apply existing infringement tests and to incorporate new provisions. These new statutes nevertheless altered the scope of copyright protection and impacted the way that litigation could unfold.

CONCURRENT CHANGES TO EVIDENCE LAW WITH THE FRE

The year before the new Copyright Act was made into law, in 1975, Congress enacted the FRE, which were intended to standardize the admission of evidence in federal cases and to clarify contested areas of evidence law.[8] "Neither the academic and judicial codifiers nor congressional adopters anticipated or even acknowledged the revolutionary nature of the changes proposed,"[9] particularly those rules that impacted expert witnesses. Section 7 of the FRE specifically addressed opinion evidence presented by witnesses, with Rules 702 through 706 regulating the admissibility of expert testimony. Under Rule 702, admissibility became a function of the source of the evidence, that is, the qualifications of the expert witness, as well as the nature of the question requiring expert knowledge.[10] Reinforcing tradition established by decades of practice and commentary, expert witnesses could be called when necessary: "If scientific, technical, or other specialized knowledge will assist the trier of fact to understand the evidence or to determine a fact in issue, a witness qualified as an expert by knowledge, skill, experience, training, or education, may testify thereto in the form of an opinion or otherwise."[11]

At the time, Rule 702 made no mention of the *Frye* test, instead providing a set of criteria by which to establish an expert witness as qualified and credible, such that they could present opinion evidence, and there was no requirement that the methods be "generally accepted." The *Frye* precedent stood, however, leaving contemporaneous federal courts to align common law with the new federal rules in ways relevant to specific areas of law, including copyright. While the introduction of these uniform rules thus served to standardize the admission of evidence in federal cases and to clarify contested areas of evidence law, they initially did little more to define the abstract nature of expertise.

THE SECOND CIRCUIT'S APPLICATION OF *ARNSTEIN*

Late-twentieth-century music copyright cases heard in the Second Circuit revealed enduring problems with the *Arnstein* test, particularly in managing the separation of copying and improper appropriation. While the routine presence of experts suggested that they were a strategic necessity, their influence on the outcome of each case remained limited and inconsistent between cases. Expert witnesses nevertheless continued to use many of the same analytical techniques, but their contributions grew increasingly theoretical and sophisticated. These conditions were not only likely in part due to other factors in the *Arnstein* test, particularly concepts of access and subconscious copying that were being judicially developed, but also likely in part due to the nature of the analyses that musical expert witnesses produced.

Offering musical "dissection," expert witnesses in each case applied techniques that separated music principally by melody, harmony, rhythm, and form, rather than considering it holistically, which was now the domain of nonexpert factfinders. Despite this analytical abstraction, increasing reliance on prose explanations and trial testimony created opportunities for expert witnesses to explain their processes and interpret their findings without explicitly commenting on unlawful, or improper, appropriation. These explanations often led to more esoteric dialogues, and in some instances even confrontations, regarding music theory between expert witnesses that could do as much to alienate factfinders and undermine expert credibility as to assist the court in resolving each case.

In *Bright Tunes Music Corp. v. Harrisongs Music, Ltd.*, for example, the court strictly applied the *Arnstein* test to find that Beatles guitarist George Harrison's song, "My Sweet Lord," had infringed on the pop hit, "He's So Fine," written by Ronald Mack and made famous in a 1963 recording by The Chiffons. The case turned on the repetition of two phrases to create the melody, which experts and the court labeled motives A and B. While decisive issues in the case dealt with compositional process, specifically access and notions of subconscious copying that left George Harrison at fault, the case exemplified the role that experts could play in the similarity inquiry.[12]

At trial, both parties introduced testimony from expert witnesses. The plaintiffs introduced Manhattan School of Music professor, David Greitzer; Harold Barlow, who had served as an expert for what the court described as "long in the field,"[13] offered testimony for the defendants, along with ethnomusicologist David Butler. Available expert reports and testimony demonstrated that the structural melodic motives in both songs were identical, but whether or not these motives were even subject matter for an infringement complaint became an issue.

Testifying on behalf of the plaintiffs, Greitzer presented a report that used a variety of notational schemes to convey different kinds of analytical information. The first page, which contains Greitzer's analytical diagrams, is shown in figure 4.1 as it was later reproduced as one of the defendant's exhibits. Rather than aligning the two melodies in tandem as many experts had done before, and in contrast to Barlow's report, Greitzer presented the two motives separately and then described their treatment in prose. This approach, perhaps strategically, implied the melodic congruence of the motives to foreground the idea of close copying. He also included a separate harmonic analysis using roman numerals, a simplistic "umbrella" diagram to show formal structure, with alphabetic designations to indicate the use of each motive. While Greitzer's diagram strategy separated each fundamental musical element likely in response to fulfilling "dissection," thereby making it easier to discuss the similarities with respect to each element, the symbolic reductions were more abstract and separate from the music performed or presented on sheet music. For all that Greitzer included prose explanations of his analysis to explain his graphs, his system of symbols, although commonly meaningful to his fellow experts, were undoubtedly unfamiliar to nonexpert factfinders.

On cross-examination at trial, the defendants employed a typical argument focused on stylistic commonality. In so doing, they attempted to discredit Greitzer's identification of similar motives by contending the motives themselves were unoriginal, and thus unprotectable:[14]

Q. Is it fair to say, Mr. Greitzer, from the testimony you have given here, that the presence of that motive in He's So Fine and My Sweet Lord would not in and of itself suggest to you that there has been a copying in this case?

A. The presence of the motive itself, no, sir, but—

Greitzer attempted to redirect the court's attention toward motive B and to emphasize the presence of a grace note as a unique, protectable feature of both songs, thereby being indicative of copying. He also noted the relationship between the descending melodic trajectory of Motive A in relationship to the ascending melodic trajectory of Motive B.[15]

Called by the defendants, Barlow presented the motives as unoriginal, therefore raising the possibility of independent creation regardless of any access claims, and testified that differences in the treatment of the motives resulted in different compositional effects, thereby leading to similarity that did not constitute improper appropriation. Barlow's report presented the two melodic motives aligned in the contexts of the larger melody and each other, which were intended to contrast Greitzer's representation as well as his analysis. At first, in Chart I shown in figure 4.2, Barlow identified the motives and pitches in melodic context for "He's So Fine." Then, in Chart IV shown in

1033

DEFENDANTS' LIABILITY TRIAL EXHIBIT A – COMPARATIVE
ANALYSIS OF "HE'S SO FINE" AND "MY SWEET LORD"

Page 1

Comparative Analysis – "He's So Fine" (HSF) and "My Sweet Lord" (MSL)

Melodic Analysis

Each of the songs is built on two repeated motives:

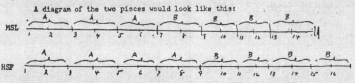

There are variations based on textual rhythms and decorative effects but essentially the two motives are treated similarly in both pieces. (This will be seen under section Musical Form)

Harmonic Analysis

The harmonization of motive A is similar in both songs:

| Minor II | Major III |
| meas. 1 | 2 |

The harmonization of motive B is varied as shown in the diagram.

HSF — Tonic chord throughout (I)

MSL — I   vi m.   I   vi m.   I   I° dim7.   II m.   IV

The alternation of tonic major with relative minor is actually anticipated in the fade out Coda of "He's So Fine". The new element in "My Sweet Lord" is the introduction of the diminished 7th chord of the 6th measure of motive B.

In conclusion, the harmonies are strongly parallel for the most part, but something new has been added in the later Harrison version through the introduction of the minor and diminished chords.

Musical Form, or Structure

A diagram of the two pieces would look like this:

MSL   A   A   A   B   B   B   B
1   2   3   4   5   6   7   8   9   10   11   12   13   14

HSF   A   A   A   A   B   B   B   B
1   2   3   4   5   6   7   8   9   10   11   12   13   14   15   16

"My Sweet Lord" extends by alternating between A and B motive sections, then by modulating up one tone.

"He's So Fine" extends by repetition of the 16 measure section. It then introduces a repeated 8 measure motive (C) and concludes with the first 16 measures.

In summation, there is a strong similarity between the two pieces in the melodic and harmonic aspects involving the A and B motives of each.

Figure 4.1 *Bright Tunes Music Corp. v. Harrisongs Music, Ltd.*, **Expert Report, David Greitzer.** Records Group 21; National Archives and Records Administration Kansas City; U.S.D.C. Southern District of New York, Civil Case Files 71-CV-602, Boxes 173, 5449, "Bright Tunes Music Corp. v. Harrisongs Music, Ltd." Joint Appendix, 1033. Credit: Author.

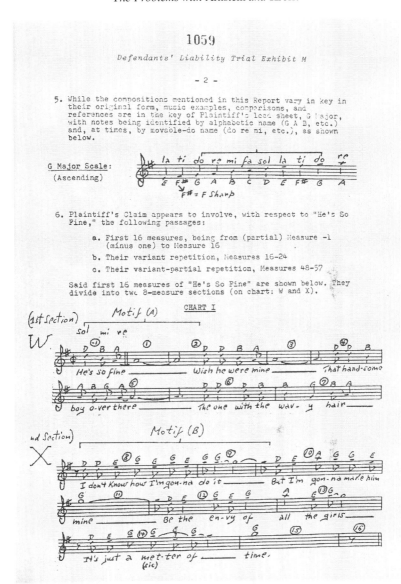

5. While the compositions mentioned in this Report vary in key in their original form, music examples, comparisons, and references are in the key of Plaintiff's lead sheet, G Major, with notes being identified by alphabetic name (G A B, etc.) and, at times, by movable-do name (do re mi, etc.), as shown below.

6. Plaintiff's Claim appears to involve, with respect to "He's So Fine," the following passages:

    a. First 16 measures, being from (partial) Measure -1 (minus one) to Measure 16

    b. Their variant repetition, Measures 16-24

    c. Their variant-partial repetition, Measures 48-57

Said first 16 measures of "He's So Fine" are shown below. They divide into two 8-measure sections (on chart: W and X).

Figure 4.2 *Bright Tunes Music Corp. v. Harrisongs Music, Ltd.*, **Expert Report, Harold Barlow Chart I.** Records Group 21; National Archives and Records Administration Kansas City; U.S.D.C. Southern District of New York, Civil Case Files 71-CV-602, Boxes 173, 5449, "Bright Tunes Music Corp. v. Harrisongs Music, Ltd." Joint Appendix, 1058. Credit: Author.

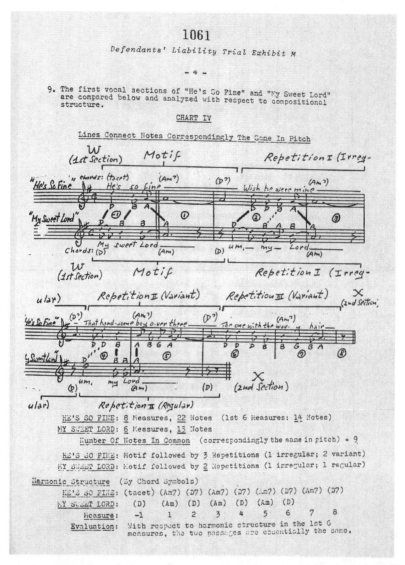

Figure 4.3 *Bright Tunes Music Corp. v. Harrisongs Music, Ltd.*, **Expert Report, Harold Barlow Chart IV.** Records Group 21; National Archives and Records Administration Kansas City; U.S.D.C. Southern District of New York, Civil Case Files 71-CV-602, Boxes 173, 5449, "Bright Tunes Music Corp. v. Harrisongs Music, Ltd." Joint Appendix, 1061. Credit: Author.

figure 4.3, Barlow indicated where congruent melodic pitches in both songs aligned and provided a quantitative analysis of those similarities.

Unlike earlier comparison charts that used coloration or circles and arrows to indicate individual note similarities but in keeping with his own analytical techniques, Barlow's charts drew comparisons with bold or dotted lines between individual pitches and he used brackets to demarcate sections of similar melodies. This notational method required viewers to interpret the chart more closely. But perhaps more meaningful to nonexpert jurors was Barlow's quantitative calculations of similarity according to measures, "notes," by which he likely meant pitch, and the number of "notes" in common.

Barlow's report relied on notated music that had legally served to embody the music for decades. Alphabetic pitch and harmony designations served to bridge the expert–nonexpert gap by assisting jurors and the court to read the music notation. This perhaps strategically retained what appeared to be a reliable representation of the music as embodied in pre-interpreted notation to guide factfinders.

The defendants also retained Butler to introduce arguments regarding prior compositions, stylistic commonality, and originality. Instead of offering musical–theoretical analysis, Butler provided context on musical style in the songs, taking an approach to similarity that emphasized the context of musical resemblance.[16] He focused specifically on the relationship between spirituals and gospel, as well as stereotypical melodic patterns and their improvisatory use. In his comparisons, Butler contended that "both [songs] are based on spiritual and traditional gospel material or music derived from those."[17] Butler used his identification of pentatonicism, syncopation, and repetitious forms to associate the musical material at issue with "African American music traditions."[18] Any chart or performance he may have used has not been retained in extant records.

Both Barlow and Butler extended their analyses to include prior compositions, in order to emphasize the unoriginal nature of the two motives. This strategy reflected a long tradition among experts usually retained by the defendants that relied on prior compositions rather than note-by-note dissimilarities. Barlow cited popular songs such as "San Fernando Valley," "Pagan Love Song," "If I Had a Hammer," and "Kind of a Drag."[19] Using this style-based context for discussion, Butler also introduced recordings of similar manifestations of motives A and B in gospel music, thereby reinforcing the argument that the musical content being compared in the lawsuit was common, fundamentally unoriginal, and thus not protectable.

In its opinion, the court focused on the melodic, rhythmic, and formal similarity, appearing to disregard any discussion of musical style. Unusually for its time, the court also incorporated notated figures of each motive in footnotes to the opinion,[20] as well as solfège vocabulary used by experts but typically avoided by previous courts, to describe the motives:[21]

He's So Fine, recorded in 1962, . . . consisting essentially of four repetitions of a very short basic musical phrase, "sol-mi-re," (hereinafter motif A), altered as necessary to fit the words, followed by four repetitions of another short basic musical phrase, "sol-la-do-la-do," (hereinafter motif B). While neither motif is novel, the four repetitions of A, followed by four repetitions of B, is a highly unique pattern. In addition, in the second use of the motif B series, there is a grace note inserted making the phrase go "so-la-do-la-*re*-do." My Sweet Lord, recorded first in 1970, also uses the same motif A (modified to suit the words) four times, followed by motif B, repeated three times, not four. In place of He's So Fine's fourth repetition of motif B, My Sweet Lord has a transitional passage . . . of the same approximate length, with the identical grace note in the identical second repetition. The harmonies of both songs are identical.

The opinion's detailed musical analyses demonstrated the essential role of expert witnesses, despite the challenges of abstract and conflicting analyses presented in their testimony. Musical expert witnesses' contributions served to contextualize the court's consideration of similarity according to repetition and the quantity of musical material based on motives as structurally relevant elements of music.

APPLICATION OF THE *ARNSTEIN*
TEST AND EXPERT ANALYSES

Application of the *Arnstein* test did not always go so smoothly. In *MCA Music v. Earl Wilson*, for example, in the Southern District of New York, the court applied the *Arnstein* test to arrive at a judgment for the plaintiff music publishing company, MCA Music. In its complaint, MCA alleged that its copyright for "Boogie Woogie Bugle Boy," was violated by Earl Wilson's "Cunnilingus Champion of Company C," one of several raunchy songs in his shocking 1974 musical, "Let My People Come: A Sexual Musical."[22]

After the plaintiffs presented their case based on meeting the elements of the *Arnstein* test, defendant Wilson introduced a series of unsuccessful arguments. Following anticipated defense arguments, including a claim that similarities constituted fair use because "Champion" was a burlesque parody of "Bugle Boy," Wilson principally denied accusations of infringement and claimed that the commonalities between the songs were unoriginal and thus not protectable.[23] In a more unusual argument, Wilson also attempted to apply the new FRE as a means to circumvent similarity analysis altogether. He argued that evidence of nonexpert lay listener perceptions of similarity should be inadmissible under the FRE on hearsay grounds, hoping instead to rely exclusively on expert analysis.[24]

At this unusual nonjury trial, the court heard testimony from routine-expert Harold Barlow, who served on behalf of both parties, as well as from conductor-composer Russell Goudey, who was called by the defendant.[25]

Using techniques similar to those used in *Bright Tunes*, Barlow's report contained copious charts reflecting melodic, harmonic, rhythmic, and recording arrangement comparisons between the two songs. At trial, Barlow offered note-by-note comparisons and concluded that "what exists in common between the two compositions in question exceeds the bounds of coincidence and defendants' song could not have been arrived at independently."[26] To elaborate, Barlow compared the two songs, claiming that they shared[27]

> a 12-bar structure which is used in repetition involving notes in the main that are 8 beats to the bar in certain areas of the melody and certain areas of the bass. There is a general harmonic similarity, and certain specialized rhythmic patterns are also in common in the two compositions, and also, additionally, certain, what in the parlance is known as breaks, which are found to be in common in the two compositions.

Barlow also presented a series of charts and a recording of him playing excerpts of the songs to explain his analysis to the court.[28] His discussion was melocentric and emphasized pitch congruence, comparing the two melodies phrase by phrase in nine separate charts. For example, the first chart was described as showing "a note-for-note comparison and the notes that are in common are shown joined by connecting lines. The notes are named by their pitch names by alphabetic designation."[29] Although the chart did not use the two-color technique of previous expert witnesses, Barlow's placement of the two melodies in tandem and marked similarities based on pitch were familiar continuations of analytical techniques.

The defendants also retained conductor-composer, Russell Goudey. As the court noted in its opinion, Goudey "vouched for the accuracy of Mr. Barlow's comparison charts,"[30] without providing any additional explanation of them. The trial transcript of his examination reflected the same statement, but suggested Goudey's reticence to concede to Barlow's analysis. Finding fault with Barlow's second chart, Goudey explained that "I don't think the parts of the song coincide."[31] Here, it appears that Barlow's comparison was indisputable according to Goudey, who struggled to fulfill his role in bolstering the defendant's case against the similarities Barlow presented.

Goudey's attempt to discredit Barlow's report in its capacity serving the plaintiff created an expert confrontation centered on abstract theoretical conceptions of melody. During cross-examination, Goudey defined melody as "a series of tones of varying pitch sounded in succession and formed rhythmically to make a recognizable musical pattern."[32] The plaintiff's attorney attempted to impeach this definition as "not a generally accepted definition" in accordance with the aging *Frye* test and its restraint on expert testimony.

They also challenged Goudey's requirement for changes in pitch by suggesting melody merely needed to be a "horizontal movement of note,"[33] that need not vary in pitch. This reflected Barlow's later definition of melody as "a succession of notes, be it as little as two or as many as infinity following consecutively on a horizontal level as opposed to harmonic structure on a vertical level."[34] This music-theoretical disagreement regarding the definition of melody seemed to undermine the opposing analyses, and likely did little to assist the court in making its decision.

Although Barlow and Goudey did not use any markedly new technique for comparing the two songs at issue in the case, the depth to which they conducted their analyses and confronted one another points toward greater analytical sophistication. Like contemporaneous cases, the expert witnesses considered not only melodic congruence and abstract theoretical notions of melody, but also the compositional construction of the songs at issue in the stylistic context of popular music. Their analyses and testimony would prove influential on the court, which ultimately decided in favor of MCA. In its evaluation of similarity, the court applied Barlow's analysis to find that "Champion" was copied from "Bugle Boy." Yet in its determination of substantial similarity, the second prong of the *Arnstein* test intended to be decided by nonexperts, the court's reasoning included evidence presented by Barlow.[35] The court later dispensed with Wilson's argument regarding fair use by relying on common law precedent to reject characterizations of the song as burlesque parody and noting that the quantity of similarity would exceed fair use.[36]

More significant to the role of expert witnesses, *Wilson* highlighted the issue surrounding reception of expert testimony under the *Arnstein* test. While Barlow's statement regarding independent creation and commonalities explicitly commented only on copying, not improper appropriation, the court applied the statement both to its evaluation of copying as well as its evaluation of improper appropriation, where such evidence should have been excluded.[37] This apparent misapplication of expert testimony pointed toward a shortcoming in the test itself, namely, that both inquiries required detailed information regarding similarity. The first prong of similarity evaluation, however, is driven by expert analysis, rather than nonexpert jurors who were not even present at the bench trial. By applying expert testimony beyond its designated prong of the similarity inquiry, the *Wilson* court proved that despite legal constraints on experts, once they have testified, their contributions cannot be forgotten or excluded. Thus, legal constraints on expert testimony did not necessarily limit the decision-making process of nonexperts as the test seemed to intend, which had implications for the unpredictability of the legal decision-making process itself.[38]

ABSTRACT ANALYSES

Even in the Second Circuit, expert analysis produced in the late twentieth century followed trends of increasing abstraction, with mixed consequences for
the influence of experts on the outcome of each case. In *Gasté v. Kaiserman*,
for example, experts produced highly abstract analyses and testimony whose
influence on the final outcome of the case is at best implicit. In this case,
plaintiff Louis Gasté alleged that his copyrighted song, *Pour Toi*, which
appeared as part of the soundtrack for the French film, *Le Feu Aux Poudres*,
was infringed by Morris Kaiserman's more popular song, "Feelings."[39] At
trial, the plaintiffs called music theorist Anthony Ricigliano, who at the time
served as chair of the music theory department at the Manhattan School of
Music.[40]

Ricigliano's expert report showed an increased level of abstraction in
analysis, producing both more common comparison charts based on music
notation with various arrows, lines, and brackets to direct the attention of
factfinders, as well as melodic contour graphs. These graphs visually demonstrated comparisons of the shape of the two melodies, with each melody line
distinguished by color, but reduced the music to its melody while retaining at
least some of its rhythmic and metrical context. The graphs applied analytical
abstraction strategically by representing musical information in a form that
retained most of the same information as western notation but presented pitch
and interval content in a change-over-time format more easily perceived by
nonexperts.

In addition, Ricigliano introduced a separate chart for harmonic analysis
that provided abbreviated lead sheet symbols for each of the harmonies in
both songs, arranged in tandem and demarcated by bar lines. Removing
the music from its context in western notation seemed to abstract similarity
from the musical material, but it also simplified the comparison process by
reducing harmonic information into separate graphs. Then, at trial, Ricigliano
defined melody,[41] rhythm,[42] and form,[43] which not only served to ground
his analysis but also to assist factfinders in making sense of his theoretical
testimony.

The defendants introduced Irwin Coster at trial, who did not produce
any of his own charts or independent analyses. Coster's testimony instead
served primarily to rebut Ricigliano's analysis. In addition to distinguishing between the pitches in the melodies of the two songs, Coster presented
rhythm as a critical characteristic separating the two songs. He also drew
attention to harmonic differences in the songs and indicated that the harmonic resolutions and voicings were "not unique." Thus, Coster's testimony
problematized analytical focus on melody and pitch congruence, signaling

that rhythm and harmony could also be determinative of musical similarity or difference.[44]

The jury verdict favored Gasté, which the Second Circuit would later affirm.[45] The court's decision relied on the high level of similarity presumably influenced by Ricigliano's testimony, but his explicit influence remains undefined. The decision established that "if two works are so strikingly similar as to preclude the possibility of independent creation, 'copying' may be proved without a showing of access."[46] Thus, factfinders may infer access based on a high level of copying. The court went on to establish that in cases involving popular music, the level of copying required is particularly high, given "the limited number of notes and chords available to composers and the resulting fact that common themes frequently appear in various compositions."[47]

In effect, *Gasté* increased the stakes for expert testimony by requiring a higher threshold for similarity in cases involving popular music, which for a variety of reasons dominated music copyright litigation. Because of "the limited number of notes and chords available to composers and the resulting fact that common themes frequently reappear in various compositions, especially in popular music,"[48] plaintiffs would need to show more similarity, now "striking" similarity, between the two songs in order to elicit an infringement finding.[49] This higher threshold for infringement would prove to be significant in later cases and put pressure on experts to produce analyses that found greater quantities, or seemingly more obvious, similarities in comparisons of popular music for factfinders.

THE SECOND CIRCUIT MOVES INTO
THE NEW MILLENNIUM

Early-twenty-first-century cases heard in the Second Circuit reveal the ongoing nature of problems rooted in the legacy of aging, flawed decision-making processes. Yet despite these issues, many musical expert witnesses continued to apply similar analytical techniques to separate and compare musical elements, often presenting graphic analyses of their conclusions through representations with written notation. At the same time, expert witnesses increasingly incorporated idiomatic stylistic context based on their genre identification of the songs at issue, adding another layer of sophistication to their analyses.

In the Second Circuit, for example, was the case of *Tisi v. Patrick*, in which plaintiff songwriter Michael Tisi alleged that Nine Inch Nails and Filter guitarist Richard Patrick unlawfully copied from Tisi's song, "Sell Your Soul," with his own alt-rock anthem, "Take a Picture."[50] The case involved music theorist Lawrence Ferrara and composer-professor Michael White as expert witnesses. In an unusually collegial negotiation, the experts agreed to analyze the music given the same criteria, identified the same similarities and differences, and yet arrived at opposite conclusions. They agreed that the melodies were dissimilar but then drew opposite conclusions as to the harmony, rhythm, and form of the two songs. Their arrival at different analytical conclusions, despite using the same premise and criteria, could likely have been influenced, at least in part, by their party affiliation.[51]

The court ultimately resolved the dispute in favor of Patrick, finding that the similarities were "insignificant and incidental and can be attributed to common musical practices in rock and pop music."[52] In its opinion, the court foregrounded expert contributions, even acknowledging that the court was "unfamiliar with the genre" prior to receiving testimony from Ferrara.[53] After reviewing their analyses in detail, including lead-sheet-notation discussions of the harmonies in each song and compositional conventions in rock and popular music, the court introduced the notion of "superficial similarity," which considered issues of stylistic idiom and prior compositions in relation to categorizing putative similarities:[54]

> For the uninitiated, much of rock music sounds the same, and a hasty comparison of ["Sell Your Soul"] and ["Take A Picture"] could result in a finding of *superficial similarity*, as both songs employ a standard usage in rock music: an introduction, verse, chorus, and bridge, with harmonic and rhythmic similarities common to many musical genres, including pop rock. A closer review of the two compositions reveals, however, that they are significantly different.

Although notions of superficial similarity were not new, given emphases on evaluating similarity based only on original, protectable elements, the *Tisi* court's explication provided judicial validation to the approach. It fueled the application of a higher striking similarity standard, such that plaintiffs would need to overcome superficial similarities between the works at issue. The court did not, however, define the practical contours of these terms, thereby limiting any practical refinement of the similarity inquiry.

The agreement between expert witnesses in *Tisi* was less the norm than growing tensions between witnesses retained by opposing parties. During this period, expert witness confrontations throughout litigation raised issues about opposing experts' techniques and theories. More than representing differences in analytical techniques, these confrontations served to undermine the credibility of experts and to promote the partisan goals of the party to which each expert served.

THE SEVENTH CIRCUIT'S PROBLEMS WITH
THE EXPERT-ORDINARY LISTENER DIVIDE

Like the Second Circuit, Seventh Circuit courts in the late-twentieth century encountered issues with applying the *Arnstein* test, particularly in balancing the roles of experts and nonexperts. In *Selle v. Gibb*, for example, the court applied the *Arnstein* test to result in a jury finding for plaintiff Ronald Selle, but with defendant members of the BeeGees ultimately winning the lawsuit based on a post-trial motion. In *Selle*, locally known musician Ronald Selle alleged that his song "Let It End," was infringed by the BeeGee's disco ballad, "How Deep Is Your Love," as featured on the soundtrack to the film, *Saturday Night Fever*.[55] Selle claimed that his song was recorded, copyrighted, submitted to eleven music publishing companies, and performed a few times at local Chicago events, therefore, the BeeGees had access to the song and copied it. The BeeGees countered by providing their compositional process for the song and challenging Selle's argument of "inferred access" as being conflated with similarity.[56]

The trial for this case was unusual in that both parties hired expert witnesses to offer their analyses but only one presented in court. Selle hired expert Arrand Parsons, a music professor at Northwestern University, and renowned film composer David Raksin, who provided testimony at trial; the BeeGees consulted Harold Barlow, whose testimony was not given at trial and whose preliminary report is not included with extant court records. Selle had also retained Harold Barlow as an expert witness to introduce at trial on rebuttal, but he does not appear in extant court records to have been called.

Raksin prepared a report using notated sheet music as well as tape recordings of the songs in order to produce prose explanations and nine charts, a few of which were exhibited at trial but which were not retained in the court records.[57] His testimony explained his research and analytical process for prior compositions as well as comparing the two songs at issue. In his analysis, Raksin continued expert witness traditions of melocentric comparison, placed in context of phrasing and form: "there was one factor in this case which I did not encounter and don't recall ever having encountered in any other case before, and that is, the matter of in this case there are two separate parts of the song which are similar, not just one, but two, Phrase A and Phrase B. They are in the same place in the song, and that struck me as being very important."[58] Using his own labels to refer to melodic themes, Raksin emphasized that the similarity between the two songs, when considered in context, became legally relevant. Later in his examination, Raksin presented a similar technique by swapping melodies and chord progressions between songs, asserting that because the melody of one song could align with the harmonic progressions of the other, the songs should be considered similar. In addition to this hypothetical cross-over, Raksin provided descriptions of general compositional practices, from melodic sequences to serialism to rhythmic pulse and articulations. During one such explanation, Raksin was prompted to explain that melody was often the most important feature to popular songs, including those at trial.[59]

Parsons' contributions to the lawsuit signaled a significant diversion from cumulating practices of expert evaluations, both in his analytical techniques and abstract visual aids. In his report and testimony, Parsons emphasized pitch and rhythmic similarities between the two songs, which began with a computer-aided analysis of the melodies in each song:[60]

> I lined up the music first. I took the Selle lead sheet, the Bee Gee [*sic*] lead sheet, copyrighted both. I took the published score. . . . I then arranged for a computer specialist to print out the pitches of the melody so that this report would be understood by someone who did not read notation. I had the computer print out the notes by pitch names, note names, and to print out the rhythmic elements, the note values. I did that for the same three songs. I put that all together in a composite of my analysis.

At trial, he demonstrated the extent of pitch and rhythmic overlap using mylar overlays attached to printed cards, which also were not retained in court records.[61] When overlaid, the court could ostensibly see where the two melodies were the same or different because matching pitches on the overlay appeared in red.[62] The colorful overlap likely made similarities clearer than comparing the two melodies in tandem, even despite western music notation. This means of indicating musical similarity required little interpretation on the viewer's part, seeing the note for note alignment and hearing it reinforced aurally through live courtroom performance.

Parson's graphical method opposed the abstraction of contemporary expert witnesses, like what Raksin and Barlow prepared, by retaining western notation yet representing it in a novel format. Parsons's testimony addressed the quantitative extent of similarity, which the district court summarized in its opinion with little revision:[63]

> the first eight bars of each song (Theme A) have twenty-four notes out of thirty-four and forty notes in plaintiff's and defendants' compositions, respectively, that are identical in pitch and symmetrical positions. Out of thirty-five rhythmic impulses in plaintiff's composition and forty in defendants', thirty are identical. In the last four bars of both songs (Theme B), fourteen notes in each are identical in pitch. Of the fourteen rhythmic impulses in Theme B of both songs, eleven are identical. Finally, both Theme A (the first eight bars) and Theme B (the last four bars) occur in the same position in each composition.

As Parsons explained, "the two songs had such striking similarities that they could not have been written independent of one another,"[64] later reiterating, "the similarities are so great, the similarities are so vivid and striking that they would preclude independent composition."[65]

Rather than calling Barlow as a witness for examination at trial, the defense sought to undermine Parsons's testimony by impeaching him for a lack of familiarity with popular music, specifically with the BeeGee's stylistic idiom.[66] This strategy required the defendants to rely primarily on their testimony regarding creative process, with only a sophisticated prose discussion of music to rebut Parsons. They argued that the quantitative similarities that Parsons identified alone were not conclusively indicative of copying, especially given the BeeGees' evidence of independent creation and lack of access to Selle's music during their songwriting process. In keeping with the *Arnstein* test, however, Parsons did not comment on the relevance of these similarities to infringement findings.

The jury proved to be unconvinced by the defense and decided in favor of Selle. The appellate court later overturned their verdict, however, pursuant to a motion notwithstanding the verdict filed by the members of the BeeGees that challenged the sufficiency of the evidence produced at trial. Most notably, the BeeGees argued that testimony given by each member of the group regarding their compositional process had indicated independent composition could not be overridden by an inference presented by an expert witness—in this case, Parsons.[67] Selle then appealed the ruling, only to have it affirmed. The Seventh Circuit majority indicated that "the plaintiff must always present sufficient evidence to support a reasonable possibility of access because the jury cannot draw an inference of access based upon speculation and conjecture alone."[68] Where there is a lack of access, as the defendants showed, there was no need to advance to similarity analysis.

In addition to its landmark ruling regarding access and striking similarity, the *Selle* court proved the appeal process to be the strongest check on the subjective nature of nonexpert jury decisions. More than reversing the jury verdict, the Seventh Circuit's decision on appeal refined the relationship between access and similarity. It altered the role of expert witnesses by imposing further legal limitations on the scope of their influence in circumstances where proof of access is high, creating a legal climate where expert witnesses would be more relevant in situations where access was difficult to prove or dispute.

THE NINTH CIRCUIT AND PROBLEMS
WITH EXTRINSIC ANALYSIS

Despite the majority of circuits relying on the *Arnstein* test, the Ninth Circuit set out applying the *Krofft* test. Courts and expert witnesses alike struggled to apply the standard, particularly with regard to applying detailed analysis of the "musical idea" in the works at issue. In its attempt to keep the test applicable across categories of expressive works, the *Krofft* test had not offered any hint as to where to distinguish a musical idea or how it should be evaluated by expert witnesses.[69] The notion of underlying, not protectable musical material lent itself to reductive analytical techniques, which likely contributed to increases in the abstraction and sophistication of forensic analyses produced by expert witnesses. These methods, however, separated expert analyses from the music at issue and the holistic comparisons made by nonexpert jurors.

In *Baxter v. MCA*, Leslie T. Baxter sued film-score composer John Williams, alleging that the musical score to the movie *E.T.: The Extra Terrestrial* infringed on Baxter's copyright to his song "Joy." Baxter's song was part of a seven-song collection titled, *The Passions*. In the lawsuit, Baxter claimed that Williams had participated in an unrelated performance of "Joy" during a concert at the Hollywood Bowl decades earlier, therefore, he had access to the song and copied a six-note motive. To prove similarity, Baxter argued that a six-note motive constituted a "small but qualitatively important portion" of "Joy" that had been allegedly appropriated.[70]

In response to a motion for summary judgment filed by the plaintiffs seeking a judicial ruling without trial based on the facts of the case, Williams conceded that the two musical ideas were similar by conceding access to "Joy." In a comparable approach to the relationship between similarity and access taken in *Selle*, expert testimony was limited due to Baxter's convincing proof of access. Because *Krofft* had limited expert testimony to only the extrinsic test, or analysis of the similarity between the ideas behind the two works, experts were no longer legally available. Instead, the only issue at trial had to do with the intrinsic test, whether there was similarity between the expressions of these ideas between the two works.[71]

The trial court handed down its decision in favor of the plaintiffs. On appeal, however, the Ninth Circuit found summary judgment improper under *Krofft*, which reopened the case, and in so doing, effectively reopened legal space for expert testimony. The court also noted that "no bright line rule exists as to what quantum of similarity is permitted before crossing into the realm of substantial similarity"[72]; therefore, the six-motive on which Baxter relied to argue access could not constitute a substantial enough portion of the song. More importantly, the court stated that granting summary judgment on these grounds necessarily required the present perceptions of the judge without expert testimony, which did not fully consider the intrinsic test that addressed the expression of each idea. Thus, the Ninth Circuit remanded the case to the district court with new instructions.[73]

At the new trial, the plaintiffs called musicologists Robert Winter and Phillip Springer, while the defendants called musicologists Earl Spielman and Harold Barlow. Their analyses accounted for the relationship between

melody and harmony and the nature of similarity as indicative of independent creation or copying, comparable with the precedent in *Selle v. Gibb*
and earlier stages in the litigation process of the current case. The two
expert witnesses called by the plaintiffs emphasized the melodic contour
and aural performance of the music, but did not introduce any graphic
exhibits. In contrast, the two experts called by the defendants relied more
heavily on such charts. To that end, Springer created impromptu charts on
a blackboard at trial that were intended to accompany his live courtroom
demonstrations at the piano, but were not rendered in permanent form to be
retained in court records.[74]

Spielman produced an unusually abstract chart that compared the music at
issue in a new way. His "chromatranscription" demonstrated a high level of
abstraction used to show similarity of musical idea in a symbolic way, completely separated from the context of western notation or live performance.
Despite this abstraction, the chart appeared to retain concepts of pitch and
rhythmic duration for each melody represented in rows of quadrilaterals.
Where colors and patterns matched, there was similarity, or what Spielman
called "simultaneous pitch occurrences."[75] Drawing from the long expert
tradition of using color to demarcate similarity, the chart relied on color to
symbolize similarity. In so doing, this chart completely removed western
notation, trading it instead with a more abstract graph intended for viewers ostensibly unable to read western music notation. Although Spielman's
impact on the jury cannot be definitively evaluated, a verdict ultimately found
that the six-note motive from "Joy" was not protectable on its own and therefore the theme from *E.T.* did not infringe on it.

Legally, *Baxter* highlighted issues with expert testimony in the *Krofft*
test. As the summary judgment motion demonstrated, there were valid legal
means to bypass the extrinsic test altogether because of the limited contributions of expert witnesses. Thus, the *Baxter* court seemed to introduce a *de
facto* "ordinary listener" test, where infringement is determined exclusively
based on the evaluation of nonexpert witnesses.[76] This decision could be
applied strategically by attorneys to maximize the subjective nature of
jury-centric inquiries, thereby assisting parties attempting to avoid the influence of experts that might reveal similarity otherwise potentially missed by
nonexperts.

MUSICAL IDEAS AND THE ORDER OF EVALUATIONS

Contemporaneous courts attempted to define criteria for the legal concept of
a musical idea as it pertained to extrinsic analysis, with problematic effect.
In *Thompson v. Richie*, for example, Gene Thompson and Tracy Singleton

sued Lionel Richie, claiming infringement with his own "Sela," "Stuck on You," and "Deep River Woman."[77] Prior to any trial, the district court initially granted a motion for summary judgment for Richie, having applied the *Krofft* test to determine a lack of similarity in the ideas, according to evidence from the plaintiff's expert witness, Robert Winter, and the expression of the songs at issue.[78] The Ninth Circuit later reversed and remanded the decision on grounds that it had questionably applied the test, finding that similarity between the musical ideas constituted a question of fact.[79]

As a result of the appellate decision, the case was finally sent to trial, but with an unusual trifurcation order that separated and reordered the hearing of each issue, such that the trial court was to consider intrinsic similarity before extrinsic, and the matter of access was to be resolved last.[80] According to the plaintiff's attorney, however, the order was flawed, because a finding of substantial similarity according to the intrinsic test would necessarily mean that their underlying ideas would be similar and extrinsic analysis would be complete without contributions from expert witnesses. The court accepted this reasoning, declared a mistrial, and at the new trial, it more strictly followed the *Krofft* test.

During the evaluation process for intrinsic similarity in the new trial, where all evidence was heard first and then issues were decided, expert witnesses disagreed about theoretical conceptions of a musical idea, revealing substantive legal ambiguity. The plaintiffs retained expert witness Garnett Brown, who considered a musical idea to manifest when it is expressed in musical form.[81] Conversely, the defendants retained Ricigliano, who testified that a musical idea was a self-contained entity, but generally represented only a portion of a larger musical work, which on a whole contains multiple musical ideas. The musical elements that make up such ideas reflected the elements used by expert witnesses for over a century to assess similarity: "(1) a single line of pitch or rhythm (melodic); (2) a vertical group of pitches (harmonic or chordal); (3) a series of time values without pitch (rhythmic); or (4) a combination of pitch, rhythm, and chord(s)."[82] In the context of the case, however, the resulting expert confrontation pitted Brown's statement that the music contained similar ideas as forms of popular music against Ricigliano's statement that the musical ideas were distinct.[83] Although the jury ultimately found a lack of access on Richie's part, such that they did not address substantial similarity, it is unlikely that this expert confrontation would have elucidated musical similarity for them. Despite the confusion, the case was ultimately resolved in favor of the defendants.

After *Baxter* and *Thompson*, experts were left grasping at a means to analyze music that addressed fundamental ideas outside the context of their expression manifested in the music at issue. Although contemporaneous cases had attempted to define the contours of the underlying "idea" in an expressive work, their criteria, such as "plot, themes, dialogue, mood, setting, pace, characters, and sequence,"[84] were ineffective as applied to music. "Pitch, harmony, and tempo," as criteria offered in *Thompson*, hardly clarified matters. The testimony of musical expert witnesses in these cases thus reflects their attempts to adapt to new legal constraints, particularly attempting to present analyses that reflected only the ineffable musical idea of the music at issue without mentioning the expression of that idea.

Over time, the Ninth Circuit continued to incorporate criteria for assessing the underlying idea at issue under the *Krofft* extrinsic test. As a result, courts decreasingly relied on the extrinsic test that strictly evaluated only the ideas behind a work, seeming to "stray[] from *Krofft*'s division between expression and ideas."[85] In *Shaw v. Lindheim*, a case involving the copyright of television scripts, the court revised the scope of its extrinsic test and attempted to offer clarification as to the two prongs.[86] Noting that "[a]ny test for substantial similarity is necessarily imprecise,"[87] the court reconceived of the test as "more sensibly described as objective and subjective analyses of expression."[88] Thus, the extrinsic test was now considered a legally objective test for evaluating the expressions of the works at issue, contrasted with the intrinsic test, now as a subjective evaluation of them. This linguistic refinement has had minimal practical effect in deciphering the test, however, and failed to account for inherent subjectivities in analyses produced by expert witnesses.

THE NINTH CIRCUIT MOVES INTO THE NEW MILLENNIUM: *SWIRKSY V. CAREY*

For the Ninth Circuit, the case of *Swirsky v. Carey* was illustrative of ongoing issues with the *Krofft* test, particularly surrounding experts' extrinsic, legally objective, analyses. In this lawsuit, songwriter plaintiffs Seth Swirsky and Warryn Campbell sued Mariah Carey, along with her songwriting team and other music industry entities, alleging that they had profited from the release of plaintiff's "One of Those Love Songs," as recorded by female vocal group Xscape, with Carey's "Thank God I Found You." Both songs were mastered by engineer Bob Ludwig and both albums on which the songs appeared were produced by Sony and distributed by Columbia Records.[89]

Robert Walser, called by the plaintiffs, made transcriptions from the recordings to produce a series of visual representations, including one that isolated and reduced the chorus melodies of both songs from their embellished performances according to stylistic conventions of R&B. Although the melodies were aligned in tandem, somewhat unusually, he provided no additional designation to signify points of congruence. As Walser would later explain, his graph was "designed to show certain relationships, certain musical details, but it is not a performance score. And to then take this and perform from it inevitably involves making—putting things in that are not notated here."[90]

The defendants challenged Walser's analysis, arguing that both its method and representation were improper and should have been excluded as evidence. According to them, Walser allegedly relied too heavily on his own reductive decisions not readily discernable by the court, thereby ignoring potential differences in pitch and rhythm by selectively removing musical content. Not only did Walser's method appear to exaggerate melodic similarities, they argued, but the reductions were also based on his own perceptions via transcription and analytical decision-making. The core of the defendant's argument was a contention of implicit subjectivity in the expert's analysis, which, according to the defendants, belied the objective prong of the legal test.

Applying *Krofft*, the district court agreed with, and thus found in favor of, the defendants. On the issue of substantial similarity, the court focused on Walser's analysis, summarizing and quoting from it directly to outline its own opinion and to address one of the main disputes between the parties. Its reasoning identified Walser's analysis as defective for being "selective," and relying more on his individual perceptions rather than purportedly objective, extrinsic analysis. Instead, the district court relied on note-by-note, solely melodic comparisons on full transcriptions of the choruses in each song. After finding that the melodies were either dissimilar or not protectable, "given the lack of melodic similarity between the two songs, any alleged similarity in key, harmonic structure, tempo, or genre, between [the two songs] is not sufficient"[91] to constitute a material issue, so the court granted summary judgment in favor of the plaintiffs.

On appeal, however, the Ninth Circuit found Walser's testimony to be admissible. The court interpreted the legal prong, "[o]bjective analysis of music," ostensibly aided by musical expert analyses, such that it "cannot mean that a court may simply compare the numerical representations of pitch sequences and the visual representations of notes to determine that two choruses are not substantially similar, without regard to other elements of the compositions."[92] In its reversal and remand, the majority opinion acknowledged that although there are differing methods and approaches to analysis, they must account for similarities across musical elements in an integrated way:[93]

> Certainly, musicological experts can disagree as to whether an approach that highlights stressed notes, as Dr. Walser's does, is the most appropriate way to break down music for substantial-similarity comparison, but no [analytical] approach can completely divorce pitch sequence and rhythm from harmonic chord progression, tempo, and key, and thereby support a conclusion that

compositions are dissimilar as a matter of law. It is these elements that determine what notes and pitches are heard in a song and at what point in the song they are found. To pull these elements out of a song individually, without also looking at them in combination, is to perform an incomplete and distorted musicological analysis.

The court further emphasized the *ad hoc* nature of forensic similarity analysis, explaining that:[94]

there is no one magical combination of these [musical elements] that will automatically substantiate a musical infringement suit; each allegation of infringement will be unique. So long as the plaintiff can demonstrate . . . that the similarity was "substantial" and [original to the] work, the extrinsic test is satisfied.

Thus, Walser's analytical method and conclusions fulfilled the court's expectations and were ultimately considered as evidence. The case ultimately settled out of court in 2006, but the legal treatment of Walser's contributions have continued to serve as precedent for separating musical ideas from expressions and the legal role of expert testimony.

PROBLEMS WITH THE LEGAL INQUIRY

Despite changes in the analytical techniques that expert witnesses used and the legal scope of their influence, the role of musical experts in the late twentieth and early-twenty-first centuries continued on a similar trajectory: marking points of similarity and difference so that factfinders might be better equipped to distinguish between lawful commonality and unlawful appropriation. After *Arnstein*, experts were limited to copying as the first prong of similarity analysis and were prevented from commenting on whether that similarity constituted infringement. The legal invocation of expert "dissection" coincided with a rise of more sophisticated techniques that placed melody in its formal and harmonic context before identifying congruence. In turn, this shift legally and analytically altered the criteria for similarity, such that melodic congruence needed to coincide with harmonic and formal congruence in order to meet the threshold of musical similarity.

The *Krofft* decision furthered a legal trend toward narrowing the role of expert witnesses and drove changes in the analysis and the similarities they located. Experts under *Krofft* were now limited to "extrinsic" aspects of similarity, referring to the musical idea legally thought to be capable of being identified through analysis. As *Baxter* and *Thompson* demonstrated, experts and courts alike struggled to set widely applicable criteria for defining or locating a musical idea, separate from its expression through live or recorded performance or in commonly used western notation, and then evaluating the similarity between those musical ideas. The legal quest for the musical idea lent itself well to abstract musical analyses and symbolic representations, as well as to reductive techniques that sought to dispense with surface-level musical material deemed by the expert witness to be inessential to musical identity for the purposes of similarity. But these techniques had an inconclusive effect in assisting courts to determine infringement. Even with the modification of *Krofft* under *Shaw*, which supposedly brought the extrinsic test more closely in alignment with *Arnstein*, the application of expert testimony remained limited. Early twenty-first century cases, especially *Swirsky v. Carey*, likewise highlighted many of the fundamental problems with these legal tests, demonstrating both the essential role of musical experts and the issues that riddle their contributions to litigation.

Cases heard in the late twentieth and early twentieth-first centuries identified through application the problems generated by presumptions of objectivity, abstract legal conceptions of a divide between musical ideas and expressions, and convoluted tests for evaluating similarity that divided experts and nonexperts. Rather than overturning these tests entirely, courts instead introduced a variety of refinements that did more to confound than simplify the decision-making process. This legal climate, when combined with the sweeping reforms in the 1976 Copyright Act and the introduction of new musical technologies and styles predicated on digital sampling, brought about a critical juncture for evaluations of music as intellectual property.

NOTES

1. *1971 Sound Recording Act*, 85 Stat. 391, § 1(a).

2. *Copyright Act of 1976*, 17 U.S.C. § 302.

3. 17 U.S.C. § 102(a).

4. 17 U.S.C. § 408.

5. In the later case of *Lenz v. Universal Music Corp.*, 801 F.3d 1126 (9th Cir. 2015), the court would recast fair use as an authorized right rather than an excuse for use that might otherwise amount to infringement.

6. See *Folsom v. March*, 9 F.Cas. 342 (C.C.D. Mass. 1841).

7. 17 U.S.C. § 107.

8. Josh Camson, "History of the Federal Rules of Evidence," *Proof*, Last modified Spring 2010, https://apps.americanbar.org/litigation/litigationnews/trial_skills/06 1710-trial-evidence-federal-rules-of-evidence-history.html.

9. Mark I. Bernstein, "Jury Evaluation of Expert Testimony Under the Federal Rules," *Drexel Law Review* 7 (Spring 2015): 259.

10. Rule 702 has applied to all expert testimony, and is therefore governed by principles of FRE 104(a), which required that the court decide preliminary questions, including whether a witness is qualified, as part of the admissibility process. Federal Rules of Evidence, Public Law 93–595, Rule 104(a) (January 2, 1975) (amended 2011).

11. *Federal Rules of Evidence*, Public Law 93–595, Rule 702 (January 2, 1975) (amended 2011).

12. *Bright Tunes Music Corp. v. Harrisongs Music, Ltd.*, 420 F. Supp. 177, 177 (S.D.N.Y. 1976).

13. *Bright Tunes*, 420 F. Supp. at 180 n.11.

14. *Bright Tunes v. Harrisongs*, Transcript, 95 (Greitzer). Records Group 21; National Archives and Records Administration Kansas City; U.S.D.C. Southern District of New York, Civil Case Files 71-CV-602, Boxes 173, 5449, "Bright Tunes v. Harrisongs."

15. *Bright Tunes v. Harrisongs*, Transcript, 96–97 (Greitzer).

16. See *Bright Tunes v. Harrisongs*, Transcript, 486–90 (Butler).

17. *Bright Tunes v. Harrisongs*, Transcript, 493 (Butler).

18. *Bright Tunes v. Harrisongs*, Transcript, 494 (Butler).

19. *Bright Tunes v. Harrisongs*, Transcript, 435–44 (Barlow).

20. *Bright Tunes*, 420 F. Supp. at 178n.1.

21. *Bright Tunes*, 420 F. Supp. at 178; see also *Bright Tunes v. Harrisongs*, Transcript, 39 (Greitzer).

22. *MCA Music v. Earl Wilson*, 425 F. Supp. 443, 443 (S.D.N.Y. 1976).

23. *Wilson*, 425 F. Supp. at 450.

24. The court noted that under FRE 803(1), present sense impressions, such as those of nonexpert listeners upon hearing two songs, are exceptions to the hearsay rule and that regardless of the evidence's introduction, final decisions regarding infringement are at the court's discretion. *Wilson*, 425 F. Supp. at 450–51. The argument would ultimately fail. See *Wilson*, 425 F. Supp. at 446–54.

25. *MCA v. Wilson*, Transcript, 16 (Barlow). Records Group 21; National Archives and Records Administration Kansas City; U.S. Court of Appeals 2d Cir. Case Files 80-771-80-7776, Box 122, "MCA v. Wilson."

26. *Wilson*, 425 F. Supp. at 449; *MCA v. Wilson*, Transcript, 25 (Barlow).

27. *Wilson*, 425 F. Supp. at 449; *MCA v. Wilson*, Transcript, 25 (Barlow).

28. *MCA v. Wilson*, Transcript, 26 (Barlow).

29. *MCA v. Wilson*, Transcript, 28 (Barlow).

30. *Wilson*, 425 F. Supp. at 449.

31. *MCA v. Wilson*, Transcript, 363 (Goudey).

32. *MCA v. Wilson*, Transcript, 376 (Goudey).

33. *MCA v. Wilson*, Transcript, 377 (Goudey).

34. *MCA v. Wilson*, Transcript, 401 (Barlow).

35. *Wilson*, 425 F. Supp. at 449.

36. *Wilson*, 425 F. Supp. at 452–54.

37. *Wilson*, 425 F. Supp. at 449 (S.D.N.Y. 1976); see also Alice Kim, "Expert Testimony and Substantial Similarity: Facing the Music in (Music) Copyright

Infringement Cases," *Columbia – VLA Journal of Law and the Arts* 19 (Fall 1994–Winter 1995): 116.

38. Kim, "Expert Testimony," 116.

39. *Gasté v. Kaiserman*, 669 F. Supp. 583 (S.D.N.Y. 1987).

40. *Gasté v. Kaiserman*, Transcript, 456 (Ricigliano). Records Group 21; National Archives and Records Administration Kansas City; U.S. Court of Appeals 2d Box 144, Cir. Case Files 88–7367, "Gasté v. Kaiserman."

41. Melody included interval content, rhythm, basic shapes, and structure. See *Gasté v. Kaiserman*, Transcript, 457 (Ricigliano).

42. "Rhythm is the organization of time values or duration." *Gasté v. Kaiserman*, Transcript, 468 (Ricigliano).

43. "Form refers to the organization of the musical ideas." *Gasté v. Kaiserman*, Transcript, 466 (Ricigliano).

44. *Gasté v. Kaiserman*, Transcript, 495 (Coster).

45. *Gasté v. Kaiserman*, 863 F.2d 1061, 1063 (2d Cir. 1888).

46. *Gasté*, 863 F.2d at 1068.

47. *Gasté*, 863 F.2d at 1068.

48. *Gasté*, 863 F.2d at 1068–69 (citing *Arnstein v. Edward B. Marks*).

49. *Gasté*, 863 F.2d at 1068–69.

50. *Tisi v. Patrick*, 97 F. Supp.2d 539, 541 (S.D.N.Y. 2000).

51. *Tisi*, 97 F. Supp. at 543.

52. *Tisi*, 97 F. Supp. at 545.

53. *Tisi*, 97 F. Supp. at 541.

54. *Tisi*, 97 F. Supp. at 543 (emphasis added).

55. *Selle v. Gibb*, 567 F. Supp. 1173, 1176 (N.D. Ill. 1983).

56. See *Selle*, 567 F. Supp. at 1176–77; 1180–81.

57. *Selle v. Gibb*, Transcript, 11–12 (Raksin). Records Group 21; National Archives and Records Administration Chicago; U.S.D.C. Chicago, Civil Transcripts Case 78–3656, Boxes 7–8, "Selle v. Gibb."

58. *Selle v. Gibb*, Transcript, 45 (Raksin).

59. *Selle v. Gibb*, Transcript, 147–48 (Raksin).

60. *Selle v. Gibb*, Transcript, 9 (Parsons).

61. *Selle v. Gibb*, Transcript, 222–23, 226–27, 232–34 (Parsons).

62. Reynolds, *Music Analysis*, 142, 613–14.

63. *Selle*, 567 F. Supp. at 1178.

64. *Selle v. Gibb*, Transcript, 202 (Parsons) (cited in opinion).

65. *Selle v. Gibb*, Transcript, 237 (Parsons).

66. *Selle v. Gibb*, Transcript, 266–72 (Parsons).

67. *Selle*, 567 F. Supp. at 1175; 1182.

68. *Selle*, 741 F.2d 896, 901 (7th Cir. 1984).

69. See also Avsec, "'Nonconventional' Musical Analysis," 353.

70. *Baxter v. MCA, Inc.*, 812 F.2d 421, 422-24 (9th Cir. 1987).

71. *Baxter*, 812 F.2d at 423–24.

72. *Baxter*, 812 F.2d at 425.

73. *Baxter*, 812 F.2d at 424–25.

Chapter 4

74. Reynolds, *Music Analysis*, 212.

75. Reynolds, *Music Analysis*, 923.

76. *Baxter v. MCA, Inc.*, 812 F.2d 421, 424 n.2 (9th Cir. 1987).

77. *Thompson v. Richie*, No. CV 85-1583 (C.D. Cal. March 7, 1985). See also Stephanie Jones, "Music Copyright in Theory and Practice: An Improved Approach for Determining Substantial Similarity," *Duquesne Law Review* 31 (Winter 1993): 278n.7.

78. *Thompson*, No. CV 85-1583; see also Jones, "Music Copyright," 278n.7.

79. *Thompson v. Richie*, 820 F.2d 408 (9th Cir. 1987).

80. Jones, "Music Copyright," 297–98.

81. Jones, "Music Copyright," 278.

82. Ricigliano, as summarized in Jones, "Music Copyright," at 301.

83. Jones, "Music Copyright," 278 n.7, 299–300.

84. *Shaw v. Lindheim*, 908 F.2d 1353, 1359 (9th Cir. 1990).

85. *Shaw*, 919 F.2d at 1357.

86. *Shaw*, 919 F.2d at 1355–56.

87. *Shaw*, 919 F.2d at 1356.

88. *Shaw*, 919 F.2d at 1357.

89. *Swirsky v. Carey*, 376 F.3d 841 (9th Cir. 2004).

90. *Swirsky v. Carey*, Walser Deposition, 117–18.

91. *Swirsky*, 226 F. Supp.2d at 1234.

92. *Swirsky*, 276 F.3d at 847–48.

93. *Swirsky*, 276 F.3d at 848.

94. *Swirsky*, 276 F.3d at 848.

Chapter 5

Sampling Cases and the
Digital Audio Revolution

Congressional reforms of federal statutory copyright law throughout the twentieth century attempted to bring laws in closer sync with rapid technological innovations, particularly for music. Most notably, the Digital Millennium Copyright Act, passed in 1998, attempted to modernize the 1976 Copyright Act to address concerns with digital media and rampant piracy.[1] The Digital Performance Right in Sound Recordings Act of 1995 similarly granted public-performance rights to sound recording copyright holders.[2] These late-century legislative acts seemed to promise greater protection for sound recordings. Yet legal emphasis on adapting to innovations in audio technology seemed to do more to address use than to redefine the scope of copyright protection itself, instead reifying divisions between copyrights for musical compositions, and recordings of them, than to accommodate music created first on record.

By the last three decades of the twentieth century, emerging musical styles proved to revolutionize existing conceptions of the copyrightable musical work and, in turn, the contours of musical similarity when infringement claims inevitably arose. In particular, the cultivation of hip-hop out of 1970s DJ culture, which pioneered borrowing short instrumental breaks to link sets and create overlapping grooves for dancing or backgrounds to poetic interludes, introduced creative practices more closely aligned with "'open source' culture" than the exclusivity of federal copyright.[3] The rise of music technologies in the 1980s, such as samplers, sequencers, synthesizers, drum machines, and software designed to process sound, enabled collage-style compositional techniques to flourish. To creators, almost any sonic material could be considered useable, including samples from already copyrighted musical works.

Infringement litigation that involved these techniques arose in the 1990s and has continued to present courts and musical experts alike with new musical, analytical, and legal terrain. In addition to problematizing the relationship between musical compositions and recordings, these cases have caused courts to reconsider thresholds for legal similarity. Because samples typically involve brief segments of recorded audio, the small quantity of copyrighted material involved has raised legal questions about whether the amount of material at issue is so insignificant that it might constitute a *de minimis* exception or similarly trigger fair use as an affirmative defense.[4] Furthermore, given that musical material at issue in each lawsuit is nearly, if not entirely, congruent, these cases presented new questions regarding the best evidence and techniques for forensic similarity analysis, the criteria for assessing similarity, interpretations of the legal thresholds for copyrightability and infringement, and even musical expertise itself.

STARTING *UPRIGHT*

Although infringement claims involving alleged use of unlicensed samples had already been presented by 1990, including the now-famous lawsuit over a melodic line featured in Vanilla Ice's "Ice Ice Baby" being sampled from "Under Pressure," by Queen and David Bowie, most of these cases settled out of court.[5] But the case of *Grand Upright Music, Ltd. v. Warner Bros. Records, Inc.* brought questions of copyright ownership and sampling culture to the courtroom. In this case, Raymond Edward O'Sullivan, a popular Irish singer-songwriter known as Gilbert O'Sullivan, and his publishing company sued rap artist and producer Marcel Theo Hall, known professionally as "Biz Markie," and his publishing company, Warner Brothers, for sampling melodic and lyrical content from O'Sullivan's song, "Alone Again (Naturally)," in Biz Markie's similarly titled "Alone Again," off his album, *I Need a Haircut.*[6] The sample of an accompaniment pattern in O'Sullivan's song appears throughout "Alone Again," starting from the beginning of the track. Although Warner and Biz Markie had sought permission to use the recording during their creation process, O'Sullivan had denied granting a license. Trial Judge Duffy ruled in favor of O'Sullivan, famously beginning his opinion with the dicta, "[t]hou shalt not steal,"[7] and referring the case for criminal prosecution, which the U.S. Attorney never pursued.

In his opinion, Judge Duffy addressed O'Sullivan's valid copyright and his performance on the master recording, but the judge ultimately found the defendant's actions, rather than the quantity and originality of the content in question, most persuasive. During production, Biz Markie and his team unsuccessfully sought a license for their use of "Alone Again (Naturally)."

Evidence of this attempt, along with testimony from the defendants indicating that they knew they were obligated to obtain a license, indicated the presence of the sample and that it was unlawfully borrowed for economic gain.[8] No discussion was introduced regarding fair use as a potential affirmative defense.

The case famously resulted in O'Sullivan receiving 100 percent of royalties and an injunction against continued release of "Alone Again," but the decision had far-reaching practical implications for future sampling practices. The decision generated a legal climate that made licensing samples for collage-style composition expensive, if not cost preclusive, for many creators. With the correlating effect of rampant unlicensed sampling, it also promoted new techniques that were at times compatible with copyright practices and at other times not. Interpolation, or the process of recreating a sample using new instruments and sounds and paying only to use the composition rather than for a mechanical license for the recording, became one viable solution. Another involved careful editing of a sample, created either to obscure detection of it or simply to integrate the borrowed material into the musical texture of the new song. While these techniques could be used to avoid infringement claims, they did not insulate creators from potential legal problems.

Grand Upright ignited legal discourse surrounding copyright protections for instances of digital sampling. Several cases involving similar claims followed, including *Jarvis v. A & M Records*.[9] In 1982, Boyd Jarvis composed the early house anthem, "The Music Got Me," to be recorded with his ensemble, Visual, and released the following year on Prelude Records.[10] Seven years later, in 1989, Robert Clivilles and David Cole wrote and recorded their own house track, "Get Dumb! (Free Your Body)," featuring rap artist Freedom Williams, to be released on A&M Records and Vendetta Records as singles for themselves and for the groups, Seduction (under the title "Heartbeat"), and the Crew (under the litigated title). Clivilles and Cole admitted to including samples from "The Music Got Me" in all three formats, however, which redirected the focus of the lawsuit away from copying.[11]

Because the defendants admitted to copying, little, if any, attention to musical similarity as analyzed by expert witnesses seemed necessary. The court instead moved directly to the second prong of similarity analysis to determine whether the sampling amounted to improper appropriation. Borrowing its reasoning from *Grand Upright* and citing a legal treatise for language, the *Jarvis* court labeled sampling cases "fragmented literal similarity." As the presiding judge opined about what he called "literal verbatim similarity," "the copied parts could not be more similar—they were digitally copied from plaintiff's recording."[12] By classifying the infringement claim this way, the court shifted their inquiry away from an ordinary listener standard typically applied in legal similarity analysis to one focusing more on the quantitative and qualitative values of the purportedly original sampled content. The complex of legal claims resulted in a partial grant and a partial denial of the defendant's collection of a motion to strike and motions for summary judgment, but the opinion reinforced reasoning from *Grand Upright* and added to the cultivation of jurisprudence surrounding copyright and sampling.

Grand Upright and *Jarvis* both involved evidence of direct copying, meaning that musical expert testimony would not have been necessary to contribute to evaluations of access or similarity to assess whether the borrowing amounted to infringement. While testimony regarding creative processes in hip-hop as distinct from previous styles of music encountered by courts might have elucidated matters of originality, extant records do not appear to have included contributions from expert witnesses in this way. Yet the apparently reduced role of expert witnesses in these cases did not become normative for future sampling cases.

FORENSIC ANALYSIS OF SAMPLING CLAIMS

Not all sampling cases have involved a direct admission of copying, and, as at least one musical expert has noted, rarely have samples appeared unaltered in later compositions.[13] As a result, musical expert witnesses have continued to serve an essential function in cases that involve this category of infringement claim by contextualizing and interpreting increasingly detailed musical comparisons for the court. Functioning within existing legal schemes for evaluating copyright infringement, expert witnesses were challenged to develop analytical techniques to compare, and contextualize, elements that would be, by their very nature, similar according to recognized legal parameters of melody, harmony, and rhythm. While some expert witnesses continued to apply traditional forensic analytical techniques based on written notation, others attempted to account, to various extents, for matters relevant to the digital processing involved in altering samples. The latter increasingly relied on audio-based assessments of similarity, often aided by audio specialists with qualifications new to expertise in music copyright cases.

Although musical expert witnesses had been using computerized analysis for decades to reach beyond the confines of western notation and traditional analytical techniques, comparisons aided by audio technology have proven to be critical to the minute details between samples. Increasingly refined technologies can facilitate the production of brief aural examples isolated for factfinders that seem to offer greater consistency than live courtroom performance, as well as waveform graphs that have provided a more descriptive sonic representation of the music distinct from the prescriptive visual representation of western notation. Often produced by audio specialists, these highly detailed analyses have offered a critical set of techniques that have been applied in court alone, in conjunction with, and at times in opposition to, notated corollaries.

Waveform comparison and phase inversion in particular have been used primarily in the context of digital sampling cases. Using specialized software, such as Audacity, Audiodesk, Digital Performer, iZotope, and Pro Tools, experts can reduce the speed of a recording to hear minute details, and they can use various techniques to isolate, manipulate, and even in some cases recreate, sections of recordings for the purposes of comparison. Like transcriptions and graphs representing notated similarities, these analyses have been represented visually for factfinders during litigation via graphs introduced as exhibits. By focusing on as a little as a few milliseconds and using phase cancellation to isolate a sample from other accompanying sounds, experts have identified the same sound source in the two songs at issue in a case.[14]

Similar to forensic audio analyses used in non-copyright cases, experts have also used spectrographic analyses, but with less frequency. These techniques compare variations over time to locate similarities in frequency. Yet as expert witness Alexander Stewart explained, "in [his] experience, music spectrograms seldom seem to offer conclusive evidence though they may still be valuable for corroborative purposes."[15] Together, such aural comparisons can seem to account more precisely for similarity by incorporating musical parameters critical to listener perception, yet typically treated as secondary in previous copyright infringement cases, such as timbre, tempo, rhythmic variance, and dynamics.[16] These analyses can also appear to provide forensic quantification and replicability that might simultaneously seem to mystify and to instill a sense of objectivity in factfinders, especially when introduced alongside, or in opposition to, notated corollaries.

The case of *Newton v. Diamond* provides an example of the contrasts between notated and aural analytical techniques introduced by expert witnesses. Avant-garde art music composer James Newton sued members of The Beastie Boys for sampling a six-second, three-note sequence of his flute composition "Choir," in their song, "Pass the Mic," the first single off their third rap-rock hybrid album, *Check Your Head*.[17] The Beastie Boys had obtained a license from ECM records to sample from Newton's recording of "Choir" lawfully in 1992, under which they constructed their song.[18] The six-second sample they selected, which involved a flutist playing a C while vocalizing a C-D-flat-C melody into their instrument, was looped throughout "Pass the Mic," which itself was approximately four and half minutes long. Plaintiff Newton contended that in sampling from his recording, defendant members of the Beastie Boys drew not only the three-note sequence that their license covered, but also the distinctive musical sound that the plaintiff had developed as part of the unlicensed musical composition.[19] In response, the defendants argued that the sample was not protectable and was so minimal that it could not constitute copyright infringement.

Expert reports produced for this case illuminated the costs and benefits of various analytical techniques for sampling in the wake of new musical styles and creative processes. The plaintiffs relied on expert reports from musicologist-composer J. Christopher Dobrian and composer Olly Wilson, while the defendants relied on music theorist Lawrence Ferrara. Each expert presented his own analyses of the two songs to identify the sample and addressed the key issues of the case. One of the main sources of contention between the experts, and for the outcome of the case, was whether Newton's vocalization, or multiphonic technique, could be considered unique to his composition, not simply as it was performed on the recording. Experts agreed that the technique of vocalizing into a flute while playing was not unique to Newton's composition, but rather a technique used in some sub-Saharan African musics and in other late-twentieth-century avant-garde compositions.[20] But Newton's response was that although the technique itself was not unique, his performance of it in "Choir" was unique to him and the composition, despite an absence of description in the score of how his technique was distinct from that used in any other piece or by any other performer. Rather, the score merely showed the notation and general indications to perform such vocalization.

In his report, Dobrian argued against the application of traditional forensic analyses that focused on melody, noting that:[21]

[a]pplying traditional analysis to this brief excerpt from Newton's "Choir" . . . a theorist could conclude (erroneously, in my opinion) that the excerpt contains an insignificant amount of information because it contains a simple "neighboring-tone" figure: C to D-Flat and back to C. That might possibly be true if this were a melody from the baroque or classical periods . . . . If, on the other hand, one considers the special playing technique described in the score (holding one fingered note constant while singing the other pitches) and the resultant complex, expressive effect that results, it is clear that the "unique expression" of this excerpt is not solely in the pitch choices, but is actually in those particular pitches performed in that particular way on that instrument. These components in this particular combination are not found anywhere else in notated music literature, and they are unique and distinctive in their sonic/ musical result.

Dobrian explained here that analyses in this case required nontraditional techniques, which he believed would account better for timbre and the complex relationships between flute and voice, using computer-produced spectral plots to demonstrate the "dissonant conflict between voice and flute that creates new frequencies, turbulence, and the unique sound."[22] He further described the aural analysis of "Choir":[23]

> The plots show time going from the "front" of the picture toward the "back." Frequency is left-to-right from 100 Hz to 2000 Hz (0.1 KHz to 2.0 KHz). Amplitude is shown by the height and color at each frequency at each moment in time. The picture called "Choir Excerpt" shows the excerpt that the Beastie Boys extracted, as it originally appears in Newton's recording. Note that it has no less than seven(!) prominent frequency bands, each one changing amplitude at a different rate, including many harmonics of the main tone, some energy that's even lower than what he played (caused by different tones and/or turbulence), and additional low level energy distributed throughout the spectrum. The main point here is that there are seven distinct main regions of energy in the frequency range being analyzed, and that the regions evolve with a great deal of independence. This is the result of Mr. Newton's refined breath control for interpretive use of tone color. The independent prominences of the different component frequencies can be likened to 7-part counterpoint, demonstrating that the sound (notated rather simply in the score) is in fact way more complex than a normal single flute note.

Dobrian also included in his report a screen capture of his analyses that he called "One Flute Note," to serve as a point of comparison. It was intended to "show how simple the spectrum of a single focused normal flute note looks. It shows energy in a single frequency band (with a tiny bit of extra stuff at the beginning during the grace note)."[24] Wilson's complementary report similarly contended that, in the recording, Newton was "not simply using a technique that is common in contemporary musical practice, but rather creating a specific musical event in the composition *Choir* that reflect[ed] his specific artistic vision."[25]

In contrast, Ferrara contended that Newton's application of the multiphonic vocalization technique offered nothing distinct from any other avant-garde composition that called for the same technique. Furthermore, Ferrara noted that Newton's performance was "qualitatively different than what is scored"[26]; therefore, protection of Newton's composition could not extend to his recording of it as licensed to the Beastie Boys. He instead recommended that it should have been limited to content represented on sheet music. As Ferrara said of Dobrian's timbral analysis, "[t]hat entire analysis is irrelevant. The qualities and attributes of the 'sound' and 'performance' of the composition must be peeled away from the analysis, in view of the fact that the Beastie Boys licensed"[27] the recording. Dobrian's response was that Ferrara approached the score with "an erroneous idea of the role of notation . . . an extremely restrictive view of the interpretive qualities a performer—especially a composer/performer—may bring to notated music, and perhaps on an incomplete understanding of the practical technical details of the performance."[28] The core of the experts' disagreement was not only about matters of analytical technique and the medium of comparison, but the musical criteria by which each song should be compared. But despite this expert confrontation, the district court found in favor the defendants, and the Ninth Circuit eventually affirmed.[29] In addition to a review of these analyses, the opinion relied on other sampling cases decided in the same year,[30] and earlier cases with similar fact patterns,[31] to reason that the three-note sequence of the sample was not protected because it lacked originality.

The Ninth Circuit's reasoning, however, has proven pivotal to the legal decision-making process for sampling cases. Because "music sampling will often present cases where the degree of similarity is high,"[32] the court applied notions of fragmented literal similarity undoubtedly inspired by the decision in *Jarvis*:[33]

> fragmented literal similarity exists where the defendant copies a portion of the plaintiff's work exactly or nearly exactly, without appropriating the work's overall essence of structure. Because the degree of similarity is high in such cases, the dispositive question is whether the copying goes to trivial or substantial elements. Substantiality is measured by considering the qualitative and quantitative significance of the copied portion in relation to the plaintiff's work as a whole.

The *Newton* court then introduced a distinction between substantial use and use that is *de minimis*, meaning too minimal to constitute material infringement. This exception, by this time nearly a century old, had been initially introduced by stalwart Judge L. Hand to emphasize substantiality in federal copyright claims. As the *Newton* court explained, "use is *de minimis* only if the average audience would not recognize the appropriation."[34] Relying on established standards for evaluating similarity, the court determined that a sample would have to be recognizable enough according to a nonexpert standard for any similarity to result in an infringement finding.

Even beyond these legal precedents, differences between analytical techniques in the *Newton* lawsuit highlighted significant changes to forensic similarity analysis necessitated by allegations of unlawful sampling. For decades, expert witnesses had presented western notation-driven analytical dissections using various graphical means, but most commonly ones that separated musical elements using notation. With waveform analyses, musical elements were released from the confines of that notation, instead being presented as a totalizing representation of sonic data, including additional information such as timbre that would be otherwise left unwritten.

Many of the same legal and forensic musicological practices, increasingly reliant on audio-based comparisons, were applied in Second Circuit cases that overlapped with *Newton*. Two related copyright cases involved plaintiffs Ralph Vargas and Bland-Ricky Roberts, who sued defendants Brian Transeau and Pfizer, Inc., among others, regarding the use of rhythmic themes from their composition, "Bust Dat Groove Without Ride," in Transeau's composition, "Aparthenonia," and in a campaign for the arthritis drug, Celebrex.[35] The copyright registration for "Bust Dat Groove without Ride," from the album *Funky Drummer vol. II*, included a one-measure percussion pattern using high-hat cymbal, snare drum, and bass drum performed live by Roberts and then looped 27 times.[36] The plaintiffs contended that the combination of instrumentation and rhythmic pattern were sufficient to be unique and original, such that its similarity to a rhythmic phrase from Transeau's "Aparthenonia," and as it was recreated for use in a Celebrex commercial, constituted infringement. The plaintiffs therefore alleged that Transeau unlawfully sampled and manipulated "Bust Dat Groove Without Ride."[37]

Musical experts in both cases compared the original recorded versions of each song as well as a recreated version of "Apartheonia" associated with the commercial. During litigation, the defendants hired Richard Boulanger, a professor of music synthesis, to conduct waveform as well as spectral analyses, to compare "Bust Dat Groove" and "Aparthenonia" to identify whether the latter sampled from the former. Boulanger used these computer-driven audio appraisals to locate rhythmic congruence in the "drum strikes" between the recreated "Aparthenonia" and "Bust Dat Groove" recordings, finding none. As the court recounted from Boulanger's report, "the audio source material in Aparthenonia is unique and original and is not at all based on or copied or derived from [BDG]."[38] Anthony Ricigliano, who was also retained by the defendants, similarly conducted his comparisons based on waveform graphs of each recording produced on Pro Tools and transcriptions into western notation. Using these materials, Ricigliano identified a percussive groove track in "Bust Dat Groove," consisting of four individual tracks, the rhythms for which he classified as "so basic that [it] can be found in elementary drum set books dating back to the 1960's."[39] Offering a characterization of this musical content that evinced a common argument among defendants since the nineteenth century, Ricigliano declared, "therefore, the rhythm patterns in Bust Dat Groove do not, singly or in combination, contain any original rhythm patterns that rise to the level of protectable musical expression."[40]

Perhaps representing an unusual level of impartiality, conclusions reached by expert witnesses hired by the defendants were confirmed by the plaintiff's expert, Stephen Smith.[41] The plaintiffs also hired percussion expert Matthew Ritter, who produced both transcriptions and audio recordings as exhibits to demonstrate what he identified as a high level of similarity between the two songs. Ritter contended, however, that "Aparthenonia" contained digitally edited elements of "Bust Dat Groove without Ride."[42] Offering greater support of Ritter's claim, the plaintiffs' sound engineer and sampling expert, Ivan Rodriguez, likewise claimed that "Aparthenonia" was created by importing and manipulating drum beats from "Bust Dat Groove," to ensure that the sample was not identical.[43]

The expert witnesses agreed on neither method nor representation, however, leading to confrontations outlined in supplemental expert reports. For example, Ritter challenged Ricigliano's analysis for his use of "Xs" rather than traditional note-heads to indicate the drum patterns in his transcriptions of the rhythmic patterns. Ricigliano defended his notation decision by associating note-heads with definite pitch and distinguishing the instruments heard on the recordings, specifically the snare drum, as producing indefinite pitch.[44] Ritter also challenged Ricigliano's analysis regarding instrumentation, disagreeing about the identification of a separate tom-tom rhythm, which Ritter had alternatively classified as "ghost notes" associated with the snare drum line. By highlighting differences in expertise and analytical approaches, these disagreements externalized potential subjectivity in audio-based analyses that belied legal conceptions of forensic objectivity that seemed to surround it.

The court ultimately decided in favor of the defendants because the plaintiffs were unable to establish striking similarity, applying a heightened similarity standard introduced in *Tisi v. Patrick*. The opinion tacitly pointed toward expert witnesses that cast doubt on the similarity of the two songs, thereby demonstrating that the plaintiffs did not meet the striking similarity threshold and that the defendants' motion for summary judgment could be granted. Similar to *Newton*, notation- and audio-based analyses in the *Vargas* cases led to disagreements between experts, but the latter techniques also offered unparalleled insight into the relationship between the two songs in cases of sampling, which proved to be influential on court decisions.

COMBINING ANALYTICAL TECHNIQUES

In early twenty-first century infringement cases over sampling claims, audio-based analytical techniques were often presented against notation-based forms of musical analyses, creating evidentiary conflicts as much about the production of analysis as the interpretation of it for legal purposes. These new appraisals seemed to promise more precise points of comparison for musical material otherwise seemingly congruent according to notation-based, melocentric analytical techniques. Yet as sampling cases swept across the United States, some cases demonstrated how notation-based techniques could work harmoniously with audio-based techniques. They also signaled the importance that prior compositions and style analysis could have in contextualizing the nature of musical similarities.

The cataclysmic case of *Bridgeport Music, Inc. v. 11C Music* precipitated the presiding court to sever complaints into 476 separate lawsuits, many of which involved claims of unlicensed sampling that seemed to narrow the use of expert analyses altogether.[45] Overlapping with the *Vargas* lawsuits was one of these separated cases: *Bridgeport Music, Inc. v. Dimension Films*. This case analyzed the use of a two-second guitar sample from the beginning of George Clinton and Parliament-Funkadelic's funk anthem, "Get Off Your Ass and Jam," which members of Public Enemy later altered and looped to be used in N.W.A.'s uptempo rap song, "100 Miles and Runnin'," later used in the soundtrack to the film, *Hook Up*. Although the sample involved a three-note descending melodic figure, its repetition, location at the beginning of the Parliament-Funkadelic song, and prominence in the recording mix highlighted the importance of the figure to the identity of "Get Off Your Ass and Jam."[46] The plaintiff's expert, Alexander Stewart, relied on this analysis to contextualize the sample in "100 Miles and Runnin'" as intentionally intertextual, thereby drawing from the original value of "Get Off Your Ass and Jam."

The trial court applied a *de minimis* exception to the use of the sample, emphasizing the pitch quantity of the figure with less attention to its function in the song. On appeal to the Sixth Circuit, this decision was famously reversed, with the majority claiming that such an exception should never have been introduced. As a result of this decision, the Sixth Circuit panel established that sound recording owners had an exclusive right to sample the recordings they controlled, without evaluation according to a *de minimis* exception or substantial similarity. In short, as the court declared, "[g]et a license or do not sample."[47] Despite copious critiques from scholars across disciplines and multiple courts, the *Bridgeport v. Dimension Films* decision has not been overturned.

This landmark decision has served to raise the legal stakes for copyright holders and creators alike by pushing infringement via sampling toward something similar to a strict liability scheme, thereby countering legal characterizations of sampling as a *de minimis* exception. While this bright line rule might seem to challenge the contemporary legal relevance of expert analyses, their role has continued to be central to the infringement inquiry. Because samples are rarely borrowed without revision, even to simply align differences in tempo or to layer in a recorded mix, musical expert witnesses have remained necessary, not only to identify and contextualize similarities but also to locate the sample in a recording according to audio-based appraisals.

While differences in analytical information created by notation-based and audio-based techniques pitted experts against one another in previous sampling cases, they also have been used to achieve complimentary results for one party. In *Bridgeport Music, Inc. v. Justin Combs Publications*, for example, Bridgeport owned copyright to the song, "Singing in the Morning," by funk group, the Ohio Players, which they claimed was sampled in Notorious B.I.G.'s hip-hop track of his debut album, "Ready to Die," the rights to which were held by Justin Combs Publications. Although experts figured significantly in the litigation process, of particular note were the analyses presented by Alexander Stewart and Mark Rubel for the plaintiffs.[48]

Stewart's report combined his own transcriptions and notated comparisons of the implicated section in both songs with an auditory evaluation of the sound quality in the respective recordings to demonstrate that the passages were duplicated exactly: "In addition to the parameters of melody, rhythm, instrumentation, and harmony," which would have been represented by notation, "the passages match in rhythmic and intonational subtleties, timbre or tone color, and inflection."[49] Because of these likenesses, he "consider[ed] the possibility extremely remote that the producers of 'Ready to Die' assembled the exact same instrumentalists (guitar, winds, and vocalists), and managed to duplicate not only the transcribed parameters . . . timbres, inflections, and other details, but also the analog sound quality and studio ambiance of the recording."[50] Stewart contextualized this allegedly borrowed section of "Singing in the Morning" according to its originality and centrality to the song's structure, as well as the significance of its placement and repetition in "Ready to Die" as evidence of the significance of these similarities.[51]

The plaintiffs introduced Stewart's analysis alongside aural analysis produced by Mark Rubel. Using Audiodesk to compare small sections of each recording, Rubel isolated the six-second sample from "Singing In The Morning" and compared it to various sections in "Ready to Die" with perceptibly similar "syncopated horn patterns and vocal singing."[52] Even though Rubel did not include visual images of his waveform analyses for the court, he did include a CD of the audio inputted into Audiodesk with his report for factfinders to conduct their own aural comparisons. When Rubel compared a sample from 2:34–3:40 from "Singing in the Morning" to a passage beginning at 1:05 after the first hook in "Ready to Die," not only did pitch and rhythm align, but also the idiosyncratic tempo of the original and the alleged sample: "'Singing in the Morning' was recorded at a time when music was not usually played metronomically, so its tempo varies quite a lot. That makes it even more notable that the tempo readily matches the loop of 'Ready to Die.'"[53] Whereas matters of tempo in other cases were often relegated to secondary parameters, for digital sampling cases, minute similarities and dissimilarities in tempo locatable through digital audio analysis were revealing.

On appeal, the court's decision hinged on damage allocation, but expert witness contributions likely influenced the initial jury award to the plaintiffs.[54] The majority opinion in particular referenced Stewart's emphasis on context, that the "significance of the passage" must be considered beyond the "strictly mathematical" quantitative evaluation of the amount sampled from the original song when calculating damages.[55] Despite the court's focus on matters of legal procedure, this case nevertheless demonstrated that these two analytical techniques, although providing different information regarding forensic similarity to factfinders, could provide complimentary, and compelling, expert evidence.

SAMPLING AS FAIR USE AND THE
ROLE OF EXPERT WITNESSES

Although in some cases, the musical content sampled was considered so small that it was subject to the *de minimis* exception without further analysis, in other cases, the court conducted fair use analysis. Reliance on expert testimony to contextualize the significance of the sample to the song and to broader stylistic features continued. In yet another Bridgeport Music case, this time against UMG Recordings, Inc., the court evaluated whether Public Announcement's song, "D.O.G. in Me," which was released on their 1998 album, *All Work, No Play*, infringed on George Clinton and Parliament Funkadelic's song, "Atomic Dog." The sample involved the lyrics "bow wow wow, yippie yo, yippie yea" and repetition of the word "dog" as well as the sound of rhythmic panting.[56]

Similar to related *Bridgeport* cases, factfinders relied on expert testimony—Stewart on behalf of the plaintiffs and Ricigliano on behalf of the defendants—to understand the significance of "Atomic Dog" in funk communities as well as the prominence and recognizability of the sampled sections.[57] After trial, a jury verdict found in favor of the plaintiffs, that "D.O.G. in Me" infringed on Bridgeport's rights to "Atomic Dog." On appeal, the Sixth Circuit panel addressed UMG's argument that jurors should have been instructed to consider fair use as an affirmative defense, claiming that the samples were included as "homage" to "Atomic Dog."[58] After conducting similarity analysis and establishing that "D.O.G. in Me" was similar to "Atomic Dog," the court continued to consider fair use, applying the four factors to determine that the samples were not excusable according to fair use:[59]

"D.O.G. in Me" is certainly transformative (first factor), having a different theme, mood, and tone from "Atomic Dog." However, as an original musical composition, "Atomic Dog" is clearly within the core of copyright protection (second factor). Moreover, although the scope of use by "D.O.G. in Me" consisted of relatively small elements of the song, testimony at trial indicated that they were the most distinctive and recognizable elements of "Atomic

Dog" (third factor). Finally . . . [g]iven the fact that "Atomic Dog" is one of the most frequently sampled compositions of the Funk era, Bridgeport could lose substantial licensing revenues if it were deprived of its right to license content such as that used by UMG.

As a result, the Sixth Circuit affirmed the district court's opinion. Although expert witnesses did not appear to contribute any additional substantive information regarding similarity analysis, the stylistic context they provided regarding the structure of the sample and of the songs, as well as the relevance of the sample to funk communities, proved pivotal, specifically in this case to balancing the first, third, and fourth fair use factors.

CURRENT CIRCUIT SPLIT

While sampling cases have been heard in other appellate jurisdictions, their decisions have often hinged either on other areas of music copyright,[60] or simply applied existing tests for substantial similarity.[61] In conjunction with discrepancies between the Sixth and Ninth Circuits' approaches to copyright, appellate circuits are divided as to the best approach to evaluating sampling infringement claims. In particular, the 2016 case of *VMG Salsoul, LLC v. Ciccone* brought about a significant jurisprudential challenge to the *Bridgeport* decision's severe consequence for unlicensed sampling and *de minimis* exceptions.

In *VMG Salsoul*, Plaintiff VMG Salsoul alleged that Madonna Ciccone and her producer, Shep Pettibone, sampled a segment of their song, "Ooh I Love It (Love Break)," featuring a horn blast, in both the radio edit and the compilation version of her song, "Vogue."[62] Both artists worked with Pettibone on these projects, although creation occurred a decade apart from one another. The origins of the horn part were traced to "Chicago Bus Stop (Ooh, I Love It)," a song written and produced in 1975 by Vincent Montana, Jr. to be recorded by the Salsoul Orchestra. Approximately seven years later, in 1982, Pettibone sought permission to use "Chicago Bus Stop" as inspiration for a remix that would become "Love Break." In creating "Vogue," Pettibone and programmer Alan Friedman claimed to have generated a horn hit sound using a proteus emulator with prerecorded, factory-installed, live sounds, an Akai S1000 processor to integrate individual synthetic instrumental sounds, alongside other studio techniques. The plaintiffs alleged that these horn hits in "Vogue" were sampled from an instrumental version of "Love Break."

Both parties' arguments relied on contributions from expert witnesses regarding similarity. Following traditions of expert testimony, the plaintiff's expert witness, Alexander Stewart, transcribed the relevant sections of both songs, consisting of one chord or "horn hit" that appeared in single or doubled patterns, and then aligned the notation for the court. He also identified the presence of single- and double-horn hits from "Love Break" in two places in "Vogue," noting that although the musical content was quantitatively small, amounting to four pitches each, the call and response formal function of the horn hit remained the same in "Vogue." In response, the defendants' expert witness, Gage Averill, recast the horn hit as a percussive stylistic feature common not only to the Salsoul Orchestra but also to other popular music artists, such as James Brown.

The district court initially found the horn hits to be unoriginal for the composition and the sound recording, and thus not on their own protected by federal copyright. Even if the horn hits were protectable, the court continued to explain in its opinion, according to an "ordinary observer" standard, the segment was so small that any copying would be *de minimis.*[63] Addressing Stewart's analysis in detail, the court found the horn hit not only excluded from the sheet music for "Vogue" but also that the musical content of the hit was quantitatively insignificant, consisting of four notes, and it characterized the call and response function of the hits as an unprotectable musical idea. On appeal, the Ninth Circuit affirmed the decision in favor of the defendants, explicitly setting their jurisdiction apart from the Sixth Circuit: "We recognize that the Sixth Circuit held to the contrary in *Bridgeport Music, Inc. v. Dimension Films* . . . like the leading copyright treatise and several district courts—we find Bridgeport's reasoning unpersuasive."[64] Finding that a *de minimis* exception applied, the panel established that courts should account for the size and nature of implicated samples and conduct substantial similarity analysis.

The circuit split after *Salsoul* not only reopened conversations regarding the function of samples in music, but it also reinforced the relevance of expert analyses of those samples. While the Sixth Circuit rule might seem to have contributed to a practical elimination of expert analysis, except perhaps to identify a sample and qualify its value to the composition as a whole, *Salsoul* reinforced the need to evaluate both the content of the sample and its context in the implicated musical works to determine whether a *de minimis* exception applies or to move forward with similarity analysis. Thus, even in cases where musical congruence is nearly guaranteed, musical expertise is still necessary to contextualize it based on musical factors beyond melody, harmony, rhythm, and form.

MUSIC COPYRIGHT AND DIGITAL SAMPLING

Despite the Sixth Circuit's strict rule seeming to reduce need for musical expertise, its recent circuit split with the Ninth Circuit and the nature of digital sampling infringement claims appear instead to reinforce the necessity of experts. These cases have also adjusted not only the nature of expert witness contributions but also notions of expertise itself. No longer simply a matter of industry experience or academic musicological credentials, expertise has also come to include the professional and academic experience of audio specialists. While contributing to existing legal procedures for similarity inquiries, audio specialists introduce new analytical techniques designed to identify minute sonic features not typically designated through western notation. Due to the nature of sampling claims, audio-based analytical techniques recast musical similarity by introducing matters previously dismissed, such as tempo, key, and instrumentation, as well as sonic elements not easily notated but perceptible on record, such as timbre, texture, vocal or instrumental technique, and studio production. In so doing, experts might identify similarity and distinguish between the presence of a sample or mere replication. They can also comment on the function of a sample within a typically multilayered sound recording as well as the relevance of the sampled section and entire song to a particular style history.

As a result, the role of musical expertise in digital sampling cases has expanded according to new mediums of musical evidence and analysis. Alongside notation-based analyses typically produced by academically credentialed musicologists and theorists, audio-based analyses produced by audio specialists might seem to offer more precise, or scientifically objective, representations of music for the court. Yet cases across appellate circuits have demonstrated that samples rarely appear unaltered in latter compositions, and it is often difficult to prove their incontrovertible presence using these seemingly "scientific" means. Expert witnesses that present notation-based analyses can meanwhile continue to serve an important function by interpreting and contextualizing this data in terms of theoretical analysis and musical style. This diversification of expertise has proven to be complementary in cases, offering more detailed evidence of musical similarity where melodic, rhythmic, or harmonic congruence are nearly guaranteed.

More than instances of small or legally inconsequential copying, cases involving digital sampling have presented a novel and significant legal problem to previous copyright holders and new creators. Relying to varying extents on decades-old systems for evaluating and classifying similarity according to musical congruence and notation-based analytical techniques, courts were initially ill-prepared to assess new forms of musical production at least partially dependent on similarity for layers of intertextual meaning. Their solutions to date, including applications of similarity analysis as well as *de minimis* and fair use exceptions, have only marginally bridged these gaps. Yet even in light of mounting jurisprudence, courts have continued to rely on the contributions of musical expert witnesses to contextualize musical structures and styles, clarifying new boundaries between musical works.

NOTES

1. *Digital Millennium Copyright Act*, 112 Stat. 2860 (1998).

2. *Digital Performance Right in Sound Recordings Act*, 109 Stat. 336 (1995).

3. Justin A. Williams, *Rhymin' and Stealin': Musical Borrowing in Hip Hop* (Ann Arbor, MI: University of Michigan Press, 2014), 1.

4. The legal maxim *"de minimis non curat lex"* serves to establish that "the law does not concern itself with trifles," or seemingly small, inconsequential matters. See *West Pub. Co. v. Edward Thompson Co.*, 169 F. 833, 861 (E.D.N.Y. 1909) ("Even where there is some copying, that fact is not conclusive of infringement. Some copying is permitted. In addition to copying, it must be shown that this has been done to an unfair extent").

5. See, for example, David Moser, *Music Copyright for the New Millennium* (Artistpro, 2001), 62.

6. *Grand Upright Music, Ltd. v. Warner Bros. Records, Inc.*, 780 F. Supp. 182 (S.D.N.Y. 1991).

7. *Grand Upright*, F. Supp. at 184.

8. *Grand Upright*, F. Supp. at 184–85.

9. *Jarvis v. A & M Records*, 827 F.2d 282 (D.N.J. 1993).

10. The opinion uses both "The Music's Got Me" and "The Music Got Me" as the title of Jarvis's song. See, for example, *Jarvis*, 827 F.2d at 286, 293–94.

11. *Jarvis*, 827 F.2d at 282.

12. *Jarvis*, 827 F.2d at 281 (citing M. Nimmer & D. Nimmer, *Nimmer on Copyright* § 12.03[A][2]).

13. Stewart, "Been Caught Stealing," 342.

14. See also Jordan S. Gruber, Fausto Tito Poza, and Anthony J. Pellicano, "Audio Recordings: Evidence, Experts and Technology," *American Jurisprudence Trials* 48 (2013): 1–586.

15. Stewart, "Been Caught Stealing," 347.

16. See Jamie Lund, "An Empirical Examination of the Lay Listener Test in Music Composition Copyright Infringement," *Virginia Sports and Entertainment Law Journal* 11 (Fall 2011): 137–77.

17. *Newton v. Diamond*, 204 F. Supp.2d 1244, 1246 (C.D. Cal. 2002). See also Kembrew McLeod and Peter DiCola, *Creative License: The Law and Culture of Digital Sampling* (Durham, NC: Duke University, 2011), 136–38.

18. *Newton*, 204 F. Supp.2d at 1246.

19. *Newton*, 204 F. Supp.2d at 1246–49.

20. *Newton v. Diamond*, Dorian Report, 1; Wilson Report, 20–21; Ferrara Report, 7–8, *James Newton v. Michael Diamond*, Accession 021-06-10001 FRC 10031831 Box 11, San Bernardino, CA (both cited in 204 F. Supp.2d at 1250).

21. *Newton v. Diamond*, Dobrian Report, 6.

22. *Newton v. Diamond*, Dobrian Report, 7.

23. *Newton v. Diamond*, Dobrian Report, 7.

24. *Newton v. Diamond*, Dobrian Report, 8.

25. *Newton v. Diamond*, Wilson Report, 21; see also *Newton*, 204 F. Supp.2d at 1256.

26. *Newton v. Diamond*, Ferrara Report, 1–2.

27. *Newton v. Diamond*, Ferrara Report, 1–2.

28. *Newton v. Diamond*, Dobrian Report, 1.

29. See *Newton v. Diamond*, 349 F.3d 591 (9th Cir. 2003).

30. See *Jean v. Bug Music, Inc.*, 2002 WL 287786 (S.D.N.Y. 2002).

31. *McDonald v. Multimedia Entmt, Inc.*, 20 U.S.P.Q.2d 1372 (S.D.N.Y. 1991).

32. *Newton*, 388 F.3d at 1195.

33. *Newton v. Diamond*, 388 F.3d 1189, 1195 (9th Cir. 2003) (citations omitted).

34. *Newton*, F.3d at 1193.

35. *Vargas v. Pfizer, Inc.*, 418 F. Supp.2d 369, 370 (S.D.N.Y. 2005) [hereinafter *Pfizer*].

36. *Pfizer*, 418 F. Supp.2d at 370; *Vargas v. Transeau*, 514 F. Supp.2d 439, 441 (S.D.N.Y. 2007) [hereinafter *Transeau*].

37. *Transeau*, 514 F. Supp.2d at 439, 441–42.

38. *Transeau*, 514 F. Supp.2d at 444 (citing Boulanger Report, 61).

39. *Vargas v. Pfizer*, Ricigiliano Declaration, 1.

40. *Vargas v. Pfizer*, Ricigiliano Declaration, 1.

41. *Transeau*, 514 F. Supp.2d at 444.

42. *Transeau*, 514 F Supp.2d at 444–45.

43. See *Transeau*, 514 F. Supp.2d at 445.

44. *Vargas v. Pfizer*, Ricigliano Supplemental Declaration, 2 (referencing Ritter Declaration, 24–25).

45. *Bridgeport v. 11C Music*, 202 F.R.D. 229 (M.D. Tenn. 2001).

46. *Bridgeport Music, Inc. v. Dimension Films*, Stewart Declaration, 5–7.

47. *Bridgeport Music, Inc. v. Dimension Films*, 410 F.3d 792, 801 (6th Cir. 2005).

48. *Bridgeport Music, Inc. v. Justin Combs Pub.*, 507 F.3d 470 (6th Cir. 2007). The opinion notes that at trial, Plaintiff's counsel "implied that defendants' expert [Dr. Ferrara] was 'a fancy guy from New York.'" 507 F.3d at 479.

49. *Bridgeport v. Combs*, Stewart Report, 4.

50. *Bridgeport v. Combs*, Stewart Report, 4.

51. *Bridgeport v. Combs*, Stewart Report, 4–5.

52. *Bridgeport v. Combs*, Rubel Report, 3.

53. *Bridgeport v. Combs*, Rubel Report, 3.

54. See *Bridgeport Music, Inc. v. Justin Combs Pub.*, 507 F.3d 470 (6th Cir. 2007).

55. *Bridgeport v. Combs*, 507 F.3d 470, 484 (6th Cir. 2007).

56. *Bridgeport Music, Inc. v. UMG Recordings, Inc.*, 585 F.3d 267, 267 (6th Cir. 2009) [hereinafter *UMG*].

57. *UMG*, 585 F.3d at 273.

58. *UMG*, 585 F.3d at 278.

59. *UMG*, 585 F.3d at 278.

60. See, for example, *Sarregama India v. Mosley*, 635 F. 3d 1284 (11th Cir. 2011).

61. See, for example, *TufAmerica, Inc. v. Warner Bros. Music Corp.*, 67 F. Supp. 3d 590 (S.D.N.Y. 2014).

62. *VMG Salsoul, LLC v. Ciccone*, 824 F.3d 871, 875–76 (9th Cir. 2016).

63. *VMG Salsoul*, 824 F.3d at 874.

64. *VMG Salsoul*, 824 F.3d at 874 (citation omitted).

Chapter 6

New Standards of Musical Expertise

The rise of digital sampling cases in the 1990s and continuing into the twenty-first century revealed deepening fractures in aging legal decision-making processes for copyright infringement. But even lawsuits heard at this time that did not involve sampling depicted courts grappling with subjectivities in assessments of similarity and inconsistent outcomes across cases and jurisdictions. Judges and attorneys in some of these cases have appeared to adapt to these fundamental legal problems by redefining standards of expertise, both in the infringement decision-making process as well as the qualifications and contributions of expert witnesses.

Some courts have sought solutions that refine existing legal procedures by introducing heightened standards for factfinders evaluating similarity according to matters of audience. Short of introducing new kinds of expert testimony, these decisions have blurred historic divisions between experts and nonexperts, codified in *Arnstein* and reified in *Krofft*, by revising the hypothetical ordinary listener standard to emphasize presumably shared musical knowledge among the audience of the works at issue in each case. In so doing, these courts have expanded what had been a binary opposition according to judicial perceptions of musical skill into a spectrum of legally recognized listener acuity. Although these standards have not changed the prescribed legal role of expert witnesses, they may impact the practicalities of expert contributions and the information factfinders must consider when distinguishing between stylistic commonality and copying.

Concurrently evolving legal standards for expert witness qualification in the late twentieth century appear to have coincided with strategic emphasis in music copyright cases placed on experts' academic credentials and their methodologies to mitigate ongoing concerns about evidentiary precision and objectivity. In light of these changes to federal evidence law and circuit splits about decision-making processes, legal practitioners appear to be adjusting their litigation strategies. Relying on deep historical roots traceable to the nineteenth century, recent attorneys and witnesses have both propelled forensic musicology as an emergent area of expertise specific to music copyright, with a growing number of expert witnesses claiming a combination of academic credentials in musicology coupled with forensic experience. While this subject matter remains largely untheorized, attorneys and witnesses have invoked notions of a standard procedure for forensic similarity analysis in pretrial pleadings and reports that seems to insinuate credibility and consistency across expert witnesses and their contributions.

These recent innovations demonstrate courts and attorneys alike appealing to expertise for at least a partial solution to fundamental issues in music copyright and perennial questions of how, and by whom, similarity should be assessed. Heightened legal listener standards and coalescing conceptions of forensic musicology both promise greater acuity in evaluations of musical similarity. Although the far-reaching impact of these new standards has yet to be determined, they serve to reinforce the essential, and evolving, role of musical expertise in federal copyright litigation.

HEIGHTENED LISTENER STANDARDS

By the late twentieth century, each circuit had settled on its own process for separating similarity from infringement, creating what has been recognized as an incoherent plurality of concurrent tests that have created inconsistencies between circuits and have done little to reduce inconsistencies across case outcomes. Although most tests can be traced to *Arnstein* in some way, each circuit has its own refinements that diversified the field of copyright law and slightly altered the role of experts. The First, Second, Third, Fifth, Sixth, and Seventh circuits have adopted *Arnstein* in its original formulation or in some variant; the Ninth Circuit has retained the *Krofft* test with refinements, which was also adopted by the Eighth Circuit. Other jurisdictions, however, began to refine the *Arnstein* test in ways that, like *Krofft*, effectively introduced new tests for similarity. In most circuits, these new tests focused attention either on managing nonexpert jurors or on the content evaluated in similarity analysis and the process by which it was evaluated, with implications for expert contributions.

The Tenth Circuit, for example, adopted the "Abstraction-Filtration-Comparison" test. Drawing inspiration from the Second Circuit's development of a separate test to evaluate similarity in copyright cases over computer software that accounted for its idiosyncratic and highly specialized creative process,[1] the Tenth Circuit applied that test to all categories of expressive works, including music.[2] Under this new decision-making process, a court would still divide copying, based on access and similarity, from improper appropriation, and would approach copying according to an "inverse ratio rule." The court would follow a new process that brought determinations of infringement back to being a question of law:[3]

> At the abstraction step, we separate the ideas (and basic utilitarian functions), which are not protectable, from the particular expression of the work. . . . Then, we filter out the nonprotectable components of the product from the original expression. Finally, we compare the remaining protected elements to the allegedly copied work to determine if the two works are substantially similar [*sic*].

This convoluted test was applied to music in *McRae v. Smith*, a case that involved singer-songwriter Maree McRae suing to protect her rights in the country love song, "Every Minute, Every Hour, Every Day," which was allegedly infringed by Gerald Smith and Wayne Perry's similarly styled "Every Second."[4] Here, the new legal test filtered out stylistic idioms common to country music, such as the "two-step" rhythm and meter, lyrical themes of first-person love, harmonic progressions, and verse-chorus formal structure as not copyright protectable.[5] What protectable musical elements remained could then be compared. For the *McRae* case, the comparisons that the plaintiffs produced did not follow the legal process of analysis and failed to rebut dissimilarities that the defendants identified, which resulted in the court granting their motion for summary judgment.

The Tenth Circuit's adoption of the Abstraction-Filtration test seemed to promote legal reliance on expert witnesses, both reinforcing their role in the decision-making process and clarifying the nature of their contributions. The filtration step in particular seemed to invite reductive analyses that embraced comparisons of structural melody, harmony, rhythm, and form, while offering a more definitive legal mechanism to coping with matters of stylistic commonality. But the process still relied on historic divisions between music experts and nonexperts, with final legal decisions regarding infringement left to nonexperts.

NEW STANDARD: "INTENDED AUDIENCE"

While the Tenth Circuit applied a different test that honed analyses of similarity, other jurisdictions retained existing legal tests and instead revised the standard by which factfinders would assess similarity.[6] In the Fourth Circuit, for example, the court introduced an "intended audience" standard that served to narrow the hypothetical pool of ordinary nonexpert listeners, such that similarity would be evaluated by listeners with greater acuity and contextual knowledge of musical style and tradition specific to the songs at issue. In so doing, the court seemed to respond to issues with the ordinary listener standard without completely overturning a decades-old decision-making process.

In the landmark 1990 case of *Dawson v. Hinshaw Music*, plaintiff composer-conductor William L. Dawson alleged that his unaccompanied choral arrangement of the spiritual, "Ezekiel Saw De Wheel," was infringed by an arrangement of the same piece created by Gilbert Martin. Although the song was originally copyrighted in 1940 by John W. Work in a collection of spirituals, folk songs, and hymns, Dawson registered his arrangement in 1942, and sold thousands of copies of it until Kjos assumed control in 1967 as Dawson's exclusive agent. In 1980, Gilbert Martin composed an arrangement of the same spiritual and granted Hinshaw Music, Inc. control over it. The corporation then registered the arrangement for copyright in 1981. Before filing suit in 1986, Dawson contacted Hinshaw to inform them of potential infringement over his arrangement.[7] The nature of the lawsuit as revolving around two competing arrangements of the same song, which would inevitably be perceptibly similar, called for careful musical and legal attention to subtler points of comparison not necessarily distinguishable to all ears.

At the bench trial, where the judge served as factfinder in place of a jury, five musical expert witnesses were retained, including Robert Campbell and Herndon Spillman for the plaintiff, and Alice Parker, Wilton Mason, and Joel Carter for the defendant. Presiding Judge Ward claimed on the first day of trial that he would rely on these experts, stating:[8]

> I am not a musician. I was exposed to it a couple of years when I was a teenager. I appreciate good music. I appreciate music whether it's good or bad, for the most part. But this is a very technical thing and I am going to rely on experts with reference to the substantial similarity test. Also I think I have enough experience to not depend on expert testimony when they go beyond their field of expertise.

Despite this statement, and in light of evidence that Martin had access to Dawson's arrangement and the testimony of experts indicating copying-in-fact, Judge Ward decided in favor of Hinshaw. His seemingly peculiar decision turned on Dawson's failure to enter into evidence recordings of the competing arrangements in court—a presentation of the music in a way that the judge believed would be perceived better by nonexpert, ordinary listeners.

On appeal, the Fourth Circuit court remanded the decision, noting that the relevant point of comparison was sheet music, not recorded performance. More importantly, it observed that "courts have been slow to recognize explicitly the need for refining the ordinary observer test in such a way that it would adopt the perspective of *the intended audience*."[9] Although the court recognized that for certain popular songs, evaluations from the general public, presumed to be comprised of ordinary listeners, might be most appropriate, other cases required a different standard. Finding fault with the existing standard, the court noted that "[o]nly a reckless indifference to common sense would lead a court to embrace a doctrine that requires a copyright case to turn on the opinion of someone who is ignorant of the relevant differences and similarities between two works."[10] Instead, the court established that "where the intended audience is significantly more specialized than the pool of lay listeners, the reaction of the intended audience would be the relevant inquiry."[11] Thus, for instances where an audience was presumed by the court to have specialized knowledge, a narrower standard based on revised conceptions of musical skill arguably offered a more accurate representation of the market audience. This new model relied on scholarly commentary on copyright that "'[i]f the works in issue are directed to a particular audience, then the "spontaneous and immediate" reaction of that audience is determinative.'"[12] While the *Dawson* court offered no definition for audience or specialized musical knowledge, or even what constitutes a reaction from them, it did identify that an intended audience could often be the general public. In the present lawsuit, however, the audience was comprised of a narrower pool of choral directors. This intended audience was legally determined to be focused more closely on sheet music than recorded performance, so the trial court's decision needed to be revisited.

Although the Fourth Circuit seemed to overlook that choral directors might easily be admitted as musical experts—who could then be qualified to conduct both prongs of similarity analysis—and that its evidentiary distinction between sheet music and recording excluded devoted audience members that would only listen to live or recorded performances from the arrangements, the court did introduce the idea that similarity might be analyzed differently by various groups of nonexpert witness listeners. It attached legal significance to matters such as repertory and style as well as practices of composition and arrangement in dispositive analyses of similarity. Thus, a subtle difference in harmonic voicing or phrasing that might be perceptibly similar in the totalizing comparisons of an ordinary listener might present a distinguishable difference to the overall effect for an intended audience member. Although these issues proved to be more broadly applicable, the inherent similarities between competing arrangements in *Dawson* undoubtedly shed new light on matters of audience and listener acuity.

The legal construction of an intended audience posed new questions about the appropriate standard for nonexpert evaluations of similarity. While an intended audience might bring about more precise results, its make-up would be different across cases, thereby thwarting attempts at consistency. Not only would determining an intended audience prove difficult, but that listener pool could also be separate from an "actual" audience in ways that a composer, publisher, or even a court, could not anticipate. The introduction of this new standard, while retaining the presence of expert witnesses and *Arnstein's* divided similarity analysis, nevertheless altered what was previously considered a binary opposition between experts and nonexperts by generating a spectrum of expertise that empowered at least some listeners according to implicit criteria, such as market participation or musical training. This new standard allowed the court to retain musical expert witnesses, as well as constraints on their analyses to the first prong, and to preserve the holistic comparisons made by nonexperts, while seeming to reduce problems caused by seemingly ill-equipped "ordinary" nonexperts.

NEW STANDARD: "DISCERNING OBSERVER"

Although not yet pristine, the more recent "intended audience" standard has proven to be influential on contemporary infringement cases involving music as well as other copyrightable media in and beyond the Fourth Circuit.[13] Jurisprudential movement away from the ordinary listener standard identified by other courts as "inherently subjective" and "out-of-date," seems to recognize not only musical knowledge held among individuals otherwise categorized as nonexperts but also to acknowledge a greater diversity of musical skills among this large, legally categorized group. These contemporary cases continue to revise the decades-old model established in *Arnstein*, but they still retain a bifurcated approach to similarity analysis.

Two cases decided in 2015 in the Southern District of New York— *McDonald v. West* and *Lane v. Knowles-Carter*—offer contemporary examples of the incorporation of such a revised standard. In both cases, the presiding court applied a similar "discerning observer" standard, introduced in an earlier copyright case involving quilt squares.[14] In these cases, it was recordings, rather than notated sheet music, that served as tangible representations of the songs at issue and provided central points of comparison for the courts. This distinction, and any perceptual discrepancies among experts or nonexperts that may have resulted from comparing recordings as opposed to sheet music, was legally less relevant to the decision-making process than elevating the standard of musical skill required for nonexpert comparison.

McDonald v. West hinged on a procedural argument indicating that local musician-plaintiff Joel R. "Joel Mac" McDonald's claim to his groove-driven R&B song, "Made in America," was infringed by a song of the same name on R&B-hip-hop performers Kanye West and Jay-Z's album, *Watch the Throne*. The court engaged in substantial similarity analysis, with emphasis on shared similar lyrical themes, including references to influential Black American activists Martin Luther King, Jr. and Malcom X and alliterated with the word "made" in the hook, and shared stylistic elements with few melodic or rhythmic congruences. The case was resolved for the defendants, with the court finding that the plaintiff had failed to state a claim for which legal relief could be granted—a decision that was affirmed by the Second Circuit.[15] Similarly, in *Lane v. Knowles-Carter*, plaintiff Ahmad Javon Lane sued R&B star Beyoncé over the use of "X&O" as shorthand for "kisses and hugs" in the title and lyrical content of her song—copying Lane's "XOXO" in her own "XO" off her self-titled album—as well as similarities in the beginnings of the two songs.[16] Both cases were resolved, perhaps unsurprisingly, in favor of the defendants, but it is the method for approaching the legal evaluation of musical similarity that is significant to understand judicial conceptions of expertise.

In some ways more specific than the intended audience standard, the "discerning observer" standard these cases applied requires a higher level of awareness and understanding among nonexperts to permit their discernment between relevant points of comparison and stylistic commonality. This test calls for nonexperts to separate protected and unprotected elements before making holistic comparisons of the protected elements with regard to putative infringement. As the court explained in *McDonald*:[17]

> When a plaintiff alleges infringement of a copyrighted work that incorporates significant elements from the public domain, however, the "ordinary observer" test must become "more discerning.". . . [A] court applying the "more discerning observer" test may not simply "dissect the works at issue into separate components and compare only the copyrightable elements." This would narrow copyright too much, and render protection for the selection and arrangement of public domain elements a dead letter. When applying the "more discerning observer" test, the Court must make sure to engage in a holistic comparison of the two works, looking for substantial similarity that is apparent "only when numerous aesthetic decisions embodied in the plaintiff's work of art—the excerpting, modifying, and arranging of [unprotectible components] . . .—are considered in relation to one another."

According to the new test, a court must consider the source of similarity when examining works comprised of both protectable and nonprotectable material, which would be typical of many popular music styles. Although the dispositive, totalizing evaluation made by nonexperts remains intact, this elevated legal standard requires a higher level of awareness and understanding of matters including style, genre, and tradition to permit the discernment between protected and unprotected musical elements when evaluating improper appropriation.

Despite the introduction of alternative standards, the ordinary listener standard, with deep roots in early-twentieth-century copyright cases and judicial conceptions of musical skill, continues to influence forensic similarity analysis across circuits. The notion that members of a public listening audience lack musical training but constitute the majority of a commercial music market paralleled arguments for a contemporaneous music appreciation movement and notions that music requires the cultivation of listening skill to understand. When considered in conjunction with a legal tradition in and beyond copyright law of consulting expert witnesses and underlying copyright policy based on creators' economic control over their works, these ideas contributed to the development of a redundant legal process that relied on holistice valuations of similarity by "lay," "average," or "ordinary" listeners expressly because of their perceived lack of musical expertise coupled with their purchasing power.

Since the late-twentieth century, courts have begun to reinterpret musical expertise to reflect a diversity of listening skill and acuity among nonexpert listeners. Whether an "intended audience" or a "discerning observer" is introduced, these legal standards have begun to reimagine the "ordinary" listener in ways that acknowledge musical skills possessed by nonexpert listeners as a kind of expertise relevant to legal inquiries still separate from that of an expert witness. While courts have not established definitive contours for these hypothetical, specialized, but still nonexpert, listeners, they appear to have recognized a spectrum of listening skill and knowledge that influences comparisons of allegedly similar musical works.

The continued application of these heightened standards promises to reveal any practical impact on expert testimony. Neither the "intended audience" standard, nor the "discerning observer" standard, narrow, or even eliminate, the contributions of expert witnesses to determinations of copying. These standards might impact the practicalities of expert testimony, however, as future courts may require additional contextual evidence to establish the shared musical knowledge among the relevant audience and theoretical explanations about that knowledge as it pertains to the music at issue in each case.

NEW CASES, SAME STANDARDS

Questions regarding the nature and relevance of musical expertise have not always resulted in new standards. A lawsuit over Lady Gaga's song, "Judas," in *Francescatti v. Germanotta*, provides an illustrative example.[18] In this case, Chicago-based singer-songwriter plaintiff Rebecca Francescatti, a Chicago-based musician, alleged that her song, "Juda," was infringed by defendant Stefani Germanotta, known professionally as Lady Gaga, in her song "Judas," a single from her hit synthpop album, *Born This Way.* Francescatti wrote "Juda" in 1998 and registered a version of the song with guitar and vocals the following year, in 1999. In 2005, Francescatti registered a new recording that included drums, bass, strings, background vocals, sound mapping, and self-made samples. To create the new recording, Francescatti had enlisted help from defendant-musician Brian Gaynor. Five years later, in 2010, Gaynor became creatively involved with members of Lady Gaga's creative team, including Paul Blair, who collaborated with Gaga on content for *Born This Way.*[19]

Both parties hired expert witnesses, notably including Yasser Shehab and Dale Cockrell for the plaintiff and Lawrence Ferrara for the defendant. All three experts relied on their own transcriptions of the songs to conduct comparisons as to melody, harmony, rhythm, formal structure, and lyrical content. The pretrial litigation process, however, involved seemingly partial attacks on expert methodologies, specifically the classification of intervals according to numerals and qualitative labeling as "large" or "small." The plaintiff introduced an argument that Ferrara's transcription and analysis were "outdated" because they relied on notation-based, rather than computer-driven, audio-based appraisals more typically applied in cases that involved sampling. They went on to challenge Ferrara's comparisons to prior copyrighted songs "that may be known by baby boomers . . . as if they are relevant to understanding computer audio music files that have been compiled into a sound recording."[20] Although their argument was presented undoubtedly to undermine Ferrara's credibility as a seasoned expert witness and his references to prior compositions, it still reinforced critical differences between methods applied to similarity analyses.

In addition to dismissing the plaintiff's argument regarding methodology, the defendants took a different, yet equally as challenging, approach to the role of expert analysis. They called for application of the Seventh Circuit's interpretation of the *Arnstein* standard in *Atari, Inc. v. North American Philips Consumer Electronic Corp.*, which emphasized the second prong of substantial similarity analysis reliant on ordinary listeners, over the first prong, which involved expert witnesses.[21] Based on *Atari*, the expert contributions should become less relevant to the outcome of the case than those of an ordinary listener, even at the expense of the defendant's own expert contributions.[22] The plaintiffs responded that expert analyses were not only important to the infringement decision-making process, but that they were essential in this particular case, which involved "[c]omputer generated EDM [electronic dance music that] requires computer analysis,"[23] as opposed to what they characterized as "side by side comparisons"[24] of music featured in other cases. Thus, expert testimony was essential, but only if it applied computer-driven, and presumably audio-based, analytical techniques.

Disagreement over the legal application of expert testimony drew attention to the adversarial system in which expert analyses are introduced alongside enduring questions about the role of expert testimony in evaluations of similarity. The court opinion outlined a detailed discourse of the relevant standards and approaches to substantial similarity and their use in music copyright cases. Rather than introduce a new standard or revised test, the court applied an "extrinsic–intrinsic" analysis, following *Krofft* and *Swirsky*, while declining to "filter out" unprotectable elements. After determining that expert testimony would be informative as to putative musical similarities, the court also rejected the plaintiff's attempt at distinguishing an essentially electronic compositional process for the songs at issue from any other process. "[T]he legal standard does not change with the musical genre; electronically-created music 'still consists of melody, harmony, rhythm and lyrics, even if created electronically.'"[25] For the second prong, the court reviewed new standards of expertise presented in earlier cases, but it ultimately followed the precedential ordinary observer standard because it determined that listeners of both songs would have no specialized musical expertise. Because the court determined a lack of substantial similarity, the defendant's motion for summary judgment was ultimately granted.

Despite the introduction of new listener standards in some circuits, they continue to be limited in their application based on jurisdiction and subjective criteria applied at the judge's discretion in each case. The *Lady Gaga* case in particular highlights a contemporary circuit split surrounding heightened listener standards, with some courts reticent to introduce new precedents in the evaluation of similarity. Recent cases nevertheless have signaled shifting legal perceptions of listener acuity away from century-old conceptions of musical knowledge associated with western art music and notation-based analyses toward a recognition of the proliferation of musical styles, information, and analyses across the United States. These heightened standards of expertise thus present new approaches to mitigating the specialized, *ad hoc* nature of music copyright infringement lawsuits with the goal of more accurate evaluations of similarity according to musical skill and listener acuity.

REVISIONS TO EVIDENCE LAW AND THE CERTIFICATION OF EXPERTS

The introduction of new listener standards for factfinders in music copyright occurred alongside concurrent revisions in other areas of federal law, with significant implications for the qualification and function of expert witnesses. The enactment of the FRE in 1975 loomed over the application of expert testimony, as courts struggled to reconcile the decades-old *Frye* test and the new codes introduced by Congress. In 1993, the Supreme Court offered a solution in *Daubert v. Merrell Dow Pharmaceuticals, Inc.*[26] The unanimous decision galvanized the application of the FRE for the admission of scientific expert testimony. In addition to urging judges to conduct preliminary inquiries into the extent of expertise of a witness and the methods they used to arrive at their testimony, the Supreme Court introduced four factors courts should consider regarding the reliability of evidence introduced by experts:[27]

> faced with a proffer of expert scientific testimony, then, the trial judge must determine at the outset . . . whether the expert is proposing to testify to (1) scientific knowledge that (2) will assist the trier of fact to understand or determine a fact at issue. This entails a preliminary assessment of whether the reasoning or methodology underlying the testimony is scientifically valid and of whether that reasoning or methodology properly can be applied to the facts in issue . . . . Many factors will bear on the inquiry, and we do not presume to set out a definitive checklist or test. But some general observations are appropriate.

The checklist included four "considerations," or factors, that the Court believed would be "[o]rdinarily" relevant, including (1) whether the expert's theory or technique could and had been tested; (2) whether the theory or technique had been subject to peer review; (3) whether an accepted error rate was applicable; and (4) whether the method was generally accepted in the field.[28] In effect, the *Daubert* factors broadened the scope of the court's discretion from what it had according to the *Frye* test. Although it offered seemingly more concrete criteria, the decision placed discretion to determine relevance and credibility of expert testimony in the hands of judges, rather than on the specialized acceptance of other experts within the field as proven by attorneys. The decision also left two open questions: first, how to reconcile the court's focus on an expert's "principles and methodology, not on . . . conclusions," with the call for judges to decide whether the "methodology properly can be applied to the facts in issue"[29]; and second, the extent of application of the factors to nonscientific testimony.

The Supreme Court would address nonscientific expert testimony two years later, in *Kumho Tire Co. v. Carmichael.*[30] It is at this point that all expert witnesses officially fell under the explicit rule of evidence law. In its unanimous decision that the evidence was admissible, the Supreme Court reinforced *Daubert*, noting that a court's "'gatekeeping' obligation, requiring an inquiry into both relevance and reliability, applies not only to 'scientific' testimony, but to all expert testimony."[31] In addition to establishing the applicability of the

Daubert factors to all types of expert witnesses, the court explained that not all factors were always relevant to the specific nature of the expert testimony. Again, the Supreme Court left determinations of the relevancy of each factor, and thus the admissibility of the witness as an expert, to the court's discretion.

Although these new criteria have rarely become an explicit point of contention in music copyright cases, they have shaped the qualification process for expert witnesses as well as efforts by opposing parties to impeach them according to both qualification and methodology. Already concerned with vague processes for finding infringement and inherent subjectivity in the similarity inquiry itself, courts have focused instead on interpreting precedent and more specific factual matters in each case. Nevertheless, party strategy in recent cases has included witness impeachment, which even when unsuccessful, undoubtedly undermines the contributions of the impeached expert in the eyes of the court.

FORENSIC MUSICOLOGY

Refinements to evidence law surrounding expert testimony introduced by *Daubert* and *Kumho Tire* have contributed to contemporary litigation strategies that increasingly prefer expert witnesses with both academic credentials and past forensic experience in addition to expert witnesses with music industry experience. These evolving legal practices have coincided with the codification of forensic musicology as an emergent subdiscipline of musicology. Outside isolated use of the term "forensic" in the earliest lawsuits involving music, "forensic musicology" has been used with increasing frequency only in the past three decades, usually to refer to individuals who have cultivated specialized skills to serve as musical expert witnesses in copyright infringement cases. The term appears to acknowledge a distinction between the practices and goals of expertise as required by federal copyright law and those recognized by academic music communities.

To date, limited academic scholarship has been produced by forensic musicologists, mostly for one another or for predominantly legal audiences, that outlines analytical methods and analyzes the stakes of the discipline. Its practitioners instead do more to assist the litigation process than to offer academic study of expertise or legal issues with music copyright litigation examined through a musicological lens. The term, encapsulating mostly the activities associated with expert analysis and testimony but which might be expanded to include the preparation and signing of *amicus curiae* briefs, thus seems to imply its own specialized expertise within music necessary to conduct analyses for courts, encompassing work produced both by musicologists with various specialties and music audio specialists.[32]

During examinations in past cases, expert witnesses have provided limited insight into their understandings of forensic musicology, the role of musical expertise in copyright litigation, and the unique challenges it presents. As expert witness Robert Walser noted in a 2002 deposition for *Swirsky v. Carey*, for example:[33]

> When you are analyzing music for a book or an article, you are doing it in order to make a contribution to an already ongoing scholarly conversation. You are responding to what other people have done in their scholarship, and you are trying to refine the methodology, proposing insights, and your analytical techniques are guided by those goals, the goals of the discipline of musicology . . . . I'm often responding to analyses that don't proceed in the way that academic analyses proceed. And I'm also responding to the legal context that may be quite different from the academic context.

One reason for this distinction is that legal rules structure the way litigation proceeds, including the admissible evidence available for musical analysis and the place of that analysis in the legal decision-making process. For music copyright cases, statutory requirements of tangibility, which prior to the 1976 Copyright Act meant the deposit of sheet music, have contributed to reliance in litigation on notation-based comparisons.[34] In many cases, expert witnesses conduct their analyses according to sheet music deposited with the U.S. Copyright Office or, more recently, transcriptions of audio-based recordings usually of their own creation. Rules for evidence and civil procedure, as well as common law decision-making procedures, offer what Walser described as a "legal context" that control how, when, and what kind of information musical expert witnesses can offer.

Another distinguishing feature between academic and legal spaces is the audience for which expert witnesses produce their analyses, which in this context entails the nonexpert factfinders tasked with legal decision-making. As a result, expert witnesses are hired to contribute to a conversation that is more adversarial than scholarly, structured by legal procedure and driven by partisan attorneys. Yet in keeping with expectations established by legal similarity tests, expert witnesses have described their contributions as ostensibly impartial, providing information to aid, rather than convince, factfinders. Expert witness and forensic musicologist Alexander Stewart explained regarding the application of different analytical practices for traditional interpolation and digital sampling cases, "as an expert witness, my charge is not to take sides in these debates but rather to offer unbiased and objective analyses that attempt to keep these analytical strands separate and clear."[35] The history of forensic musicology demonstrates, however, that even the most apparently impartial analyses are cast into an adversarial system with different stakes than academic musicology.

Despite these limitations, musical expert witnesses over the course of copyright history have applied their comparisons to assess putative similarities and dissimilarities for the presiding court, typically by applying one of a few common analytical techniques. Because the music being compared will undoubtedly share at least some stylistic commonalities, expert witnesses have often placed greater analytical weight on pitch- and rhythm-based melodic congruence in the structural context of harmony and form, with the goal of producing close, often note-by-note, comparisons. They have often applied their own schemas to isolate melodies by removing embellishments to locate a structural melody and essentializing harmonic structures to their abstract qualities. Expert witnesses can, and typically have, adjusted for discrepancies in key, tempo, and meter, and contextualize their analyses according to matters of phrasing and instrumentation. The resulting analyses have tended to focus primarily on surface-level evaluations of congruence. While applying many of the same theorizations of musical structures, this approach differs from academic counterparts that tend to cast melody as a result of counterpoint, with various models used to reveal compositional process or stylistic innovation and convention.

Forensic similarity analyses are often accompanied by graphic representations introduced in reports and as trial exhibits. These graphs have most commonly placed songs in tandem, representing structural melody and rhythm via western notation with alphabetic designations and abbreviated symbols, typically either Roman numerals or lead-sheet-style chord symbols, to indicate harmonies. Isolated or sequential congruences are often indicated with coloration, arrows, X's, or brackets to direct factfinders' attention.

Although these diagrams can serve an important explanatory function as visual aids, they also can reinforce legal reliance in copyright law on notation-based musical evidence. Techniques that emphasize surface-level pitch and rhythmic similarities in a song's melody have been used consistently by expert witnesses with increasing levels of detail since the nineteenth century, driven at least in part by the ways a plaintiff characterizes the alleged infringement in their initial complaint. As scholars have noted, however, privileging melody as the key feature of similarity and originality has been propelled by decades of judicial opinions, due in part to "long-standing musical practices in the West,"[36] as well as deference to precedent set by previous cases and the analytical specialty of the experts themselves.[37] As a result, contemporary "courts pay little attention to rhythm, harmony, or other elements of music. They mention them, if at all, as support for their findings."[38] Legal treatises, which do not constitute binding law but can be consulted by legal practitioners for reference, are less explicit, but still emphasize a hierarchical approach to musical elements that privilege melody as a primary analytical parameter: "a musical work consists of rhythm, harmony and melody—and that the requisite creativity must inhere in one of these three."[39] In most cases, expert witnesses have focused their attention on these factors. This attention likely has as much to do with evidence and legal constraints on expert analyses in the decision-making process as it does with meeting the needs of a nonspecialist factfinder audience tasked with determining infringement.

As Walser noted in *Swirksy v. Carey*, however, reliance on notation in western music has generated analytical problems when interacting with more recent musical works:[40]

> If you are dealing with classical music or a Tin Pan Alley popular song, you have a song that's written, that's the primary text. It may be recorded in many different versions, but there is still the sense that the song is the written thing. That's not the way music has operated in the last half of the 20th century, especially in the last couple of decades with new technologies. So one big topic, as I said, has been moving away from the idea that notation is some sort of master system for representing musical—music comprehensively, and seeing that it is, in fact, "tactical," that it reveals certain things and conceals other things; that it—that all analyses and all transcriptions do that and have certain purposes.

Despite legal emphasis on notation-based analyses, musical expert witnesses hired in more recent cases have also begun to incorporate audio-based comparisons produced by audio specialists, often focusing on waveform comparison and phrase inversion. These techniques have been applied most commonly in the context of infringement cases involving digital sampling, where attention to minute sonic detail is critical to legal evaluations of similarity.

While the litigation process carefully controls the ways that forensic similarity analyses are applied to legal evaluations of similarity, the analytical techniques available to expert witnesses remain comparatively unchecked. Yet for myriad reasons, forensic musicologists tend to apply a few analytical techniques seemingly better suited to locating musical similarities relevant to matters of intellectual property, often in the context of written evidence. These techniques specifically respond to the essential task of forensic musicology, that is, to identify and contextualize for courts the nature of shared musical terrain between musical works in each case.

"STANDARD MUSICOLOGICAL PROCEDURE"

As forensic musicology coalesces, expert witnesses and legal practitioners alike have referred to it, or at least the invocation of the field of musicology broadly defined, as a signal of specialized skill and experience. Despite recent critiques that this discipline lacks a codified methodology,[41] its emergence has happened alongside the rise of legal references to analytical techniques used to conduct forensic similarity analysis described as "accepted practice for musicological analysis"[42] or "standard musicological procedure."[43] Although there are no legally defined criteria for musical analysis or a codified set of best practices "generally accepted in the field," common, often notation-based, analytical techniques used by expert witnesses across cases appear to have influenced these notions of normative analytical practice. Even expert witnesses have begun to use the term, as well as variations on it, such as "musicological comparison" and "musicological analysis." Aside from the presence of common analytical trends across past cases, its use may be a response to standards for witness and evidence admissibility established by the FRE and the *Daubert* factors. It might also be that strategically invoking the expertise associated with musicology as a credentialed, academic profession seems to lend forensic credibility. In so doing, attorneys, courts, and even some experts, have attempted to imply standardization in forensic similarity analyses across cases. Yet notions of standardization have revealed issues not only for experts tasked with the practicalities of aiding courts, but also for legal presumptions of analytical objectivity and expert witness impartiality.

In *Brainard v. Vassar*, for example, plaintiff songwriters David Brainard, Dustin Evans, and Tim Mathews sued defendant songwriters Phil Vassar and Craig Wisemen, along with multiple music publishing and production companies, alleging that the plaintiffs' country song, "Good Ol' Days to Come" was infringed by the defendants' own song, "Good Ole Days."[44] The plaintiffs claimed that they collaborated on writing the song in October 2003, which was recorded by Dustin Evans the following January, and then the team began "pitching" the song to various music companies before it was featured on Evans' July 2004 album by the same name.[45] It was during this time, in early 2004, that the defendants allegedly gained access to the song, which they denied, claiming that they began to write their song in March for release in September the same year. The plaintiffs retained Gerald Eskelin and the defendants retained "forensic musicologists" Anthony Ricigliano and Dan Dixon to serve as expert witnesses.[46]

Their reports followed a long tradition of analytical techniques, the age and general acceptance of which likely seemed to embody notions of standard musicological procedure. Ricigliano's report outlined the musical elements central to his comparison, placing melody, harmony, structure, and lyrics as the "principal aspects" of comparison, followed by key, meter, and tempo.[47] In keeping with many analyses proffered in previous cases, including those prepared by Ricigliano, transcriptions of the two songs were transposed to be in the same key. Rather than merely stating as much, Ricigliano noted that such transposition was "standard musicological procedure": "To facilitate comparison of the musical elements the musical examples are notated in the same key of G major (*standard musicological procedure*). Also, where applicable, the scale-step designation for each melodic pitch is shown by the number under each melody note."[48] While they did not apply the expression "standard musicological procedure," Eskelin and Dixon also used "musicological" to describe their analytical methods. Eskelin's report began with an explanation that "[i]t contain[ed] a *musicological comparison* of the above named songs in regard to possible copyright infringement."[49] The report continued with Eskelin's comparisons and conclusions without outlining any further analytical technique. Nonetheless, his conclusions referred to tonal harmony designations, including "dominant chord," melodic scale degrees, and phrasing, suggesting that he followed a similar procedure used by many other musicologists. In a similar way, Dixon used the phrase "comparative *musicological* analysis" to refer to his use of many of the same analytical techniques, except that Dixon's report placed greater emphasis on rhythm.[50]

The court found in favor of the defendants by granting their motion for summary judgment.[51] In its opinion, the court indicated that "[d]espite similar titles, the two songs, recordings of which were provided to the court, sound different in many ways."[52] In its discussion, the court relied on experts to indicate that "experts in this case essentially agree"[53] that similarities between the two songs were "the result of common usage in the industry and that they are not indicative of copying."[54] The analytical techniques used by the experts, however, were not mentioned, rendering unclear the impact that invocations of standard practice may have had on the court's interpretation of their contributions.

Legal notions of a standard procedure for music analysis appeared again in 2011 in the case of *Straughter v. Raymond*. Here, musician-producer Lee Straughter sued defendants Usher Raymond, Jermaine Dupri Mauldin, Bryan-Michael Paul Cox, and multiple music production companies, alleging that they infringed on Straughter's song, "The Reasons Why," with their own R&B song, "Burn."[55] The plaintiff claimed that his song appeared under the title "No More Pain" on R&B group Reel Tight's 1999 album, *Back to the Real*. In response, the defendants claimed that they co-wrote "Burn" in 2003, which was then featured as the second single off Usher's hit March 2004 album, *Confessions*.[56] Musical expert witnesses, including Cheryl Keyes retained for the plaintiffs while George Saadi and Lawrence Ferrara were retained by the defendants, applied two different methods to conduct their analyses, which became a point of legal confrontation during the pretrial process.

Unlike in *Brainard*, the invocation of standard procedure appeared not in any expert report, but in a memorandum used to impeach the plaintiff's expert witness. The defendants claimed that Keyes "substitute[d] her own subjective views for *long-standing, fundamental, widely accepted musicological principles.*"[57] In addition to arguing that Keyes' analysis was not grounded in "reliable principles and methods,"[58] the defendants' argument centered on terminology, calling into question Keyes's use of terms such as "motif" and "harmonic rhythm."[59] In her subsequent declaration, Keyes responded by presenting a list of alternatives and claimed that her use of the term derived from a desire for consistency in communication. She furthermore outlined the basis for her more qualitative "coding" analysis as rooted in music theory and ethnomusicological techniques Keyes had developed herself through studies of hip-hop and rap.[60]

Keyes's testimony was ultimately excluded from the lawsuit because of the contingent basis of her participation, not because of her methodology.[61] But the pretrial disagreement nevertheless signaled reliance on notions of standard procedure not simply as an abbreviation and appeal to past common practice among musical expert witnesses, but rather in a more partial attempt at witness impeachment. "Standard musicological procedure" instead served as a means to undermine expert credibility and qualification. This argument proved unsuccessful in the *Straughter* case, but it has perilous implications for future cases where alternative techniques might more acutely evaluate putative similarities, and dissimilarities, between musical works.

Although academically and legally undefined, recent invocations of "standard musicological procedure" raise questions not only about applicable analytical techniques for music copyright litigation, but also about the potential development of "best practices," or the *Daubert* factors' requirement that expert analytical methods are "generally accepted in the field," meaning in music copyright, among forensic musicologists. This emerging practice appears to focus on a legal quest for objectivity through development of at least quantifiable techniques and at best an incontrovertible method. As an emerging legal notion, it relies on recognition of forensic musicology as a credentialed discipline and appeals to higher standards of witness specialization to denote expertise with the promise of impartial objectivity. But its application in litigation has yet to guarantee greater clarity or consistency across cases, let alone greater analytical precision. In some instances, the term instead appears to represent strategic efforts toward legitimizing, and in some cases delegitimizing, expert contributions.

The adversarial legal context generates subjective questions for forensic musicologists surrounding their methodological choices and their ostensibly impartial role informing factfinders about music. On the one hand, standardization of analytical techniques might promise fewer confrontations over expert analyses, thereby informing courts with less disagreement or esoteric theoretical discourse. On the other, existing procedures may not address the unpredictable nature of future lawsuits, evolving musical styles, or the agency of legal factfinders, who ultimately can, and do, weigh all evidence on their own. "Standard musicological procedure" has thus far proven to expose, more than to resolve, issues fundamental to forensic musicology and the contributions of expert witnesses to music copyright infringement cases.

Although music copyright infringement lawsuits can hinge on issues external to similarity, analyses produced by forensic musicologists have often become a critical point of the legal process. In their role as expert witnesses, forensic musicologists can apply a variety of analytical techniques that aim to assist factfinders, but that also respond to ongoing legal challenges generated by the lack of a bright-line threshold between lawful commonality and unlawful appropriation, as well as the variability in decision-making processes across jurisdictions. Yet their contributions, which are treated by both expert witnesses and courts alike as ostensibly impartial, are introduced into a legally constrained, adversarial system propelled by partial attorneys and interpreted subjectively by nonexpert factfinders. These circumstances differentiate the essential tasks and analytical methods of forensic musicology from its broader academic field, thereby introducing specialization surrounding contemporary musical expertise.

REFINING MUSICAL EXPERTISE

Recent music copyright cases have led legal practitioners, both judges and attorneys, along with expert witnesses, to reinterpret notions of musical expertise throughout the litigation process. The development of heightened listener standards across jurisdictions has introduced a spectrum of listener acuity that has required courts to recognize, and better account for, audience expertise. The coinciding refinement of evidence law surrounding expert witnesses and appeals to forensic musicology as an emergent discipline with standard methodologies reflect a concurrent forensic quest for analytical precision and objectivity. Both manifestations of expertise reveal courts seeking to resolve inconsistencies and subjectivities in music copyright infringement cases through more acute sensitivity to the perception and evaluation of musical similarity. In so doing, they have reaffirmed the essential role of musical expertise in copyright litigation that can extend beyond expert witnesses.

NOTES

1. See *Comput. Assoc. Int. Inc. v. Altai Inc.*, 982 F.2d 693 (2d Cir. 1992).
2. *Country Kids 'N City Slicks, Inc. v. Sheen*, 77 F.3d 1280, 1284 (10th Cir. 1996).

3. *McRae v. Smith*, 968 F. Supp. 559, 563 (10th Cir. 1997) (citing *Country Kids*: "At the abstraction step, we separate the ideas (and basic utilitarian functions), which are not protectable, from the particular expression of the work. Then, we filter out the non-protectable components of the product from the original expression. Finally, we compare the remaining protected elements to the allegedly copied work to determine if the two works are substantially similar.").

4. *McRae*, 968 F. Supp. at 560.

5. *McRae*, 968 F. Supp. at 566–67.

6. Portions of this section and the one following have been previously published in, or are adapted from, Leo, "Musical Expertise."

7. *Dawson v. Hinshaw Music, Inc.*, 905 F.2d 731, 732 (4th Cir. 1990).

8. *Dawson*, Transcript, 16–18 (also cited in Philip C. Baxa and M. William Krasilovsky, "Dawson v. Hinshaw Music, Inc.: The Fourth Circuit Revisits Arnstein and the 'Intended Audience' Test," *Fordham Intellectual Property, Media, and Entertainment Law Journal* 1, no. 2 (1991): 91–115).

9. *Dawson*, 905 F.2d at 734 (emphasis added).

10. *Dawson*, 905 F. 2d at 735 (referring to *Whelan Associates v. Jaslow Dental Laboratory*, 797 F.2d 1222 (3d Cir.1986)).

11. *Dawson*, 905 F. 2d at 733.

12. *Dawson*, 905 F.2d at 733 (citing M. Nimmer & D. Nimmer, *Nimmer on Copyright* § 13.03[E], 13–62.4 n.202 (1989)).

13. See, for example, *Kohus v. Mariol*, 328 F.3d 848, 857 (6th Cir. 2003) (introducing a "target audience" standard).

14. *Boisson v. Banian, Ltd.*, 273 F.3d 262, 272 (2d Cir. 2001).

15. *McDonald v. West*, 2015 WL 5751197 (September 30, 2015), aff'd 2016 WL 5864029 (October 7, 2016).

16. *Lane v. Knowles-Carter*, 2015 WL 639540 (October 21, 2015).

17. *McDonald*, 2015 WL 5751197 at *4 (citations omitted).

18. *Francescatti v. Germanotta*, WL 2767231 (June 17, 2014) [hereinafter *Lady Gaga*].

19. *Lady Gaga*, WL 2767231 *1–*2 (June 17, 2014).

20. *Lady Gaga*, Plaintiff's Memorandum in Opposition to Defendants' Motion for Summary Judgment, 13.

21. *Atari, Inc. v. N. American Philips Consumer Electronic Corp.*, 672 F.2d 607, 614 (7th Cir. 1982).

22. *Lady Gaga*, at *7–*8.

23. *Lady Gaga*, at *8 (citing Plaintiff's Reply, 25).

24. *Lady Gaga*, at *8.

25. *Lady Gaga*, at *10 (citing Defendant's Reply, 1).

26. *Daubert v. Merrell Dow Pharmaceuticals, Inc.*, 509 U.S. 579, 587 (1993).

27. *Daubert*, 509 U.S. at 592–93. There is a vast scholarly literature evaluating these factors. See, for example, Susan Haack, "The Expert Witness: Lessons from the U.S. Experience," *Humana Mente Journal of Philosophical Studies* 28 (2015): 51–52.

28. See *Daubert*, 509 U.S. at 592–94.

29. *Daubert*, 509 U.S at 593; see also David S. Caudill and Lewis H. LaRue, *No Magic Wand: The Idealization of Science in Law* (Lanham, MD: Rowman & Littlefield, 2006), 8 (citing *Daubert*).

30. *Kumho Tire Co. v. Carmichael*, 526 U.S. 137 (1999).

31. *Kumho Tire*, 526 U.S. at 137.

32. Christopher Beam, "What's a Forensic Musicologist?" *Slate*, November 12, 2010, http://www.slate.com/articles/news_and_politics/explainer/2010/11/what s_a_forensic_musicologist.html; Sandra Haurant, "How Do I Become a Forensic Musicologist?" *The Guardian*, January 20, 2015, http://www.theguardian.com/mon ey/2015/jan/20/how-become-forensic-musicologist.

33. *Swirsky v. Carey*, 226 F. Supp.2d 1224, 1225 (C.D. Cal. 2002); Walser Deposition, 35:18–36:10.

34. See, for example, Selfridge-Field, "Substantial Musical Similarity," 249–83.

35. Stewart, "Been Caught Stealing," 361.

36. Joanna Demers, "Melody, Theft, and High Culture," in *Modernism and Copyright*, ed. Paul K. Saint-Amour (Oxford: Oxford University Press, 2011), 130.

37. See, for example, Joseph P. Fishman, "Music as a Matter of Law," *Harvard Law Review* 131 (May 2018): 1861–921.

38. Cronin, "Concepts of Melodic Similarity," 188 (citing *N. Music Corp. v. King Record Distrib. Co.*, 105 F. Supp. 393 (S.D.N.Y. 1952) & *Tempo Music, Inc. v. Famous Music, Corp.*, 838 F. Supp. 162 (S.D.N.Y. 1993) that melody is often the primary criteria for similarity). See also Mark Osteen, "Rhythm Changes: Contrafacts, Copyright, and Jazz Modernism," in *Modernism and Copyright*, ed. Paul K. Saint-Amour (Oxford: Oxford University Press, 2011), 98–113; Finell, "Using an Expert Witness," 5–6.

39. Melville Nimmer, *Nimmer On Copyright* § 2.05[D] (New York, NY: Matthew Bender, 2011).

40. *Swirsky v. Carey*, Walser Deposition, 117.

41. See, for example, Durand R. Begault, Heather D. Heise, and Christopher A. Peltier, "Audio Criteria for Forensic Musicology," Presented at *21st International Congress on Acoustics*, Last modified June 2013, http://www.audioforensics.com/ PDFs/ICA_Musicology2013.pdf, 1–2.

42. See *Tisi v. Patrick*, 97 F. Supp.2d 539, 545 (S.D.N.Y. 2000) (referring to transcription and transposition).

43. *Brainard v. Vassar*, 625 F. Supp.2d 608 (M.D. Tenn. 2009), Ricigliano Report, 1 (emphasis added).

44. *Brainard v. Vassar*, 625 F. Supp.2d 608, 612–13 (M.D. Tenn. 2009).

45. *Brainard*, 625 F. Supp.2d at 613.

46. *Brainard*, 625 F. Supp. 2d at 620.

47. See *Brainard v. Vassar*, Ricigliano Report, 1.

48. *Brainard v. Vassar*, Ricigliano Report, 1 (emphasis added).

49. *Brainard v. Vassar*, Eskelin Report, 1 (emphasis added).

50. *Brainard v. Vassar*, Dixon Report, 1 (emphasis added).

51. *Brainard v. Vassar*, 625 F. Supp.2d 608, 608 (M.D. Tenn. 2009).

52. *Brainard*, 625 F. Supp.2d at 613.

53. *Brainard*, 625 F. Supp.2d at 620.

54. *Brainard*, 625 F. Supp.2d at 620.

55. *Straughter v. Raymond*, 2011 WL 3651350 *2 (C.D. Cal. August 19, 2011).

56. *Straughter*, 2011 WL 3651350 at *2.

57. *Straughter v. Raymond*, Memorandum of Points and Authorities in Support of Defendants' Motion to Exclude and/or Strike the Opinions, Reports and Testimony of Plaintiff's Purported Expert Witness Cheryl L. Keyes, 17 [hereinafter Memo] (emphasis added).

58. *Straughter v. Raymond*, Keyes Declaration, 1.

59. *Straughter v. Raymond*, Memo, 17.

60. *Straughter v. Raymond*, Keyes Declaration, 1.

61. *Straughter v. Raymond*, 2011 WL 1789987 *1–*3 (C.D. Cal. May 9, 2011).

Conclusion

The "Blurred Lines" of Contemporary Music Copyright Litigation

The history of forensic musicology is intertwined with the evolution of federal copyright law. Since the mid-nineteenth century, legal assessments of similarity have consistently involved contributions from musical expert witnesses, certified by courts according to qualifications of music industry experience and, more recently, academic credentials. Yet judicial suspicion surrounding the ostensible objectivity of expert witness comparisons, on the one hand, and a presumed lack of listener acuity among nonexpert factfinders, on the other, has precipitated convoluted, subjective decision-making processes for separating lawful commonality from unlawful infringement. Despite revisions to the central legal similarity inquiry, from ongoing refinements of mid-twentieth-century models to introducing new standards of expertise, forensic musicologists continue to serve an essential role informing courts about the boundaries of musical identity.

The famous case of *Williams v. Gaye*, which turned on a 2015 jury verdict that hip-hop collaborators Robin Thicke and Pharrell Williams infringed on copyrights held by the estate of soul singer-songwriter Marvin Gaye and Bridgeport Music, is a result of this interdisciplinary history and the ongoing issues that contemporary forensic musicologists face. Carried out according to a complex system of procedural rules and subjective legal processes, the *Williams* case returned to perennial questions shared by forensic musicology and federal copyright law: how similarity should be evaluated; what evidence expert witnesses can, and should, consider; the analytical techniques expert witnesses apply in so doing; and the extent to which expert witnesses can, or should, impact dispositive decisions regarding infringement. Although the 2018 Ninth Circuit decision was reasoned on procedural, more than substantive, grounds, and thus did not resolve any of these questions, the case remains illustrative of them and of the blurred intellectual property boundaries between music.

THE PROCESS OF THE *WILLIAMS* CASE

In *Williams v. Gaye*, Marvin Gaye's estate alleged that Robin Thicke and Pharrell Williams, along with rap artist Clifford "T.I." Harris, Jr., infringed on Gaye's 1977 songs, "Got to Give It Up" and "After the Dance," with their own 2013 songs, "Blurred Lines," and "Love After War," respectively.[1] Although the lawsuit dealt with two pairs of songs, alleged commonalities between party anthem "Got to Give It Up" and the controversial international hit "Blurred Lines" became the focal point of the case for the parties, the court, and the media. The case featured an unusual legal procedure, with Williams and his team acting as the plaintiffs despite being the parties accused of infringement.

Expert witnesses figured prominently throughout the litigation process. In July 2013, the Gaye estate contacted Electric and Musical Industries (EMI), Gaye's music publisher, demanding that the company sue for copyright infringement. EMI refused, stating that there was no substantial similarity between the songs, so the Gaye estate retained forensic musicologist and veteran expert witness, Lawrence Ferrara, to conduct a preliminary comparative analysis. Later that same month, the Gaye estate retained legal counsel, who elicited additional analyses from veteran forensic musicologists, Peter Oxendale and Gerald Eskelin. Like EMI's internal investigation, both musicologists determined that the two songs were not similar, but their involvement with the case did not appear to continue beyond this assessment.[2] Despite these evaluations, the Gaye estate's lawyer made a demand to Williams and his team for 100-percent of royalties for copyright to "Blurred Lines," and threatened to sue.

Williams and his team responded by retaining two forensic musicologists, Anthony Ricigliano and Sandra Wilbur, both of whom concluded that there was no substantial similarity between the songs.[3] After the Gaye estate gave no response to a settlement offer extended by Williams and his team, in August 2013, the collaborators filed for a declaratory judgment, requesting a judicial decision before a formal claim could be filed, that they did not infringe on the Gaye estate's rights.[4] This led to a counterclaim filed by the Gaye estate, alleging copyright infringement, the documents for which included preliminary analysis conducted by another forensic musicologist, Judith Finell. The Gaye estate would later retain academic ethnomusicologist, Ingrid Monson, as another expert witness. The infringement litigation commenced in the Ninth Circuit, which meant that evaluations regarding infringement would follow the *Krofft* test, including ostensibly extrinsic, objective evaluations of similarity from expert witnesses.

During this pretrial process, and unsurprising given their party affiliations, Wilbur found that there were no similarities between the two songs, while Finell and Monson found the opposite, arguing that not only were there alleged similarities, but that their presence was more than mere coincidence.[5] The analytical techniques that each expert witness applied in their pretrial reports used different criteria to distinguish musical elements, particularly melody, harmony, rhythm, and form, as well as lyrical themes and vocabulary. Finell's report in particular identified "a constellation of eight substantially similar features"[6] which together "surpass[ed] the realm of generic coincidence, reaching to the very essence of each work,"[7] including "the signature phrase, hooks, hooks with backup vocals, 'Theme X,' backup hooks, bass melodies, keyboard parts, and unusual percussion choices."[8] Monson likewise located seven similar features to arrive at a complementary conclusion, that the two songs were similar according to stylistic convention and innovation. Rather than emphasizing note-by-note congruence, however, these analyses instead relied on the combination of stylistically innovative elements shared between the songs to demonstrate copying.

Early disagreements between the expert reports, documented primarily between Wilbur and Finell, emphasized differing methods and conclusions. Wilbur criticized Finell's analysis for being "primarily melodic," yet "[t]here are *no two consecutive notes* in any of the melodic examples in Finell's report that have the same pitch, the same duration, and the same placement in the measure."[9] In addition, Wilbur found fault with Finell's analysis for drawing attention to similarities in the unoriginal, nonprotectable, musical material in each song such that they would not be relevant to infringement inquiries.[10] Conversely, Finell called out Wilbur's analytical techniques, which led to conclusions that the music at issue was not similar, as being improperly "built on requiring *absolute identity* in all 3 melodic comparison factors of (A) pitch or scale degree, (B) duration, and (C) rhythmic placement for every single note in order to be similar."[11] This approach challenged a long tradition of musical expert witnesses seeking musical congruence. It instead called for a more generalized approach to assessing similarity based on the overall effect of correlating musical elements contextualized according to matters of style.

Jurors, however, would not review these reports, nor would they consider the same comparisons, because of legal distinctions between copyrights for sound recordings and compositions represented on sheet music. One of the key issues posed in the plaintiffs' motion for summary judgment was the discovery of a lead sheet for "Got To Give It Up." This notated copy was presumably created after Gaye's initial compositional process for the purpose of deposit in the U.S. Copyright Office. As a result, the deposit copy functioned as more of a sketch, including only the melody and abbreviated lead sheet symbols to represent a more complex musical composition experienced through live or recorded performance.

The plaintiffs claimed that because the defendants' copyrights in Gaye's songs were filed prior to implementation of the 1976 Copyright Act, only musical material memorialized on the lead sheet was legally protected. Therefore, according to the plaintiffs, musical material heard on the recording but not present on the lead sheet, most significantly the percussive "groove," the timbral sounds of the instruments and voices, and the background "party noise," were not protected.[12] On the contrary, the defendants argued that comparisons should not be restricted to the lead sheet because Gaye himself "did not fluently read sheet music" or transcribe his own songs; therefore, the lead sheet did not represent the song as Gaye himself conceived of it.[13] In an October 2014 ruling, presiding trial Judge John Kronstadt denied the motion, citing "significant indicia"[14] of disagreement between the parties, but found that "Got To Give It Up" as it appeared on the lead sheet would be the only musical material available for analysis at trial.[15] This evidentiary ruling not only put a limitation on the analyses that experts could produce, comparing the "Blurred Lines" recording, and transcriptions of it, to the "Got To Give It Up" lead sheet, and realizations of it, but it also limited what evidence jurors would evaluate at trial.

THE 2015 TRIAL

After a pretrial process that included conflicting reports produced by expert witnesses regarding analytical techniques and alleged similarities between the songs, the case went to trial in March 2015.[16] At trial, similarities between the songs, including the tonic-dominant harmonic progression in "Blurred Lines" compared to the dominant seventh-driven progression in "Got To Give It Up," or the pitch, rhythmic, and phrasing in melodies over the lyrics "I used to go out to parties" in "Got To Give It Up" against "and that's why I'm gon' take a good girl" in "Blurred Lines," were both verbally described and demonstrated live by expert witnesses at the keyboard in the courtroom. Rather than disputing analytical techniques or conclusions, the attorneys strategically applied the analyses presumptively to aid factfinder-jurors in assessing similarity, providing them with more detailed criteria by which to distinguish commonality from copying based on identifications of stylistic originality.

For the plaintiffs, much of Wilbur's testimony was directed toward establishing similarities as being more a matter of generic compositional practice than specific copying. By her reasoning, the harmonies in "Blurred Lines" did not reflect a simplification of the "Got To Give It Up" progression, but rather a common compositional structure. Conversely, Monson and Finell emphasized the opposite position: that shared aspects of the two songs were peculiar to Marvin Gaye, and thus more likely to reveal stylistic copying than common practice. Monson in particular focused on whether the similarities were a product of style or specific copying.[17] After defining her analytical terms at trial, Monson explained that the combination of the bass line rhythm and offbeat harmonic accompaniment played by the keyboard in "Got to Give It Up" was unique when compared with other Motown bass lines, and shared stylistic similarities to bass lines found in reggae, jazz, and ragtime.[18] According to Monson, these combined stylistic features in Gaye's song, coupled with the rhythmic and melodic similarities in the "Got to Give It Up" and "Blurred Lines" bass lines, would seem to indicate copying. Despite disagreements regarding interpretation of commonalities between the songs, expert contributions together directed the jury's attention to relevant points of musical comparison, specifically melody, harmony, rhythm, form, and lyrics, instead of matters involving timbre, key, or tempo. Their statements, however, were constrained not only by the legal procedure but also by the partiality of the attorneys' examination questions.

Seven days of testimony and two days of deliberation later, a nonexpert jury produced a finding of unwillful infringement and an award of approximately $7.3 million in damages granted to Marvin Gaye's estate.[19] Although the jury found Thicke and Williams liable, they did not find "T.I." or the other joined plaintiff parties liable. After a judicial hearing on post-trial motions, the judge reduced the damage award by approximately $2 million, but the infringement finding stood.[20]

Because the jury's confidential deliberation process may never be completely understood, it is impossible to assess thoroughly the ways and extent to which expert contributions may have impacted their decision. On the one hand, the jury verdict in favor of the Gaye estate appears to have aligned with testimony presented by Finell and Monson, suggesting that their testimony was, at least to some degree, effective. On the other hand, when considered in light of Wilbur's analytical criteria and opposite conclusions, their competing analyses likely did less to clarify the legally subjective, or intrinsic, evaluations of similarity jurors made according to the *Krofft* test in light of all evidence presented in the case.

THE APPEAL

Williams and Thicke soon filed an appeal, reiterating that the two songs were not similar and that the case should not have gone to trial despite disagreements between expert witnesses. *Amicus curiae*, or "friend" of the court, briefs were filed in 2016 to support both parties' arguments, including one submitted by over two-hundred musicians,[21] another prepared with the aid of academic and forensic musicologists in support of Williams and Thicke,[22] and conversely, yet another brief prepared by musicologists in support of the Gaye estate.[23] In addition to reinforcing the positions of each party, respectively, these briefs served to outline the policy-driven concerns of musicologists as nonparty, nonwitness experts, and to highlight the significance of the Appellate court's decision for the future of the U.S. music industry.

While the contrasting statements from nonwitness musicological experts added greater context for the court, they also served to reinforce, more than to resolve, party divisions between hired expert witnesses and heightened the adversarial, forensic context in which musicological analyses were submitted. In support of Williams and Thicke, *amici* musicologists challenged Finell and Monson's testimony as speculative, misleading, and irrelevant. They discredited putative melodic similarities identified by Finell and Monson as occurring between noncorresponding portions of the songs and relied on techniques that "distorted the duration and placement of notes in their presentation,"[24] and by highlighting the singularity of the instance of similarity Monson identified. Conversely, *amici* musicologists in support of the Gaye estate emphasized Finell's and Monson's reputations and characterized their analyses as "fully consistent with the accepted Musicological[*sic*] standards and methods,"[25] appealing to contemporary legal notions of standard analytical techniques in forensic musicology. Because these briefs were not cited in the Ninth Circuit opinion, their impact cannot be fully assessed. Their submission nevertheless highlighted another dimension of forensic musical expertise and their disagreements reinforced the inherent subjectivities of forensic similarity analysis.

On March 21, 2018, the three-judge panel of the Ninth Circuit ruled 2-1 to affirm the trial court's decision. As the majority opinion explained, rather than addressing matters of musical similarity or assuaging policy concerns regarding the protection of musical style, their conclusions instead "turn[ed] on the procedural posture of the case, which require[d] [them] to review the relevant issues under deferential standards of review."[26] This statement meant that the judicial panel focused instead on the legal weight of evidence informing the verdict, rather than reviewing that same evidence *de novo*, or as new, the same as the trial court. Because there was a "reasonable basis for the jury verdict," the majority believed that they could not overturn the jury's decision—a stance they reinforced by noting that "we are 'reluctant to reverse jury verdicts in music cases' on appeal, "[g]iven the difficulty of proving access and substantial similarity.'"[27] While the Gaye estate called the case "a victory for the rights of all musicians,"[28] the dissenting opinion paradoxically characterized it as "a devastating blow to future musicians and composers everywhere."[29]

The two-judge appellate majority grounded its opinion in legal procedure rather than clarifying matters of federal copyright or substantive elements of musical analysis. It specifically found fault with pre- and post-trial motions Williams and Thicke filed and focused on the individuals in the appropriate legal position to make infringement decisions. Although Williams and Thicke had filed a motion for summary judgment, which was denied, they had not filed for a judgment as a matter of law, so they had not preserved their right to an appeal. Nevertheless, their appeal focused on the district court's denial of the motion that they did file. But the appellate court noted that where a district court denies such a motion and then the case goes through a full jury trial, as happened in this case, that denial is not later reviewable on appeal. Even if the district court's denial of that motion was in error, the appellate majority characterized *Williams* as introducing issues not "capable of resolution with reference only to undisputed facts"[30]—a situation that, according to the decision-making process for copyright infringement, necessitated a jury, the evaluations of which could not be superseded by those of the appellate judges, or even expert witnesses.

The panel then refused to review Williams's and Thicke's argument that the trial court included evidence outside the scope of Gaye's lead sheet. The court explained that "because we do not remand the case for a new trial, we need not, and decline to, resolve this issue in this opinion. For purposes of this appeal, we accept, without deciding, the merits of the district court's ruling that the scope of the Gayes' copyright in "Got To Give It Up" is limited to the deposit copy."[31] Because of this procedural decision, the court reinforced ambiguity in the source of a copyrightable work and the potential for inequitable comparisons between essential lead sheets and the more totalizing transcriptions of recorded sound.

Williams and Thicke raised another evidentiary issue, arguing that the jury verdict went against the weight of evidence, meaning that there was insufficient proof of similarity to merit an infringement finding. In their limited capacity as a reviewing body, the Ninth Circuit majority ruled that it could not "substitute [its] evaluations for those of the jurors,"[32] noting that they would not reverse a decision unless there was an "absolute absence of evidence to support the jury's verdict."[33] Rather than weigh evidence presented by expert witnesses, the majority preserved the dispositive evaluations of nonexpert jurors. Because expert witnesses hired by the Gaye estate had testified at trial to what the appellate panel described as "multiple areas of extrinsic similarity, including the songs' signature phrases, hooks, bass melodies, word painting, the placement of the rap and '*parlando*' section, and structural similarities on a sectional and phrasing level,"[34] the panel reasoned that there could not be an "absence of evidence," so trial court's decision had to stand. There may not have been enough evidence of similarity to support the jury's infringement finding, but according to the majority, that mattered less because the two songs were not entirely dissimilar.

THE *WILLIAMS* DISSENT

As the lone dissenting judge explained, such distinctions did matter: "'Blurred Lines' and 'Got to Give It Up' are not objectively similar. They differ in melody, harmony, and rhythm. Yet by refusing to compare the two works, the majority establishes a dangerous precedent."[35] Challenging the majority's avoidance of substantive copyright issues and musical analysis, the dissent relied on contributions of expert witnesses to contend that a different legal procedure could have been followed. Thus, if the court was able to assess substantial similarity, then it should have done so without a jury. According to the dissent, the jury finding from the trial should have been vacated and the district court judge should have decided the case.[36]

The dissent's alternative procedural analysis located a legal point of entry where the majority could have delved into substantive issues of musical evidence, hinging on the essential contributions of musical expert witnesses. As it explained:[37]

> [t]he majority, like the district court, presents this case as a "battle of the experts," in which the jury simply credited one expert's factual assertions over those of another hired by the opposite party. To the contrary, there were no material factual disputes at trial. Finell testified about certain similarities between the deposit copy of the "Got to Give It Up" lead sheet and "Blurred Lines." Pharrell Williams and Robin Thicke don't contest the existence of these similarities. Rather, they argue that these similarities are insufficient to support a finding of substantial similarity.

By reframing the case as a matter of whether, in their effort to evoke a style, Williams and Thicke "took too much"[38] from Marvin Gaye, the dissent reviewed in detail the expert analyses, even providing western notation from trial exhibits, to locate and contextualize musical congruence according to the scope of copyright protection. In so doing, the dissent found a lack of overall musical similarity, and that Williams and Thicke were entitled to a decision as a matter of law, meaning one without the intrinsic evaluation of nonexpert jurors. According to the dissent, affirming the jury verdict led to the conclusion that it "allows the Gayes to accomplish what no one has before:

copyright a musical style."[39] This reasoning, however, offered little more than a counterpoint to the majority's otherwise binding decision.

The case drew to a close in December that year with a final ruling regarding damage allocation. When Williams and Thicke filed for an *en banc* rehearing, meaning a request for all judges on the Ninth Circuit bench to reconsider the decision, their petition was denied. In the final ruling on December 6, 2018, district court Judge Kronstadt ordered Williams and Thicke to pay nearly $5 million in damages—$2.9 million paid jointly, with an additional $360,000 from Williams and his publishing company and an additional $1.76 million from Thicke—and awarded the Gaye estate 50-percent of future royalties associated with the song.

CONTEXTUALIZING *WILLIAMS V. GAYE* IN COPYRIGHT HISTORY

Although the long-term impact of the *Williams* case remains indeterminate because the Ninth Circuit opinion has only begun to be interpreted and cited at the time of this publication, commentators have already offered predictions. Many have amplified the Ninth Circuit dissent's concern about a chilling effect on creativity caused by a rise in frivolous infringement lawsuits, driven at least in part by what some commentators have called "copyright trolls," alongside concerns that the case will generate a legal climate that deters creators from ever entering commercial music markets.[40] Others seem to be less worried, either supporting the trial and appellate decisions for their merits,[41] or interpreting the procedural basis for the appellate court's decision as strategically limiting its legal applicability, or even suggesting that *Williams* might prove to be a factual outlier with few analogous cases.[42] Yet even the earliest citations to court records from *Williams*, including those involving deposit copies and the scope of copyright, seem to suggest that the case may prove to be more than a factual outlier.[43]

Whether a victorious or dangerous precedent, these commentators are united in their attempts to make sense of peculiarities in the *Williams* case and the way it unfolded. Historical study of forensic musicology reveals that many of the central issues in this case actually have deep roots in cumulating legal precedent and partisan litigation strategies alongside evolving analytical techniques among ostensibly impartial expert witnesses. In light of this historical context, the litigation process in *Williams* and its outcomes might be understood better as the result of a subjective system riddled with unresolved challenges surrounding how, and by whom, evaluations of musical similarity can, and should, be conducted, and ultimately, how musical identity as intellectual property is represented.

LEGAL PROCEDURES AND LIMITS ON FORENSIC
SIMILARITY ANALYSIS IN *WILLIAMS*

Although their typical positions were reversed due to legal procedure, the parties in *Williams* introduced conventional arguments traceable to litigation practices in the nineteenth century. The party claiming infringement identified points of similarity throughout the composition, claiming that the totality, or in this case the "constellation," of resemblances, classified as similarities, amounted to infringement; the allegedly infringing party claimed that any of the musical congruences, also classified as similarities, were in unoriginal, and thus unprotectable, elements of both musical works. The fundamental disagreement, therefore, laid in determining whether those similarities constituted lawful commonality or unlawful infringement.

Because the case was heard in the Ninth Circuit, both the district and appellate courts applied a legal decision-making process for infringement according to assessments of access plus similarity, assessed according to *Krofft* and subsequent interpretations of it. The *Krofft* test, established in 1977, relied on antiquated notions of discrepancies in listener skill and judicial skepticism surrounding both the allegedly partial contributions of expert witnesses and the allegedly uninformed perceptions of nonexpert factfinders. In reinforcing *Arnstein v. Porter*, expert witnesses became limited in their contributions, prevented from offering opinions regarding final legal matters, namely conclusions regarding infringement. Nonexpert factfinders instead were tasked with weighing all evidence to make their dispositive determinations on their own. The idea-expression divide that the *Krofft* court superimposed, which famously resulted in the "extrinsic-intrinsic" test, limited expert analyses to "extrinsic" aspects of similarity, referring to a more ineffable musical idea legally thought to be identifiable through detailed analysis. Rather than seize an opportunity to contend with, and possibly clarify, the seemingly indecipherable subjectivities of this legal test as revealed by comparisons between "Got to Give It Up" and "Blurred Lines," however, the Ninth Circuit panel's opinion ultimately relied on matters of procedure.

Beyond the *Krofft* test, the statutory scope of federal copyright protection had a significant impact on the ways that evaluations of similarity proceeded. For music copyrighted prior to 1978, when the 1976 Copyright Act went into effect, sheet music served as the primary representation of a song as intellectual property. While written notation ostensibly promised legal documentation for these pre-1978 songs, and structured much of past music copyright litigation, it also proved to be problematic for music created first on record, including Gaye's "Got To Give It Up." Questions surrounding the *de facto* lead sheet and the recording in the *Williams* case—namely, what evidence should be used to conduct musical comparisons—demonstrated the role that less-easily notated features can have on the contours of a musical work, such as timbre, texture, instrumental or vocal technique, style, and many aspects of studio production. Similar to digital sampling cases, in which musical evidence is found on record and melodic, rhythmic, and harmonic congruence can be nearly guaranteed, these other characteristics seem to represent better the ostensibly original essence of musical works according to their creators. Yet these characteristics are documented differently across media formats, with implications for the material to be considered by expert witnesses, and subsequently factfinders. Despite the history of music copyright litigation having reinforced reliance on notation and features precisely captured on it, *Williams* highlighted the impact that variable compositional processes, recording technologies, and the nature of claims made in copyright disputes have evolved such that strict legal reliance on notated comparisons may no longer be as practical as they once may have been.

Musical expert witnesses, as forensic or academic musicologists, participated in this legal process from commencement through appeal, offering essential clarification as to the similarities and dissimilarities between the two songs. Yet their contributions were constrained by courts not only according to the *Krofft* test but also as to the relevant medium of evidence, and thus points of comparison, available for forensic similarity analysis. Despite, and partly because of, these challenges, expert witnesses hired by both parties produced evaluations using different criteria with conclusions well-suited to their hiring party's legal arguments, but were still treated by the court as ostensibly objective in fulfillment of extrinsic analysis.

EVALUATING MUSICAL SIMILARITY

Long-standing procedures binding the *Williams* court controlled the ways that legal similarity could be evaluated, by whom, and what evidence expert witnesses could consider. While the expert witnesses in *Williams*, as in earlier cases, were precluded legally from commenting on whether purported similarities amount to infringement, there was little, if any, restriction on the ways they could analyze similarity, including explanations of musical function and matters of stylistic convention. Given the nature of the legal arguments in *Williams*, both parties could have continued forensic musicological traditions traceable to the nineteenth century of assessing similarity according to close, note-by-note comparisons in search of musical congruence in the context of stylistic practice.

Much of the expert testimony in *Williams* did follow these patterns, set forth in cases resolved before it: expert(s) retained by the allegedly infringed party construct similarity based primarily on melodic congruence distinguishable from its formal, harmonic, and even rhythmic, contexts; while expert(s) called by the allegedly infringing party refute these analyses through their own recasting of any putative similarities as common stylistic practice. Walser's analysis in *Swirsky v. Carey*, for example, interpreted the melodies and vocal ornamentation according to stylistic practice in R&B, which informed his analytical process in locating structural melodies for comparison. Some of these characteristics can cross styles, however, thereby allowing expert witnesses to contextualize the same musical gesture differently, either into separate styles or distinguishing the extent of innovation within a shared style.[44] This qualitative analysis involved not simply the identification of musical congruence or discord, but also the classification of them according to matters of repertory. In *Newton v. Diamond*, for example, Dobrian and Wilson cast the multiphonic flute technique as a stylistic feature that distinguished the brief passage as unique, and thus copyright-protectable. Likewise, Stewart's report in *Bridgeport v. Combs* emphasized the importance of the brief shared passage to elements of funk style. Because the brief section was stylistically significant, the seemingly insignificant quantity of similarity between the two songs became dispositive of infringement.

Unlike earlier cases, however, some of the expert analyses in *Williams* produced for the Gaye estate introduced a divergence from evaluations of similarity according to musical congruence toward more generalized, cumulating musical resemblance based on stylistic commonality. According to this approach, there need not be significant sections of shared consecutive pitches, rhythms, or harmonies in order to signal copying, but instead a "constellation" of musical elements distinctive enough to highlight stylistic innovation. At least according to Finell and Monson, the combination of these elements in "Got to Give It Up," and subsequently "Blurred Lines," seemed to innovate within jazz, reggae, and ragtime styles, but because they were shared between the two songs in the lawsuit, they became indicative of similarity regardless of limited melodic or harmonic congruence. When interpreted by the 2015 jury verdict and 2018 appeal, this expert analytical approach seems to many commentators to open broad copyright protection of a "style," "feel," or "vibe" previously treated as more ineffable, and unprotectable, musical ideas, and despite a lack of consecutive musical congruence. While these analytical divisions could have undermined the credibility of expert contributions to the case, Finell and Monson's emphasis on stylistic context remained a critical point of discussion on which the case, and the dissenting opinion on appeal, ultimately hinged.

The contributions of musical expert witnesses throughout the litigation process revealed their essential, albeit legally constrained, role in music copyright litigation. Long-standing judicial precedent relied on the ostensibly objective analyses produced by those experts, which were cast into a complex, adversarial system where the subjectivities of alternate musical analyses became part and parcel of legal confrontations, or what the *Williams* dissent characterized as a "battle of the experts."[45] Far from recent legal dilemmas, ongoing issues surrounding forensic analytical techniques and impartiality have become central to forensic musicology and present rough terrain for contemporary expert witnesses to navigate.

FORENSIC MUSICOLOGY AND THE BLURRED LINES OF MUSICAL IDENTITY

The recent case of *Williams v. Gaye* encapsulated well over a century of intertwined histories of forensic musicology and federal music copyright litigation. In so doing, it highlighted the essential tasks, issues, and limitations that contemporary forensic musicologists encounter as expert witnesses. In *Williams*, as in even the earliest federal music copyright cases, "a great deal of learned musical testimony and forensic discussion"[46] presented by expert witnesses shaped legal interpretations of similarities, and dissimilarities, between music as intellectual property.

At the *Williams* trial, when asked to describe her contribution as an expert witness and forensic musicologist, Finell testified that "it's the job of the musicologist to know what's the relevant context in its entirety"[47] and that "the musicologist's job is to understand the hierarchy of important and unimportant elements in a musical work. It's my analytical description."[48] This explanation garnered criticism shortly after the trial for its implication of subjective valuation eroding musical analysis treated as presumably objective by courts.[49] Forensic similarity analyses, like the legal processes to which they contribute, are indeed not pristine. Yet Finell's contributions, alongside those of other expert witnesses called in the case, demonstrate that such musical curation can vary, and even when it is legally treated as objective, it may not always be effective in assisting jurors or judges in light of all evidence and increasingly complex legal procedures. What role then, does, and should, forensic musical expertise serve in federal copyright?

Nearly two hundred years of federal music copyright lawsuits demonstrate that musical experts serve an essential role, but one that continues to be riddled with challenges to forensic similarity analysis, the nature of expertise, and the stakes that individual musicologists or forensic musicology as a discipline should, or currently do, have in such litigation. From a legal perspective, musical expert witnesses, now often forensic musicologists, can only offer contextualized information regarding similarities, and dissimilarities, in an adversarial environment with the hope that they can influence factfinders in making the just decision. The manner and extent to which musical expertise figures into these decisions remain uncertain, but by no means do issues ongoing after *Williams* suggest that forensic musicologists have "got to give it up," in light of adversarial attorneys, unpredictable factfinders, and seemly indecipherable legal precedents that limit expert contributions. Instead, these complexities suggest that the role of the musical expert, and the discipline of forensic musicology, should be understood as serving a complex, essential function in clarifying the otherwise "blurred lines" that separate, and join, so many pieces of music.

NOTES

1. *Williams v. Bridgeport Music, Inc.*, 2014 WL 7877773 *1 (C.D. Cal. October 30, 2014) [hereinafter *Bridgeport*]. Litigation documents shall be cited as part of the case as it was named in the final Ninth Circuit opinions, *Williams v. Gaye*.
2. *Williams v. Gaye*, Plaintiffs and Counter-defendants' opposition to defendants and cross-complainants' motions for award of attorneys' fees and expenses: memorandum of points and authorities (February 10, 2016), 4–5 [hereinafter Feb. Motion].
3. *Williams v. Gaye*, Feb. Motion, 4–5.
4. *Bridgeport*, 2014 WL 7877773 at *1.
5. *Bridgeport*, 2014 WL 7877773 *2–*4 (C.D. Cal. October 30, 2014).
6. *Williams v. Gaye*, Finell Report, 1.
7. *Williams v. Gaye*, Finell Report, 1.
8. *Williams v. Gaye*, 895 F.3d 1106, 1117 (9th Cir. 2018).
9. *Williams v. Gaye*, Wilbur Report, 1 (emphasis in original); also cited in *Williams*, 2014 WL 7877773 at *3.
10. *Williams v. Gaye*, Wilbur Report, 1 (emphasis in original); also cited in *Williams*, 2014 WL 7877773 at *3.
11. *Williams v. Gaye*, Finell Declaration, 50; *Williams*, 2014 WL 7877773 at *13 (emphasis added).
12. *Bridgeport*, 2014 WL 7877773 at *6–*7.
13. *Bridgeport*, 2014 WL 7877773 at *7.
14. *Bridgeport*, 2014 WL 7877773 at *4.
15. *Bridgeport*, 2014 WL 7877773 at *10.
16. *Williams v. Bridgeport Music, Inc.*, 2015 WL 4479500 *1 (C.D. Cal. July 14, 2015).
17. *Williams v. Gaye*, Monson Transcript, 13. See also Monson, "Personal Take," 60.
18. *Williams v. Gaye*, Monson Transcript, 24–26.
19. *Williams v. Bridgeport Music, Inc.*, Jury Verdict, 2015 WL 1476803 (C.D. Cal. March 10, 2015); see also *Williams v. Bridgeport Music, Inc.*, 2015 WL 4479500 *1 (C.D. Cal. July 14, 2015).
20. *Williams v. Bridgeport Music, Inc.*, 2015 WL 4479500 *47–*48 (C.D. Cal. July 14, 2015).

21. *Williams v. Gaye*, Brief of Amici Curiae 212 Songwriters, Composers, Musicians, and Producers in Support of Appellants, 2016 WL 4592129.

22. *Williams v. Gaye*, Brief of Amicus Curiae Musicologists in Support of Plaintiffs-Appellants-Cross-Appellees, 2016 WL 4592128.

23. *Williams v. Gaye*, Brief of Amici Curiae Musicologists in Support of the Gaye Family and Arguing for Affirmance, 2016 WL 7494673.

24. *Williams v. Gaye*, Brief of Amicus Curiae Musicologists, 2016 WL 4592128, *2.

25. *Williams v. Gaye*, Brief from the Institute for Intellectual Property and Social Justice Musicians and Composers and Law, Music, and Business Professors, 2016 WL 7494673, *1.

26. *Williams v. Gaye*, 885 F.3d 1150, 1138 (9th Cir. 2018).

27. *Williams*, 895 F.3d at 1127.

28. Romano, "Blurred Lines."

29. *Williams*, 885 F. 3d at 1183 (Nguyen, J., dissenting).

30. *Williams*, 885 F. 3d at 1166 (citations omitted).

31. *Williams*, 885 F. 3d at 1165–66.

32. *Williams*, 885 F. 3d at 1172 (citation omitted).

33. *Williams*, 885 F. 3d at 1172 (citation omitted).

34. *Williams*, 885 F. 3d at 1162.

35. *Williams*, 885 F. 3d at 1183 (Nguyen, J., dissenting).

36. *Williams*, 885 F. 3d at 1183 (Nguyen, J., dissenting).

37. *Williams*, 885 F. 3d at 1183 (Nguyen, J., dissenting).

38. *Williams*, 885 F. 3d at 1186 (Nguyen, J., dissenting).

39. *Williams*, 885 F. 3d at 1182 (Nguyen, J., dissenting).

40. See, for example, Noah Feldman, "'Blurred Lines' Copyright Verdict Creates Bad Law for Musicians," *Chicago Tribune*, March 17, 2015, www.chicagotribune.com/news/opinion/commentary/ct-blurred-lines-robin-thicke-court-perspec-0317-20150316-story.html; Robert Fink, "'Blurred Lines, UR-Lines, and Color Lines," *Musicology Now*, Blog of the American Musicological Society, March 15, 2015, musicologynow.ams-net.org/2015/03/blurred-lines-ur-lines-and-colorline.html ; Jacob Gershman, "'Blurred Lines' Verdict a 'Dangerous' Threat to Creativity, Musicians Warn Appeals Court," *Wall Street Journal*, August 31, 2016, blogs.wsj.com/law/2016/08/31/blurred-lines-verdict-a-dangerous-threat-to-creativity-celebrity-musicians-warn-appeals-court.

41. Monson, "Personal Take," 58.

42. John Quagliariello, "Blurring the Lines: The Impact of *Williams v. Gaye* on Music Composition," *Harvard Journal of Sports & Entertainment Law* 10 (2019): 133–45, 141–45.

43. See, for example, *Skidmore v. Led Zeppelin*, Appellant's Petition, 9 (filed October 26, 2018); *Skidmore v. Led Zeppelin*, 16-56057 *15–*22 (9th Cir. March 9, 2020) (stating that the deposit copy defines scope of protection).

44. Mariateresa Storino, Rossana Dalmonte, and Mario Baroni, "An Investigation on the Perception of Musical Style," *Musical Perception: An Interdisciplinary Journal* 24, no. 5 (June 2007): 417–18.

45. *Williams*, 885 F. 3d at 1183 (Nguyen, J., dissenting).

46. McCormick, *George P. Reed v. Samuel Carusi*, 12–13.

47. *Williams v. Gaye*, Finell Transcript, 173.

48. *Williams v. Gaye*, Finell Transcript, 19.

49. Gregory Weinstein, "The Blurred Lines of Musicological Expertise," *Two Strikes Blog*, March 11, 2015, http://twostrikes.gregoryweinstein.com/the-blurred-lines-of-musicological-expertise/.

Bibliography

Amdur, Leon H. *Copyright Law and Practice*. New York, NY: Clark, Boardman, 1936.

An Act to Amend the Several Acts Respecting Copyrights, 4 Stat. 436 (1831) (amended 1870).

Arewa, Olufunmilayo. "Blues Lives: Promise and Perils of Music Copyright." *Cardozo Arts and Entertainment Law Journal* 27 (2010): 573–624.

———. "A Musical Work is a Set of Instructions." *Houston Law Review* 52, no. 2 (2014): 467–535.

Arnstein v. Broadcast Music, Inc., 137 F.2d 410 (2d. Cir. 1943).

Arnstein v. Edward B. Marks Corp., 82 F.2d 2775 (2d Cir. 1936).

Arnstein v. Porter, 154 F.2d 464 (2d Cir. 1946).

Arnstein v. Twentieth Century Fox Corp., 3 F.R.D. 58 (S.D.N.Y. 1943).

Atari, Inc. v. N. American Philips Consumer Electronic Corp., 672 F.2d 607 (7th Cir. 1982).

Atkinson, Benedict. *A Short History of Copyright: The Genie of Information*. New York, NY: Springer, 2014.

Avsec, Mark. "'Nonconventional' Musical Analysis and 'Disguised' Infringement: Clever Musical Tricks to Divide the Wealth of Tin Pan Alley." *Cleveland State Law Review* 52 (2004–2005): 339–371.

Baker, Maureen. "La[w] – A Note To Follow So: Have We Forgotten the Federal Rules of Evidence in Music Plagiarism Cases?" *Southern California Law Review* 65 (March 1992): 1583–1640.

Balganesh, Shaymkrishna. "The Questionable Origins of Copyright Infringement Analysis." *Stanford Law Review* 68 (2016): 791–862.

Baron v. Leo Feist, 78 F. Supp. 686 (S.D.N.Y. 1948).

Baxa, Philip C. and M. William Krasilovsky. "Dawson v. Hinshaw Music, Inc.: The Fourth Circuit Revisits Arnstein and the 'Intended Audience' Test." *Fordham Intellectual Property, Media, and Entertainment Law Journal* 1, no. 2 (1991): 91–115.

Baxter v. MCA, Inc., 812 F.2d 421 (9th Cir. 1987).

Beam, Christopher. "What's a Forensic Musicologist?" *Slate*, November 12, 2010. http://www.slate.com/articles/news_and_politics/explainer/2010/11/whats_a_f orensic_musicologist.html.

Begault, Durand R., Heather D. Heise, and Christopher A. Peltier. "Analysis Criteria for Foresnic Musicology." Presented at *21st International Congress on Acoustics*. Last modified June 2013. http://www.audioforensics.com/PDFs/ICA_Musicology2 013.pdf.

Bernstein, Mark I. "Jury Evaluation of Expert Testimony Under the Federal Rules." *Drexel Law Review* 7 (Spring 2015): 239–309.

Blume v. Spear, 13 F. Cas. 910 (C.C.S.D.N.Y. 1887).

Boisson v. Banian, Ltd., 2873 F.3d 262 (2d Cir. 2001).

Brainard v. Vassar, N. 3:07-0929 (M.D. Tenn. 2009).

Brauneis, Robert. "Musical Work Copyright for the Era of Digital Sound Technology: Looking beyond Composition and Performance." *Tulane Journal of Technology and Intellectual Property* 17 (Fall 2014): 1–51.

Bridgeport Music, Inc. v. 11C Music, Inc., (M.D. Tenn. 2001).

Bridgeport Music, Inc. v. Dimension Films, 410 F.3d 792 (6th Cir. 2005).

Bridgeport Music, Inc. v. Justin Combs, 507 F.3d 470 (6th Cir. 2006).

Bridgeport Music, Inc. v. UMG Recordings, Inc., 585 F.3d 263 (6th Cir. 2009).

Bright Tunes Music v. Harrisongs Music, 420 F. Supp. 177 (S.D.N.Y. 1976).

Camson, Josh. "History of the Federal Rules of Evidence." *Proof.* Last modified Spring 2010. https://apps.americanbar.org/litigation/litigationnews/trial_skills/06 1710-trial-evidence-federal-rules-of-evidence-history.html.

Carew v. R.K.O. Radio Pictures, 43 F Supp. 199 (S.D. Call, 1942).

Caudill, David S. and Lewis H. LaRue. *No Magic Wand: The Idealization of Science in Law*. Lanham, MD: Rowman & Littlefield, 2006.

Cholvin v. B&F Music Co., 253 F.2d 102 (7th Cir. 1958).

Comput. Assoc. Int. Inc. v. Altai Inc., 982 F.2d 693 (2d Cir. 1992).

Copyright Act of 1790, 1 Statutes at Large 124 (1790).

Copyright Act of 1909, 35 Stat. 1075 (amended 1976).

Copyright Act of 1976, 17 U.S.C. § 302 (1976).

Coulter, Jeffrey D. "Computers, Copyright and Substantial Similarity: The Test Reconsidered." *John Marshall Journal of Computer and Information Law* 14 (1995): 47–79.

Country Kids 'N City Slicks, Inc. v. Sheen, 77 F.3d 1280 (10th Cir. 1996).

Cronin, Charles. "Concepts of Melodic Similarity in Music-Copyright Infringement Suits." In *Computing in Musicology*, vol. 11, edited by Walter B. Hewlett and Eleanor Selfridge-Field, 187-209. Cambridge: MIT Press, 1997–98.

_____. "I Hear America Suing: Music Copyright Infringement in the Era of Electronic Sound." *Hastings Law Journal* 66 (June 2015): 1187–1255.

_____, ed. *Music Copyright Infringement Resource*. https://blogs.law.gwu.edu/mcir/.

Cummings, Alex Sayf. *Democracy of Sound*. Oxford: Oxford University, 2013.

Daubert v. Merrell Dow Pharmaceuticals, Inc., 509 U.S. 579 (1993).

Daus, Matthew W. "The Abrogation of Expert Dissection in Popular Music Copyright Infringement." *Touro Law Review* 8 (Winter 1992): 615–646.

Dawson v. Hinshaw Music, Inc., 905 F.2d 731 (4th Cir. 1990).

Demers, Joanna. "Melody, Theft, and High Culture." In *Modernism and Copyright*, edited by Paul K. Saint-Amour, 114–132. Oxford: Oxford University Press, 2011.

———. *Steal This Music: How Intellectual Property Law Affects Musical Creativity*. Athens, GA: University of Georgia, 2006.

Digital Millennium Copyright Act, 112 Stat. 2860 (1998).

Digital Performance Right in Sound Recordings Act, 109 Stat. 336 (1995).

Edward B. Marks v. Leo Feist, 290 F. 959 (2d Cir. 1923).

Emerson v. Davies, 8 F. Cas. 615 (C.C.D. Mass. 1845).

Federal Rules of Evidence, Public Law 93–595 (January 2, 1975) (amended 2011).

Feldman, Noah. "'Blurred Lines; Copyright Verdict Creates Bad Law for Musicians." *Chicago Tribune*, March 17, 2015. www.chicagotribune.com/news/opinion/commentary/ct-blurred-lines-robin-thicke-court-perspec-0317-20150316-story.html.

Finell, Judith Greenberg. "Scandalous Notes: A Musicologist Discusses New Developments in Music Technology that Challenge Copyright Attorneys and Expert Witnesses." *New York State Bar Association Entertainment, Arts and Sports Law Section Journal* 19 (2008). http://www2.jfmusicservices.com/scandalous-notes-a-musicologist-discusses-new-developments-in-music-technology-that-challenge-copyright-attorneys-and-expert-witnesses/.

———. "Using an Expert Witness in a Music Copyright Case." *New York Law Journal* 11 (May 1990): 5–6.

Fink, Robert. "'Blurred Lines, UR-Lines, and Color Lines." *Musicology Now*, Blog of the American Musicological Society, March 15, 2015. musicologynow.ams-net.org/2015/03/blurred-lines-ur-lines-and-colorline.html.

Fishman, Joseph P. "Music as a Matter of Law." *Harvard Law Review* 131 (May 2018): 1861–1921.

Fitzgerald, Jon. "Black Pop Songwriting 1963–1966: An Analysis of U.S. Top Forty Hits by Cooke, Mayfield, Stevenson, Robinson, and Holland-Dozier-Holland." *Black Music Research Journal* 27 (Fall 2007): 97–140.

Folsom v. March, 9 F.Cas. 342 (C.C.D. Mass. 1841).

Foster, William. "Expert Testimony: Prevalent Complaints and Proposed Remedies." *Harvard Law Review* 11 (October 1897): 169–186.

Francesatti v. Germanotta, 2014 WL 276231 (June 17, 2014).

Frank, Jerome. "Say It with Music." *Harvard Law Review* 61 (June 1948): 921–952.

Freuhwald, E. Scott. "Copyright Infringement of Musical Compositions: A Systematic Approach." *Akron Law Review* 26 (Summer 1992): 15–48.

Frith, Simon and Lee Marshall, eds. *Music and Copyright*, 2d ed. Edinburgh: Edinburgh University, 2004.

Frye v. United States, 293 F. 1013 (D.C. Cir. 1923).

Gasté v. Kaiserman, 863 F.2d 1061 (2d Cir. 1988).

Gershman, Jacob. "'Blurred Lines' Verdict a 'Dangerous' Threat to Creativity, Musicians Warn Appeals Court." *Wall Street Journal*, August 31, 2016. blogs.wsj.com/law/2016/08/31/blurred-lines-verdict-a-dangerous-threat-to-creativity-celebrity-musicians-warn-appeals-court.

Grand Upright Music, Ltd. v. Warner Bros. Records, Inc., 780 F. Supp. 182 (S.D.N.Y. 1991).

Gruber, Jordan, Fausto Tito Poza, and Anthony J. Pellicano. "Audio Recordings: Evidence, Experts, and Technology." *American Jurisprudence Trials* 48 (2013): 1–586.

Gunther, Gerald. *Learned Hand: The Man and the Judge.* Oxford: Oxford University, 2011.

Haack, Susan. "The Expert Witness: Lessons from the U.S. Experience." *Humana Mente Journal of Philosophical Studies* 28 (2015): 39–70.

Haas v. Leo Feist, 234 F. 646 (S.D.N.Y. 1916).

Hamilton, Clarence G. *Music Appreciation: Based upon Methods of Literary Criticism.* New York, NY: Oliver Ditson, 1920.

Hand, Learned. "Historical and Practical Considerations Regarding Expert Testimony." *Harvard Law Review* 15 (1902): 40–58.

Haurant, Sandra. "How Do I Become a Forensic Musicologist?" *The Guardian*, January 20, 2015. http://www.theguardian.com/money/2015/jan/20/how-become -forensic-musicologist.

Heim v. Universal Pictures, 154 F.2d 480 (2d. Cir. 1946).

Hein v. Harris, 175 F. 875 (C.C.S.D.N.Y. 1910).

Hirsch v Paramount Pictures, 17 F. Supp. 816 (S.D. Cal. 1937).

Jarvis v. A & M Records, 827 F.2d 282 (D.N.J. 1993).

Jean v. Bug Music, Inc., 2002 WL 287786 (S.D.N.Y. 2002).

Jollie v. Jaques, 13 F. Cas. 910 (C.C.S.D.N.Y. 1850).

Jones, Stephanie. "Music Copyright in Theory and Practice: An Improved Approach for Determining Substantial Similarity." *Duquesne Law Review* 31 (Winter 1993): 277–308.

Jones v. Supreme Music, 101 F. Supp. 989 (S.D.N.Y. 1951).

Kernfeld, Barry. *Pop Music Piracy: Disobedient Music Distribution since 1929.* Chicago, IL: University of Chicago, 2011.

Keyes, Michael J. "Musical Musings: The Case for Rethinking Music Copyright Protection." *Michigan Telecommunications and Technology Law Review* 10 (Spring 2004): 407–447.

Kim, Alice. "Expert Testimony and Substantial Similarity: Facing the Music in (Music) Copyright Infringement Cases." *Columbia-VLA Journal of Law and the Arts* 19 (Fall 1994–Winter 1995): 109–132.

Kohus v. Mariol, 328 F.3d 848, 857 (6th Cir. 2003).

Kumho Tire v. Carmichael, 526 U.S. 137 (1999).

Lane v. Knowles-Carter, 2015 WL 639540 (October 21, 2015).

Laroche, Guillaume. "Striking Similarities: Toward a Quantitative Measure of Melodic Copyright Infringement." *Integral* 25 (2011): 39–88.

Latman, Alan. "'Probative Similarity' as Proof of Copying: Toward Dispelling Some Myths in Copyright Infringement." *Columbia Law Review* 90 (1990): 1187–1222.

Lemley, Mark A. "Our Bizarre System for Proving Copyright Infringement." *Journal of the Copyright Society of the USA* 57 (Summer 2010): 719–735.

Lenz v. Universal Music Corp., 801 F.3d 1126 (9th Cir. 2015).

Leo, Katherine. "Musical Expertise and the 'Ordinary' Listener in Federal Copyright Law." *Music and Politics* 13, no. 1 (Winter 2019): 1–19. https://doi.org/10.3998/mp.9460447.0013.108.

Lessig, Lawrence. *Free Culture.* New York, NY: Penguin, 2004.

Livingston, Margit and Joseph Urbinato. "Copyright Infringement of Music: Determining What Sounds Alike Is Alike." *Vanderbilt Journal of Entertainment and Technology Law* 15 (Winter 2013): 227–302.

Lund, Jamie. "An Empirical Examination of the Lay Listener Test in Music Composition Copyright Infringement." *Virginia Sports and Entertainment Law Journal* 11 (Fall 2011): 137–177.

Macpherson, Stewart. *Form in Music.* London: Joseph Williams, 1930.

_____. *Music and Its Appreciation or The Foundations of True Listening.* London: Joseph Williams, 1910.

_____. *The Appreciation, or Listening, Class.* London: Joseph Williams Limited, 1936.

Manta, Irina D. "Reasonable Copyright." *Boston College Law Review* 53 (September 2012): 1303–1360.

Manuelian, Michael Der. "The Role of the Expert Witness in Music Copyright Infringement Cases." *Fordham Law Review* 57 (October 1988): 127–147.

May, Chris. "Jurisprudence v. Musicology: Riffs from the Land Down Under." *Music and Letters* 97, no. 4 (2017): 622–646.

MCA, Inc. v. Wilson, 425 F. Supp. 443 (S.D.N.Y. 1976).

McCormick, Francis M., Jr. *George P. Reed v. Samuel Carusi: A Nineteenth Century Jury Trial Pursuant to the 1831 Copyright Act.* Last modified January 2005. http://digitalcommons.law.umaryland.edu/mlh_pubs/4/.

McCormick v. Talcott, 61 U.S. 402 (1857).

McDonald v. Multimedia Entmt, Inc., 20 U.S.P.Q.2d 1372 (S.D.N.Y. 1991).

McDonald v. West, 2015 WL 5751197 (September 30, 2015).

McLeod, Kembrew and Peter DiCola. *Creative License: The Law and Culture of Digital Sampling.* Durham, NC: Duke University, 2011.

McLeod, Kembrew. "Musical Production, Copyright, and the Private Ownership of Culture." In *Critical Cultural Policy Studies: A Reader*, edited by Justin Lewis and Toby Miller, 240–252. Malden: Backwell, 2003.

_____. *Owning Culture: Authorship, Ownership, & Intellectual Property Law.* New York, NY: Peter Lang, 2001.

McRae v. Smith, 968 F. Supp. 559 (10th Cir. 1997).

Millett v. Snowden, 17 F.Cas. 374, No. 9600 (Cir. Ct. S.D. New York, NY, 1844).

Mnookin, Jennifer L. "Idealizing Science and Demonizing Experts: An Intellectual History of Expert." *Villanova Law Review* 52 (2007): 763–818.

Monson, Ingrid. "Personal Take: On Serving as an Expert Witness in the 'Blurred Lines' Case." In *The Cambridge Companion to Music in Digital Culture*, edited by Nicholas Cook, Monique M. Ingalls, and David Trippett, 58–62. Cambridge: Cambridge University Press, 2019.

Moser, David. *Music Copyright for the New Millennium.* Artistpro, 2001.

Newton v. Diamond, 388 F. 3d 1189 (9th Cir. 2003).

Nimmer, Melville. *Nimmer On Copyright*. New York, NY: Matthew Bender, 2011.

Nizer, Louis. *My Life in Court*. Garden City, NY: Doubleday, 1961.

N. Music Corp. v. King Recording Corp., 105 F. Supp. 393 (S.D.N.Y. 1952).

Osteen, Mark. "Rhythm Changes: Contrafacts, Copyright, and Jazz Modernism." In *Modernism and Copyright*, edited by Paul K. Saint-Amour, 98–113. Oxford: Oxford University Press, 2011.

Overman v. Loesser, 205 F.2d 521, 521 (9th Cir. 1953).

Packson v. Jobete, No. 28687 (Chicago, IL, 1967).

Padgett, Austin. "The Rhetoric of Predictability: Reclaiming the Lay Ear in Music Copyright." *Pierce Law Review* 7 (December 2008): 125–152.

Patry, William. *How to Fix Copyright*. Oxford: Oxford University, 2011.

Quagliariello, John. "Blurring the Lines: The Impact of *Williams v. Gaye* on Music Composition." *Harvard Journal of Sports & Entertainment Law* 10 (2019): 133–145.

Reed v. Carusi, 20 F.Cas. 431 (C.C.D.Md. 1845).

Reynolds, M. Fletcher. *Music Analysis for Expert Testimony in Copyright Infringement Litigation*. Ph.D. Diss., University of Kansas, 1991.

Romano, Nick. "'Blurred Lines' Copyright Lawsuit Ends: Robin Thicke, Pharrell Williams to Pay $5 Million." *Entertainment Weekly*, December 13, 2018. https://ew.com/music/2018/12/13/blurred-lines-copyright-lawsuit-robin-thicke-pharrell-williams-pay/.

Rose, Mark. *Authors and Owners: The Invention of Copyright*. Cambridge, MA: Harvard University, 1993.

Rosen, Gary. *Adventures of Jazz Age Lawyer*. Los Angeles, CA: University of California, 2020.

———. *Unfair to Genius*. Oxford: Oxford University, 2012.

Roth Greeting Cards v. United Card Co., 429 F.2d 1006 (9th Cir. 1970).

Samuelson, Pamela. "A Fresh Look at Tests for Nonliteral Copyright Infringement." *Northwestern Law Review* 107 (2013): 1821–1855.

Sarregama India v. Mosley, 635 F. 3d 1284 (11th Cir. 2011).

Selfridge-Field, Eleanor. "Substantial Musical Similarity in Sound and Notation: Perspectives from Digital Musicology." *Colorado Technology Law Journal* 16 (2018): 249–283.

Selle v. Gibb, 741 F. 2d 896 (7th Cir. 1984).

Shaw v. Lindheim, 908 F.2d 852 (5th Cir. 1990).

Sid and Marty Krofft Television Product., Inc. v. McDonald's Corp., 526 F.2d 1157 (9th Cir. 1977).

Simonton v. Gordon, 12 F.2d 116 (S.D.N.Y. 1925).

Sound Recordings Act of 1971, 85 Stat. 39 (1971).

Stewart, Alexander. "'Been Caught Stealing': A Musicologist's Perspective on Unlicensed Sampling Disputes." *University of Missouri Kansas City Law Review* 83 (Winter 2014): 339–361.

Storino, Mariateresa, Rossana Dalmonte, and Mario Baroni. "An Investigation on the Perception of Musical Style." *Musical Perception: An Interdisciplinary Journal* 24, no. 5 (June 2007): 417–432.

Straughter v. Raymond, 211 WL 3651350 (C.D. Cal. 2011).

Swirsky v. Carey, 376 F.3d 841 (9th Cir. 2004).

Tempo Music, Inc. v. Famous Music, Corp., 838 F. Supp. 162 (S.D.N.Y. 1993).

The New Wigmore: A Treatise on Evidence: Expert Evidence, edited by David H. Kaye, David E. Bernstein, Jennifer L. Mnookin; Richard D. Friedman. Austin, TX: Aspen Publishers, 2011.

Thompson v. Richie, 820 F.2d 408 (C.D. Cal. 1985).

Tisi v. Patrick, 97 F. Supp. 2d 539 (S.D.N.Y. 2000).

TufAmerica, Inc. v. Warner Bros. Music Corp., 67 F. Supp. 3d 590 (S.D.N.Y. 2014).

Vaidhyanathan, Siva. *Copyrights and Copywrongs: The Rise of Intellectual Property and How It Threatens Creativity.* New York, NY: New York University, 2001.

Vargas v. Pfizer, 418 F. Supp. 2d 369 (S.D.N.Y. 2005).

Vargas v. Transeau, 514 F. Supp.2d 439, 441 (S.D.N.Y. 2007).

VMG Salsoul, LLC v. Ciccone, 824 F.3d 871 (9th Cir. 2016).

Weil, Arthur. *American Copyright Law with Especial Reference to the Present United States Copyright Act.* Chicago, IL: Callaghan, 1917.

Weinstein, Gregory. "The Blurred Lines of Musicological Expertise." *Two Strikes Blog*, March 11, 2015. http://twostrikes.gregoryweinstein.com/the-blurred-lines -of-musicological-expertise/.

West Pub. Co. v. Edward Thompson Co., 169 F. 833, 861 (E.D.N.Y. 1909).

White-Smith Music Pub. Co. v. Apollo Co., 209 U.S. 1 (1908).

Whitol v. Wells, 231 F.2d 550 (7th Cir. 1956).

Williams v. Gaye, 885 F.3d 1150 (9th Cir. 2018).

Williams, Justin. *Rhymin' and Stealin: Musical Borrowing in Hip-Hop.* Ann Arbor, MI: University of Michigan Press, 2014.

Index

Note: Page references for figures are italicized.

About the Author

Katherine M. Leo, PhD, JD, is an assistant professor of music at Millikin University in Decatur, Illinois, where she teaches a variety of courses in music history and ethnomusicology. Dr. Leo's academic research on issues in U.S. music copyright and jazz history have appeared in *Music and Politics* and *Jazz Perspectives*.